Fairy Tales on the Teen Screen

Athena Bellas

Fairy Tales on the Teen Screen

Rituals of Girlhood

palgrave
macmillan

Athena Bellas
University of Melbourne
Melbourne, VIC, Australia

ISBN 978-3-319-87915-4   ISBN 978-3-319-64973-3   (eBook)
DOI 10.1007/978-3-319-64973-3

Cover illustration: Westend61 GmbH/Alamy Stock Photo

Printed on acid-free paper

This Palgrave Macmillan imprint is published by Springer Nature
The registered company is Springer International Publishing AG
The registered company address is: Gewerbestrasse 11, 6330 Cham, Switzerland

Preface

This book emerges during a period in which teen girls' screen media culture is saturated with fairy tale narratives, themes and images. These are powerful and persistent popular myths through which a range of fears, desires and hopes for the feminine rite of passage from adolescence into adulthood are staged and imagined. I am interested in this contemporary trend, particularly because it produces a range of challenging, complex and often contradictory images of girlhood. Furthermore, my fascination with the fairy tale lies in its dual capacity to be mobilised for profoundly conservative purposes, as well as for its rebellious zones of wonder and pure potential. For example, many contemporary teen revisions of the tales work to increase the agency of the heroine in interesting and complex ways, while often simultaneously cleaving to such familiar tropes as the heterosexual happily ever after as the pinnacle of success in the girl's coming of age story. The research conducted in this book is motivated by questions about how youthful femininity is constructed in both traditional, canonical versions of fairy tales, as well as contemporary teen revisions of them, and what this tells us about changing notions of girlhood in the twenty-first century. The fairy tale is about setting out limits, to be sure, but it is also about the alternatives that arise when one crosses those limits, and I am particularly interested in these possibilities. The teen screen texts under analysis in the book provide representations of girls who cross over into other worlds, disobey rules and commit unruly acts, allowing for a discussion of the fairy tale's liminal energy and powers of transgression. I endeavour to locate my attention in this space of subversion and flux to consider how received ideas about girls can be disrupted, and how alternative rituals of girlhood can be produced in their stead on the teen screen.

This book is based on my Ph.D. dissertation and I am very thankful to Dr. Wendy Haslem and Professor Angela Ndalianis, who supervised that earlier project. I am grateful, too, for the unflagging support provided by my wonderful family, Mary, Michael and Vicki, and my grandparents Athena, James, Vassiliki and George during the making of this project. Heartfelt thanks also go to my partner, Stefan Nekvapil, who lovingly encouraged me and made incredible pancakes for me as I wrote this book. I am also incredibly lucky to be surrounded by wonderful colleagues and friends who have helped me during the making of the Ph.D. and the book, especially Jodi McAlister, Mark Nicholls, Kim Clayton Greene, Elena Benthaus, Leigh McLennon, Tara Lomax, Prudence Flint and Meredith Faragher. Special thanks also go to the Weinberger family, for their friendship and support, especially during the writing of my Ph.D.

Melbourne, Australia   Athena Bellas

CONTENTS

1 Introduction: Fairy Tales on the Contemporary
Teen Screen   1

2 An Escape to the Forest in Catherine Hardwicke's
Red Riding Hood (2011)   37

3 When Sleeping Beauty Wakes: The *Twilight* Film Series,
Liminal Time and Fantasy Images   69

4 Liminal Communitas and Feminist Solidarity:
Transforming 'Bluebeard' in *Pretty Little Liars*
(ABC Family 2010–)   107

5 Cinderella's Transformation: Public Liminality and
Style as Subversion in *Gossip Girl* (The CW 2007–2012)   147

6 The Mermaid's Tale: Ultraliminality and
Feminist Futures in *Aquamarine* (Allen 2006)   189

7 Conclusion: Rituals of Girlhood Transformed
on the Teen Screen   227

Index   243

LIST OF FIGURES

Fig. 2.1   Valerie's image captured in the gaze of the father/wolf   47
Fig. 2.2   Panoramic framing and mobile camera movement in
            Red Riding Hood   52
Fig. 3.1   Bella's 'Sleeping Beauty' fantasy is visualised on a black and
            white filmstrip, emphasising her role as 'director' and creator
            of the fantasy sequence   82
Fig. 3.2   The ultraslow dissolve and spiralling camera movement in
            Twilight   86
Fig. 3.3   Edward's figure is associated with the spectacular excess of
            moonlight, pattern and lace in Bella's dream image   92
Fig. 3.4   Bella's desiring gaze at Edward as he reveals his luminous,
            sparkling body to her   95
Fig. 3.5   The camera, aligned with Bella's desiring gaze, slowly pans up
            Edward's sparkling body in a close-up shot   96
Fig. 4.1   Hanna peeps through the keyhole (4.05)   118
Fig. 4.2   Bluebeard's miniaturised bloody chamber (2.24)   119
Fig. 4.3   Hanna scrutinises the clue, zooming in on its relevant
            information and capturing it on her camera phone (4.03)   126
Fig. 4.4   The glittering pendant as decorative clue (1.20)   132
Fig. 5.1   DIY creativity and subversive ensembles made by hand (2.09)   161
Fig. 5.2   Jenny's fluorescent fashion show takes over a conservative
            adult cocktail party (2.09)   166
Fig. 5.3   Exaggerated feminine identities are revealed as playful
            masquerades (1.06)   171
Fig. 5.4   Extreme close-up on beadwork in a shop window (2.20)   178

Fig. 5.5   Tracking shots from the *flâneuse*'s point of view are
            interspersed with extreme close-up views of the shop
            window (2.20)   178
Fig. 6.1   The extreme close-up and shot reverse shot structure of this
            scene emphasises the heroines' eyes and the fragmented words
            on the page of the magazine   204
Fig. 6.2   The extreme close-up and shot reverse shot structure of this
            scene emphasises the heroines' eyes and the fragmented words
            on the page of the magazine   204
Fig. 6.3   Hyperconscious displays of femininity generate both humour
            and insightful critique of gendered performance   210
Fig. 6.4   The glitter aesthetic is revealed in the opening shots of
            Aquamarine, with the mermaid's magical powers visualised
            through images of sparkles, bubbles, iridescent colours and
            glitter   215

CHAPTER 1

Introduction: Fairy Tales on the Contemporary Teen Screen

This book explores contemporary US teen films and television series in which girls intervene in and challenge some of the limiting and prescriptive rituals of hegemonic feminine adolescence. These contemporary screen texts hybridise the fairy tale genre with the teen screen genre, and this combination of narrative forms produces new outcomes for the representation of the feminine adolescent rite of passage. There is a marked contemporary trend in retelling and revising the fairy tale on the teen screen, and this book explores how this trend is reflected in teen texts, taking *Red Riding Hood* (Hardwicke 2011), *Twilight* (Hardwicke 2008), *Pretty Little Liars* (ABC Family 2010–), *Gossip Girl* (The CW 2007–2012) and *Aquamarine* (Allen 2006) as its primary case studies. These texts are particularly notable for the shifts they enact in the representation of gender within the realm of the fairy tale, unsettling the sexist narrative economy upon which many of the tales by Charles Perrault (1697), the Brothers Grimm (1857) and Hans Christian Andersen (1837) relied. I explore the liminal moments in these teen screen rites of passage when feminine adolescent opposition and resistance occur, because these moments of opposition represent a rupture in dominant narratives of girlhood and are therefore central to a feminist reading of the teen screen.

This is the first book-length study of the relationship between the fairy tale and teen girl screen media, which is timely given that revisions of popular tales saturate girls' screen cultures in the twenty-first century. In the US context, teen girl fairy tale films include *Snow White and the*

© The Author(s) 2017
A. Bellas, *Fairy Tales on the Teen Screen*,
DOI 10.1007/978-3-319-64973-3_1

Huntsman (Sanders 2012), *Ginger Snaps* (Fawcett 2000), *A Cinderella Story* (Rosman 2004), *Beastly* (Barnz 2011), *Ella Enchanted* (O'Haver 2004), *Enchanted* (Lima 2007), *Sydney White* (Nussbaum 2007) and *Penelope* (Palansky 2006). Fairy tale narratives and tropes also abound in teen television series such as *The Secret Circle* (The CW 2011–2012), *Sabrina the Teenage Witch* (ABC 1996–2003),[1] *Buffy the Vampire Slayer* (The WB 1997–2003),[2] *Teen Wolf* (MTV 2011–), *The Vampire Diaries* (The CW 2009–2017) and *Beauty and the Beast* (The CW 2012–2016). Disney's recent films pitched at younger girls and family audiences such as *Frozen* (Buck and Lee 2013), a revision of Andersen's tale 'The Snow Queen' ([1845] 2008), *Tangled* (Greno and Howard 2010), a retelling of the Grimms' version of 'Rapunzel' (1812), along with *Cinderella* (Branagh 2015), *Maleficent* (Stromberg 2014), *Brave* (Andrews, Chapman and Purcell 2012), *Into the Woods* (Marshall 2014) and *Beauty and the Beast* (Condon 2017), demonstrate a similar preoccupation with telling girls' rite-of-passage narratives through the fairy tale.

This is not to say that the teen genre's preoccupation with revising fairy tales is only evident in the 2000s; indeed, films such as *Ever After* (Tennant 1998), *Freeway* (Bright 1996), *Edward Scissorhands* (Burton 1990) and *The Company of Wolves* (Jordan 1984) demonstrate an interest in the fairy tale long before this period. Indeed, historian Diane Purkiss traces a genealogy from fairy and nymph lore to adolescent pop culture heroines such as Buffy Summers (2000, 321). Reaching further back into teen film history, Georganne Scheiner's study of representations of feminine adolescence in early Hollywood cinema shows how silent film's representations of girls heavily relied on fairy tale subject matter (2000, 27). However, it is clear that the fairy tale has become especially popular in the twenty-first century as it continues to proliferate and multiply on the teen screen.

The question, then, is why the fairy tale has become so central to contemporary girls' visual culture. Fairy tale scholar Cristina Bacchilega argues that the fairy tale 'continues to be hypercommodified' in contemporary visual culture as it enjoys its 'renewed appeal today', but that this is not the whole story (2013, 76). She elaborates that 'the genre's social uses are—as they have been in the past—multiple and somewhat unpredictable, and...in today's convergence culture audiences are more knowledgeable and active participants' (76). As a result of this 'new economy of knowledge...today's young adult and adult public has acquired or has the potential to access a more complex and expansive sense of the "fairy tale" than what was generally available some thirty years ago' (76). These narratives are not static or reproduced in any simple sense; they are highly elastic and mutable, their meanings transforming according to the cultural context in which they are reworked and the 'economies of knowledge' that circulate around them. I argue that teen girl film revisions of the genre often express the multiplicity, complexity and expansiveness that Bacchilega identifies as central to the contemporary fairy tale. Therefore, while these popular texts certainly commodify the genre, they are also more complex than this; frequently, they shift the position of the heroine in the narratives to a more agentic role, and sometimes this shift can also undo some of the cultural myths inscribed into the girls' rite-of-passage story.

Scholarship on postfeminism and princess culture illuminates some of the key reasons why the genre has experienced a significant revival in late twentieth- and early twenty-first-century representations of girls. Ilana Nash's chapter 'The Princess and the Teen Witch: Fantasies of the Essential Self' argues that the figures of the princess and the teen witch embody the paradox of postfeminist, neoliberal Western culture. She writes that on the one hand: as commodities that exemplify 'girl power,' the princesses and witches of popular culture are offered as choices for identification and inspiration, in a cultural context where one can choose to be anything she wants. Yet at the same time, the appeal of these fantasies lies in their tropes of an inborn, pre-conscious specialness that erases a heroine's need to choose her identity at all. (2015, 21) While the heroines are permitted to have 'strong desires and [to] act upon them', they nevertheless 'still display traditional feminine goodness…and a desire—or at least a willingness—to find true love with a man' (13. See also Greenhill and Rudy 2014, 16). This speaks not only to the enduring tropes of the Perrault, Grimm and Andersen versions of the tales, but the persistent pervasiveness of Disney's iconic animations of sweet, placid, passive heroines patiently awaiting their one true love (Trites 1991; Sells 1995; Heatwole 2016). Contemporary fairy tale narratives of adolescent girlhood, therefore, are often highly ambivalent and complex, incorporating discourses of girl power while at the same time reproducing the genre's traditional representation of youthful femininity that is not only idealised, but also represented as an essence that makes the girl 'special' (21). So while the heroines of films such as *A Cinderella Story*, *Beastly* and *Enchanted* are sassy, outspoken and smart, they are simultaneously represented as intrinsically gentle, accommodating, feminine and invested in the 'happily ever after' of heterosexual romance.

Prominent fairy tale scholar Jack Zipes questions the fruitfulness of finding feminism in films such as these. Of 'Cinderella' films such as *Pretty in Pink* (Deutch 1986), he writes that:

> it is ridiculous to try to salvage the films for contemporary feminism by analysing how all the Cinderellas in these films demonstrate their talents and are active, humane, thoughtful, and assertive, as some critics have done. Such 'salvation' merely rationalises the sequence of demeaning behaviour that the female protagonist must exhibit. (2011, 189)

These films are, for Zipes, a '"horrific representation" of happiness that basically reaffirms fixed gender roles with slight touches of feminism and male benevolence' (2011, 238). While I agree that we must be critically engaged with these texts, I think that the revision of fairy tales in girls' visual cultures are more complex and polyvalent than the simple or wholesale reinscription of 'fixed gender roles' that Zipes argues for here. As Pauline Greenhill and Sidney Eve Matrix argue, fairy tale films are 'alternately conservative...and controversial' (2010, 8). If we are more attuned to the complex interactions of 'regulation and rupture' (Renold and Ringrose 2008) represented in teen fairy tale texts, perhaps we can offer more expansive readings of the role these fantasies play in the production of contemporary discourses of girlhood. The fairy tale *mise en scène* becomes an imaginative space where cultural anxieties, hopes and expectations about girls are projected, narrativised and worked through, which is particularly evident in the overwhelming abundance of teen fairy tale screen texts. Therefore, examining twenty-first-century revisions of these potent and enduring myths is especially relevant now, for they seem to be absolutely central to the construction of girlhood in contemporary media culture.

While Nash and Zipes identify the tendency for fairy tale and princess texts to be invested in essentialist representations of the girl, there are also texts circulating within girls' screen media culture that trouble this familiar terrain. The purpose of this book is to closely analyse how this unsettling produces alternative depictions of girls beyond the princess stereotype, and to consider the importance of the existence of these alternatives within the wider framework of girls' contemporary screen culture. The texts under analysis in this book all produce representations of girlhood that not only acknowledge its constructedness, but also (to varying degrees) foreground the heroines' capacity to resist the way they have been 'spoken into existence' (Pomerantz 2007, 383). They are certainly not the *only* teen fairy tale texts to do this; there are many texts in the US context and beyond that could be very fruitfully read through this lens. For this project, however, I have chosen to limit my analysis to twenty-first-century texts about which, to date, very little has been written on their feminist potential (*Pretty Little Liars* and *Aquamarine*) as well as texts that have frequently been discounted as antifeminist (*Gossip Girl, Twilight* and *Red Riding Hood*). In doing so, I hope to go beyond and complicate some of the dominant assumptions that frame mainstream and popular teen fairy tale texts as bad objects,[3] and instead look for points of resistance wherever they arise. I think that teen fairy tale narratives, even those in the mainstream, can include representations of alternative girls, and analysis of these depictions might proffer insight into the complex ways feminist politics circulate and are negotiated in teen screen media. Furthermore, I have chosen to analyse teen texts are particularly notable for their engagement with the liminal portion of their heroines' rite-of-passage journeys. While many teen fairy tale screen texts engage with moments of liminal upheaval, they often swiftly propel the narrative towards a reassuring ending that circumvents this instability and secures the girl in her 'proper' place. Meanwhile, each text under analysis in this book significantly prolongs the representation of the liminal phase and defers such a neat resolution, opening up a space to explore a range of alternative girlhoods that can be represented in the transgressive, experimental space of flux and in-betweenness.

Bacchilega argues that the fairy tale is a flexible 'web of possibilities' which 'can continue to expand and shape, weaving new problems, desires and voices in and out of it' (2008, 195). The elasticity of this web allows for the incorporation of revisions, criticisms, subversions and updates. It is in this flexibility and changeability of the fairy tale that the genre's potential for subversion lies. The incorporation of 'new problems, desires and voices' that Bacchilega identifies can work to articulate the heroine's position in the text as powerfully agentic, going beyond the limited positions offered in the classic tales. This flexibility has also allowed for feminist appropriation and revision of traditional tales, especially since the 1970s and early 1980s with the publication of important literary revisions by writers such as Angela Carter (1979), Margaret Atwood ([1983] 1986), Anne Sexton (1971), Emma Donoghue (1997).

These feminist rewritings have been driven by a desire to interrogate the patriarchal ideology embedded in the tales, and to then unsettle this ideology in order to reconfigure the tales into alternative narratives.

As Zipes writes, these revisions 'endeavour to explore possibilities to go beyond the traditional boundaries of the fairy tale and generate new worlds' (1994, 143). The traditional boundaries I am most interested in are those that limit the representation of the young female character's rite of passage, reducing her to the sexist stereotypes of helpless damsel and victim of male aggression, or a maiden patiently awaiting a Prince's kiss: Perrault's Red Riding Hood is gobbled up by the ravenous wolf; both Perrault and the Grimms' Beauty slumbers in a death-like trance, waiting 100 years for her one true love to save her; Bluebeard's wife is emotionally tortured and threatened with death in Perrault's version; Andersen's mermaid endures the excruciating pain of splitting her tail into a pair of human legs in order to attract the affections of the Prince. The 'new worlds' Zipes refers to include narratives which generate new possibilities for stories of women's rites of passage by critiquing, opposing and transforming the limited representations of women embedded in the Perrault, Grimm and Andersen tales. In her important book, *Postmodern Fairy Tales: Gender and Narrative Strategies*, Bacchilega writes that the contemporary revisions can 'expose the fairy tale's complicity with the "exhausted" forms and ideologies of traditional Western narrative, rewriting the tale of magic in order to question and recreate the rules of narrative production, especially as such rules contribute to naturalising subjectivity and gender' (1997, 23). By questioning and recreating these rules, the contemporary tale can therefore not only critique their existing ideological structures; it can also rupture them and create new narratives and representations of women in their stead.

Each text under analysis bears a different relationship to the fairy tale. In the case of *Red Riding Hood* and *Aquamarine*, a very clear and direct revision takes place. In the case of *Twilight*, *Pretty Little Liars* and *Gossip Girl*, the revision of fairy tale is perhaps less direct or obvious. There are traces and echoes of motifs, images and narrative trajectories of the fairy tale in the texts, and sometimes nods to the tales are articulated in episode titles and dialogue. The fairy tale allusions I find in some of these texts may not necessarily be intentionally foregrounded by their creators. Rather, I think that the fairy tale has become so foundational and intrinsic to the ways in which we narrativise girls' rites of passage, that traces and links to the tales can be located across a range of texts if and when we choose to look for them. As Marina Warner notes in her foundational fairy tale study *From the Beast to the Blonde* (1995), 'these are stories with staying power…because the meanings they generate are themselves magical shape-shifters, dancing to the needs of their audience' (xix–xx). Fairy tales seem to morph and weave their way through girl culture, seeping into images of feminine childhood and adolescence. This is evinced in the popularity of princess-themed garb and accessories, and in teen girl cinema's constant narrativisation of girls falling in love with boys they describe as Prince Charming, references to kissing frogs and longing for fairy godmothers. Explicitly and implicitly, the fairy tale's iconic and culturally pervasive motifs and images of the girl's rite-of-passage narrative appear again and again in contemporary tellings of feminine coming-of-age stories, even in texts that do not directly declare themselves to be invoking that tradition. I am interested in texts that display overt and more oblique references, for they all in their own way contribute to the perpetuation and transformation of the fairy tale on the teen screen.

These contemporary fairy tales work to revise the gender relations of the earlier texts by foregrounding their heroines' agency and power in the face of patriarchal oppression. I do not argue that the teen texts under analysis in this book are *straightforwardly* feminist or that they offer empowered representations of girlhood in an *uncomplicated* way. Rather, I posit that there are important moments within these texts that provide representations of girls who eschew, resist and even disrupt some of the regulatory discourses that govern their lives. In the context of the rite of passage narrative, these disruptions disallow an untroubled representation of the girl's induction into hegemonic adult femininity. The smooth veneer of the dominant narrative of girlhood is therefore unsettled in these teen texts.

The hybridisation of teen and fairy tale genres on the contemporary screen produces a confrontation between the contemporary text's heroines and the prescriptive, limiting femininities inscribed in the earlier literary text. I consider these teen texts as examples of contemporary feminist fairy tale revisions that display moments of rupture where alternative girlhoods are represented within narrative. These revisions of fairy tales not only split hegemonic gendered representations apart at the seams, but also unleash the subversive voices, narratives and identities that this hegemony has repressed. The films and television series under analysis produce representations of teen girls who, in their articulations of opposition, confront and subvert the confines of conventional femininity. These conventions include the mandatory investment in heterosexual romance; privileging an acquiescent and passive 'good girl' as the ideal expression of femininity; the display of emphasised femininity for a male gaze; and relegation to the feminine realm of the domestic. The texts under analysis produce fantasy representations of girls as hunters, travellers, adventurers and powerful storytellers and narrators of their own rite of passage. The heroines demonstrate their noncompliance by escaping from conventional culture into otherworldly spaces such as the forest or ocean (*Red Riding Hood* and *Aquamarine*); by investigating, deconstructing and exposing the exploitation and violence committed against girls and women in patriarchal culture (*Pretty Little Liars*); by constructing alternative girl group communities (*Pretty Little Liars*, *Gossip Girl* and *Aquamarine*); and by mocking, laughing at and refusing to participate in the conventions of heterosexual romance (*Gossip Girl* and *Aquamarine*).

GIRLS AND 'DOING GIRLHOOD' IN POSTFEMINIST MEDIA CULTURE

While I identify moments of subversion in these teen texts, I also acknowledge that the texts emerge within a Western, mainstream, postfeminist popular media culture. Their narratives and *mise en scènes* are populated with elements common to postfeminist media, such as fairy tale romance, consumerism and commodity culture, makeovers, fashion, sparkles, princess culture and even wedding culture. None of the texts under analysis provides representations of girls who clearly state that they identify as feminists, or girls who directly engage with feminist political activism. This speaks to our postfeminist cultural climate in which gender equality is often taken for granted as something that has already been accomplished, thus making it difficult to perceive or articulate the current necessity and relevance of feminist ideology and activism in girls' lives (see Pomerantz et al. 2013). In the texts under analysis, there is a concurrent evocation and elision of feminism: feminist politics are available in the text if we choose to look for it, but it is not explicitly labelled or declared as such.

Some feminist scholars have defined postfeminism as a backlash against second wave feminism (Faludi 1991), while others have asserted that it is 'a more complex and elastic phenomenon' than a simple backlash can account for (Waters 2011, 4. See also Genz 2009). In her book *Gender and the Media*, Rosalind Gill suggests that within contemporary media culture, feminism and postfeminism can be thought of as 'dynamic, negotiated and in the process of ongoing transformation' (2007, 251). Judith Stacey similarly delineates postfeminism as 'the simultaneous incorporation, revision and depoliticisation of many of the central goals of second wave feminism' (1990, 339. See also McRobbie 2012). As a result of this depoliticisation, the problems that girls face are construed as individual issues rather than systemic injustices perpetrated within a patriarchal culture (Kelly and Pomerantz 2009; Pomerantz et al. 2013). Furthermore, girls are positioned as empowered 'self-determined subject[s]' who can be strong and 'have it all' (Pomerantz et al. 2013, 186 and 187), but this girl power is 'only celebrated when figured in appropriately feminine terms' (Tasker 2012, 69). Film and media theorist Yvonne Tasker goes on explicate this postfeminist conundrum:

> since conventional femininities are traditionally aligned not with strength but with passivity, malleability, and a broad willingness to sacrifice self for others, the postfeminist commitment to an imagery of strong, self-defined, sexually confident yet resolutely feminine women is potentially rife with contradiction. Indeed, what postfeminist culture deems to be signs of empowerment routinely emerges as an accommodation to, and acceptance of, a diminished role for women. (69)

The girl therefore occupies a contradictory and almost impossible space within postfeminist visual culture. She is girl-powerful and framed by narratives of freedom and choice, but she also needs to cleave to the strictures of an appropriate feminine adolescent identity in order for that power to be read as positive. As Anita Harris writes on contemporary culture's construction of the 'can-do' girl, the image represents an independent, confident, successful girl who also engages with 'glamorous consumer lifestyles' (2004, 7). The flipside of this celebration of the girl is an anxiety about the risks associated with failing to accomplish these things, and an attendant focus on monitoring and governing girlhood in order to manage such deviations. Harris shows that girlhood therefore becomes a locus for a range of cultural expectations and anxieties, encouraging girl power to be primarily channelled into individual accomplishment and material gain through conspicuous consumption. As a result, as McRobbie writes, 'the new female subject is, despite her freedom, called upon to be silent, to withhold critique in order to count as a modern, sophisticated girl' (2007, 34). The contradiction appears to centre on the fact that postfeminism evokes the feminist ideal of women's 'empowerment', but that empowerment comes to be defined in limited ways, particularly in and through narratives of individualism and consumption practices.

These contradictions are in play in several of the texts under discussion in this book. To be sure, a text such as *Gossip Girl* (Chap. 5) is invested in representing a postfeminist girlhood within a neoliberal context. The girls of *Gossip Girl* are consumers of high-end fashion, and their consumption practices and beauty regimes are represented as keys to both pleasure and empowerment. Additionally, they frequently embody a stylised hyperfemininity for their own pleasure and the pleasure of others, including men. However, their performances of feminine display through fashion are not merely or straightforwardly instances of hypersexualisation and objectification for a straight male gaze. Indeed, in many instances, they subvert this system of signification from within by creating unexpected and outrageous do-it-yourself (DIY) masquerades as well as unauthorised performances that disrupt the adult masculine authority that ordinarily governs girls' school and social lives. Within this space of subversion there is a critical distance between the girl and the masquerade, and within that gap the girls engineer a number of unruly interjections into some of the conventional constructions of heterosexual, domesticised femininity. Feminist and postfeminist impulses are at work in the text, and to borrow Gill's formulation, they are in a dynamic and negotiated relationship with each other. I remain mindful of this interplay of discourses of girlhood in each of the texts under analysis, what Renold and Ringrose refer to as the potential for simultaneous reinscription and disruption of 'the postfeminist terrain' (2008, 315). And rather than predicting that the postfeminist constructions of feminine adolescence evident in these teen texts will somehow outweigh or cancel out any moments of subversion, I posit that we take seriously the multiplicities available in the narratives under analysis, including moments of feminist politics.

My theorisation of girlhood in contemporary film and television is based on the understanding that girlhood, as an identity category, is a variable construct performed and experienced in historically, socially and culturally specific contexts. As such, girlhood is not considered as an 'essential' or 'natural' identity or experience. Girlhood studies scholar Catherine Driscoll has aptly noted that:

> girlhood is made up and girls are brought into existence in statements and knowledge about girls, and some of the most widely shared or common-sensical knowledge about girls and feminine adolescence provides some of the clearest examples of how girls are constructed by changing ways of speaking about girls. (2002, 5)

If girls are 'made up and…brought into existence in statements and knowledge about girls', then girlhood can be thought of as a field of contestations in which the limits of 'acceptable' feminine adolescence are constantly negotiated, challenged, redrawn, affirmed and destabilised by girls. Relatedly, girlhood scholar Marnina Gonick points out that it is important 'to consider the institutionalised norms that regulate the boundaries of the category as well as girls' responses to them' (2006, 122), and that girls' responses can crucially work to 're-signify' girlhood (123). Therefore, the category 'girl' is a site of meanings negotiated by the regulatory and institutionalised norms as well as by girls themselves, who respond to and frequently contest these norms. This process of negotiation and contestation between girls and 'official' knowledge about girls means that the lines drawn around the category, and what it can or cannot incorporate, are constantly being redrawn, remade, and revised.

These negotiations are present in representations of girlhood, as well as the ways in which girl spectators interact with these representations as active viewers who often engage in creative prosumerist practices that can alter or activate new meanings in the text and for girlhood (Kearney 2006; Jones 2011, 439). This two-way flow of information is important to note, as it reflects how girlhood is both regulated by adult patriarchal culture, but is also subject to girls' contestations and oppositions, both onscreen and off. I am particularly interested in how the teen screen represents girls who redraw and revise these boundaries on the teen screen by opposing the official, regulatory and institutionalised knowledges about girlhood, and how this resistance could be extended into the spectatorial realm for teen girl audiences.

Girlhood agency and the concept of 'doing girlhood' are key to this book. Agency is understood, through a poststructuralist feminist lens, as a complex process which acknowledges both the limits imposed by social forces as well as the expansive possibilities of girls' 'conscious, self-directed actions' in order to account for 'what girls say and do to accomplish girlhood within limits' (Currie et al. 2009, xvii). Currie et al. make a crucial distinction between the terms 'agency' and 'choice':

> We use the term *agency* rather than *choice*, because...the common understanding of the word *choice* tends to mask the circumstances under which people make decisions...By contrast, the word *agency* spotlights human actors and social forces simultaneously. (2009, xvii original emphases)

Agency is therefore an especially useful term through which to engage a reading of teen screen heroines as actively participating in the construction of girlhood within limits, thus allowing for an account of girlhood that is both determined and constituted in patriarchal culture, while also capable of contesting the dominant power structures of that culture. It is through this form of agency that the concept of 'doing girlhood' has arisen in girlhood studies scholarship (Curie et al. 2009). Following Judith Butler's theorisation of 'doing gender' (1999), Currie et al. argue that girls do girlhood. They write that:

> femininity...is not a pre-given identity that simply emerges in young women as they age; neither is it imprinted on them by outside forces. In other words, girls are not just slaves to consumer fashion or status competition. Girls' identities are shaped as they try out different ways of being girls in various social settings. They are active in this process; they are 'doing' girlhood. (2009, xv)

The agentic potential embedded in doing girlhood is that girls may choose a variety of performances, iterations and explorations of girlhood. In negotiating these identities, they may choose performances, iterations or explorations that unsettle the limited forms of 'acceptable' girlhood set out by adult patriarchal culture. Representations of alternative, challenging or subversive ways of doing girlhood on the teen screen offer a more expansive, agentic and empowering image of girlhood as the heroines negotiate and push against the limits of patriarchal power.

This project focuses specifically on adolescent girlhood, because it is interested in teen film and television, and the kinds of girls these texts represent. Throughout this project, I work towards the recognition of challenging, agentic, resistant and powerful iterations of girlhood on the teen screen. As Sarah Projansky argues in her book *Spectacular Girls: Media Fascination and Celebrity Culture*, it is important to 'offer an optic that makes alternative versions of girlhood visible—when we choose to look for and toward them' (2014, 10). Furthermore, the recognition of these alternative versions of girlhood identifies instances in which girls can trouble and resist the patriarchal ideology which works to exclude girls' voices and stories. Projansky asserts that this feminist optic works to 'imagine as many different versions of girlhood as possible, while remaining both critical of the denigration of girls and open to—in fact, insisting on—finding queer, antiracist, feminist girls amid U.S. media culture' (2014, 99). Because the optic has a dual ability to deconstruct the governance of girlhood *and* perceive the ruptures that unsettle this governance, it is clearly rooted in a feminist poststructuralist methodology which aims to do just this. Inspired by Projansky's optic, I utilise this methodology to look for the moments in which teen screen heroines enter a liminal zone of opposition to the status quo. The feminist optic of this book searches for and charts the transformative effects of these ruptures in narratives that ordinarily relegate girlhood to the position of subordinate object.

I focus on a range of representations of girlhood across a variety of teen screens, and consider how these different screens may produce different possibilities for the representation of feminine adolescence and girlhood spectatorship. Three of the chapters are devoted to film texts (*Red Riding Hood*, *Twilight* and *Aquamarine*) and two are devoted to television texts (*Pretty Little Liars* and *Gossip Girl*). Throughout each chapter, I analyse how other screens such as mobile phones, laptops and iPads are deployed in the diegesis of these texts, and how they are used interactively with girl spectators. Contemporary youth media is structurally distributed in highly diverse and interactive ways, encouraging an engagement across a number of platforms, media and screens. Furthermore, as media scholars such as Driscoll (2002) and Sharon Marie Ross (2008) have theorised, teen film and television is organised around an aesthetic of multiplicity through which an oscillating, distracted attentiveness is built into the text and the spectatorial positions it offers. Other theorists have emphasised the quality of sharing and distribution of both commercial and girl-made media across a range of screens, suggesting that these 'cultural commodities [are not] fixed texts but...starting points for ongoing performances' (Burwell 2010, 390). Therefore, the study of multiple teen screens acknowledges the potential for more expansive representations of girlhood, as well as girls' spectatorial practices to expand into interaction, alteration and subversive redeployments. Many contemporary girlhood studies scholars recognise this and have explored how representations of feminine adolescence have emerged across a range of screen media. This includes scholarship about the presence of girls' narratives online (see Harris 2003; Polak 2006; Black 2008; Burwell 2010), on television (see Lewis 1990; Luckett 1997; Bavidge 2004; Byers 2007), and in film (see Driscoll 2002, 2011; Kaveney 2006; Brickman 2007). Throughout this book, I want to contribute to this growing field of research by considering how these multiple screens are uniquely able to revise and transform the fairy tale's gendered relations for a contemporary teen audience.

FAIRY TALE THEMES ON TEEN SCREENS: CINEMATIC AND TELEVISUAL REVISIONS

This book explores how the fairy tale provides the grounds upon which teen screen texts stage their heroine's confrontation and resistance of patriarchal power. Throughout each chapter, I consider how canonised fairy tale narratives and themes are challenged in the contemporary screen revisions, and transformed in order to rewrite the place of the girl in narrative. As Bacchilega writes, 'postmodern revision is often two-fold, seeking to expose, make visible, the fairy tale's complicity with "exhausted" narrative and gender ideologies, and, by working from the fairy tales' multiple versions, seeking to expose, bring out, what the institutionalisation of such tales for children has forgotten or left unexploited' (1997, 50). These reworkings therefore 'do not exploit the fairy tale's magic simply to make the spell work, but rather to unmake some of its workings' (23). Folklorist Cathy Lynn Preston has similarly argued that contemporary rewritings of the fairy tale can 'break or blur the genre frame and, in doing so, variously work to maintain, reproduce, transgress, or shift the boundaries of gender associated with the older fairy-tale textual tradition' (2004, 200). This is a process of refraction and revision of the earlier texts, bending the tales towards new, potentially feminist, meanings.

The fairy tale, as Maria Tatar writes, often hinges on the dual action of prohibition and violation (2004, 1–2). For example, the young bride enters her husband's forbidden chamber in Perrault's 'Bluebeard'

([1697] 2001b); Little Red Riding Hood talks to a stranger; Sleeping Beauty touches the spindle; Cinderella disobeys her stepmother. These popular texts share a common thread in their prohibition/violation narratives: each heroine is punished with either the threat of death, a 'temporary' death such as Beauty's 100-year sleep, or at its most extreme, an actual death as in Perrault's 'Little Red Riding Hood' ([1697] 2001a). At the very least, as in 'Cinderella', the heroine's liminal transgressions are ultimately contained as she is domesticised by the narrative closure of her marriage to the Prince. In these earlier texts, the violation of prohibitions was frequently met with violent reprobation, a convention that clearly worked to contain and limit the agency and power of the female rite of passage in the fairy tale. Importantly, the heroine violates the prohibition, revealing that this patriarchal power is contingent and vulnerable to subversive transgression. However, the final narrative closure that worked to confine, demean or punish women for attempting to exercise agency reaffirmed the patriarchal power that the heroine had temporarily destabilised or subverted.

The teen films and television series analysed in this book revise the traditional prohibition/violation narrative structure of the fairy tale by emphasising the transformative capacity of liminality. Whereas in the literary fairy tales under analysis, the violation of patriarchal prohibitions was configured as a punishable and therefore negative or undesirable act, the contemporary screen texts reconfigure opposition and transgression as positively transformative, where shifts in the narrative structure open up a space for the articulation of alternative feminine voices and identities. The emphasis on teen liminality as pure possibility allows the heroines of the texts to, at least momentarily, disrupt the status quo, a shift I explain in greater detail in the next section of this introduction. In these screen texts, the fairy tale becomes a terrain of possibilities onto which alternative configurations of girlhood can be mapped, explored and charted.

One of the major revisions these teen texts offer is their revaluation of the heroine's transgression of patriarchal prohibitions, and their celebration of the oppositional energy that this feminine disobedience unleashes within the narrative. Each contemporary screen text under analysis in this book places an agentic female adolescent character or characters at its centre, and she must confront the limits placed upon her as she navigates the terrain of girlhood in a culture dominated by adult masculine values and rules. These heroines are represented as hunters (*Red*

Riding Hood), authors and media producers (*Twilight* and *Gossip Girl*), investigators (*Pretty Little Liars*) and fantastic creatures with magic powers (*Aquamarine*). This creation of powerful roles for girls to take on provides a space to imagine an alternative to the 'doubly subordinated position [of] adolescent girls' in contemporary culture (Kearney 1998, 154)—in other words, being non-adult and non-male in a culture that prioritises adult male agendas—by unsettling the binary logic that defines 'girl' as a position of passivity and weakness as opposed to power and agency.

In the teen fairy tale texts under analysis, powerful girls embark upon transformative rites of passage. During this journey the girl is repeatedly called upon to be brave and heroic, and this provides an important antidote to many canonised fairy tale's helpless damsels. Fairy tale scholar Maria Garcia writes that 'the heroic journey, embarked upon in myth by medieval knights and at the movies by airborne superheroes...the much-celebrated rites of passage [are] often reserved, in literature and cinema, for boys' (2011, 32). Indeed, many feminist scholars have noted that male rites-of-passage and adventures, male directors, and male youth cultures and audiences are frequently prioritised (Inness 1998, 1; Gateward and Pomerance 2002, 13–14; Kearney 2002, 125; Short 2006, 5). For Garcia, revisions that interject into the traditional fairy tale's limited rites of passage for girls work to 'slay the dragons of girlhood confinement', and the confinement of girls' narratives (2011, 32). I strongly concur with Garcia's position on the potential for revisions of the fairy tale, and throughout each chapter I theorise the ways in which these shattering revisions can take place on the teen screen.

Opposition and Resistance in the Liminal Realm

My interest in locating moments of opposition and resistance to the status quo is informed by Michel Foucault's poststructuralist work on power and transgression. In his work, Foucault investigates the transformative capacity of disobedience within the network of power. He writes that 'power is employed and exercised through a net-like organisation. And not only do individuals circulate between its threads; they are always in the position of simultaneously undergoing and exercising this power' (1980, 98). In *The History of Sexuality (Vol. 1)*, Foucault asserts that:

where there is power, there is resistance, and yet, or rather consequently, this resistance is never in a position of exteriority in relation to power… These points of resistance are present everywhere in the power network. Hence there is no single locus of great Refusal, no soul of revolt, source of all rebellions, or pure law of the revolutionary. Instead there is a plurality of resistances, each of them a special case…the points, knots, or focuses of resistance are spread over time and space at varying densities, at times mobilising groups or individuals in a definitive way, inflaming certain points of the body, certain moments in life, certain types of behaviour. ([1976] 1980, 95–96)

Throughout this book, I redeploy Foucault's model of power and resistance in order to examine the ways in which teen screen heroines negotiate regulatory networks of power, and act upon those networks of power through resistant and oppositional means. If, as Foucault suggests, 'points of resistance are present everywhere in the power network', then it is vitally important to look for them everywhere, even in such places as girls' mainstream media texts where dominant power may at first appear untroubled.

The Foucauldian poststructuralist theorisation of power is useful in the context of a feminist analysis of girlhood on the screen. If the power network is not simply a monolithic hierarchical structure, and rather a field open to contestation and resistance, then girls can be understood as agents of power too, acting upon and contributing to the terrain of girlhood and the power relations that define it. Following Foucault, girlhood scholar Shauna Pomerantz notes that power is 'a fluid and relational process' rather than 'just a tool of coercion and subjugation', allowing for a critical understanding that 'girls can never be merely powerless in their engagement with cultural forms' (2008, 37). Pomerantz argues that feminism pushes poststructuralism 'in new directions, working to infuse [its] deconstructive aspects with a critique of gender as it intersects with race, ethnicity, class, and sexuality' (25). My redeployment of Foucault's poststructuralist methodology, like Pomerantz's, argues that representations of girls onscreen do not simply depict them as powerless, vulnerable victims at the mercy of 'bad' cultural influences—they interact with, challenge and push up against those cultural forms, exerting power too, enacting the resistance that Foucault describes as central to the power network.

In combination with Foucault's theorisation of opposition, I also invoke anthropologist Victor Turner's work on liminality as an oppositional zone. While Turner's work was originally concerned with structuralism, his work has more recently been appropriated and redeployed within poststructuralist theory. As Iver Neumann writes, Turner's work on inter- and antistructure is now being used to explore poststructuralist concepts of hybrids, margins and borders, the carnivalesque, and transversality (2012, 474). Neumann further elaborates that this signals a shift within Turnerian theory, which has moved away from the study of 'structure as ordering' and towards the poststructuralist study of 'structure as productive of margins and marginalised agents' and 'discursive margins or borderlines or boundaries and the processes and states of being one may find there' (474). Through a focus on liminal performativity, masquerade, play, margins, marginality and rupture, I hope to contribute to this poststructuralist reworking of Turner's theorisation of the liminal phase of the rite-of-passage narrative.

Anthropologist Arnold van Gennep (1960) described the rite of passage as a tripartite structure consisting of separation, transformation and incorporation. Turner elaborated on van Gennep's work and particularly emphasised the second phase, transformation or the liminal, as particularly important. As Turner writes, the pre- and postliminal belong to the regulated, structured social world, while the liminal is 'an interstructural situation' (1967, 93),[4] where one is 'neither here nor there…betwixt and between the positions assigned and arrayed by law, custom, convention, and ceremon[y]' (1977, 95). This interstructure represents a threshold or margin, a space and time situated on the edge of dominant culture, which provokes the subject of the rite of passage to question, transgress and even transform 'all the customary categories' (1967, 97) set out by the status quo. The liminal is a threshold at which hierarchies of the dominant order break down, so it is a promising concept for feminist appropriation. Because the liminal operates in the gaps or fissures, in the 'betwixt and between' (Turner 1977, 95), it is a site where conventional boundaries and hierarchies dissolve, giving way to an unsettling of the status quo. In the context of the girl's rite-of-passage narrative, the liminal represents the adolescent's phase prior to her induction into the relative stability of normative adult femininity. I locate my attention in this interstructural moment, because it's here that the teen heroines experiment with alternative and frequently oppositional ways of doing girlhood.

The passage from liminality to postliminality is an important aspect of the rite-of-passage structure. This passage represents a return to and reintegration into conventional culture. Turner's work illuminates the transformative potential of this passage. He writes that there is 'an intimate bond' (1969, 202) or 'dialectic' (203) between these two phases of the rite of passage, and that the changes made in liminality can seep back into conventional culture, making it possible 'to proceed in different directions and at different speeds in a new bout of movement' (202). Turner elaborates that liminality encourages 'periodical reclassifications of reality and man's [sic] relationship to society, nature, and culture. But they are more than classifications, since they incite men [sic] to action as well as to thought' (128–129). In this way, Turner regards society and culture as a 'process' in which the liminal and postliminal feed into and transform one another over and over (203). Jill Morawaski's work on the relevance of the liminal for feminism points the powerful capacity for the liminal as a 'yet to be settled' zone to open up 'promising actions of disobedience' (1994, 2 original emphasis). In this disobedience, Morawski argues, one can 'find where the boundaries [of the dominant order] can be moved or eliminated' (3), therefore creating post-liminal 'opportunities for substantive change in existing social arrangements' (54). Following Morawski's lead, I want to explore the yet-to-be-settled zones of feminine adolescence within narrative, and to assess the extent to which their disruptive energies can allow for representations of alternative and challenging femininities. Furthermore, I ask whether or to what extent the stories show the heroines enacting substantive social change beyond the liminal portion of the rite-of-passage narrative, when the girl reintegrates into conventional society in the postliminal.

Feminist screen theorists such as Laura Mulvey (1989), Kathleen Rowe (1995) have appropriated the concept of liminality as a way to identify moments in narrative that disrupt the dominant patriarchal order, and I take their foundational work on this topic as my starting point for theorising liminality on the teen screen. Turner's work on liminality was not feminist, nor did it address the issue of feminism; however, it provides a foundation for feminists to theorise how ruptures in dominant representational systems and narratives may occur. Mulvey's article 'Changes: Thoughts on Myth, Narrative and Historical Experience' redeploys van Gennep's tripartite rite-of-passage structure in order to theorise the liminal moments in cinematic narrative that represent 'an almost invisible breeding ground for a language of protest and resistance' and how this 'unformed language…can then develop its own signifying space' (169). Mulvey points out that narrative resembles van Gennep's tripartite structure, with the narrative's beginning and ending representative of the stability and order of the pre- and postliminal, and the middle section of the narrative representative of liminality. She writes:

> the desire and excess that characterise the middle phase of narrative represent a collectively acknowledged, but unspeakable, conflict with the codes of law that define and contain the normal course of life. This phase celebrates transgressive desire and organises it into a stylised cultural form: narrative. Just as the middle section erupts into action with disorder, so the end must integrate disorder back into stability. (170)

The liminal is a gap in the status quo that can articulate that which is 'unspeakable' and in doing so can 'develop its own signifying space'— an alterative space on the margins of the dominant narrative order that carves out a new mode of signification and representation that can in turn oppose and unsettle the status quo. While the transgressive disorder of the liminal is ultimately contained by resolution and closure, Mulvey crucially observes the potential for the liminal phase of transformation to impact upon and shift the boundaries of dominant culture in the postliminal closure—that the 'abnormal' is 'absorb[ed]…back into a sense of order that is altered but still recognisably subject to the law' (170). Therefore, Mulvey reveals that liminal moments in narrative are 'politically significant' (175) because they 'could provide the basis for change' (174) that impact upon gender relations within patriarchal cultural representations. In other words, the 'abnormal' elements produced in the liminal period are reabsorbed back into the dominant order and therefore permeate, impact upon and therefore transform it in some way. In the texts under analysis, this impact in the postliminal phase is most clearly seen in the heroines' ability to maintain aspects of the alternative feminine identities they experimented with in the liminal zone; create networks of support and solidarity between girls; and organise effective action against gendered inequality in their social worlds.

The postliminal often represents the containment of woman within the patriarchal order, what Rowe succinctly describes as 'the impulse toward social integration and renewal—by narrating the story of the woman's successful accommodation to heterosexuality and her acceptance of her proper place in the patriarchy' (1995, 210). However, in her brilliant study of women and laughter in film comedies, Rowe also identifies the liminal and carnivalesque moments in women's screen texts that disrupt this patriarchal narrative,[5] and which often emerge in representations of 'transgression and inversion, disguise and masquerade, sexual reversals, the deflation of ideals, and the levelling of hierarchies' (9). Rowe argues that it is in these disruptive, liminal moments that the power of the unruly woman as a 'site of insurgency' asserts itself most forcefully (48). The unruly woman is a figure of excess, disorder and spectacle, often characterised by an excessive appetite (both for food and sex), disruptive joke telling and laughing, and her desire to dominate men (31). In these unruly interjections that oppose woman's so-called 'proper place' in patriarchal culture, an alternative and more powerful place is made available for the feminine figure to occupy. Mulvey's theorisation of liminality in narrative and Rowe's analysis of the unruly woman provides a foundation for my analysis of oppositional and resistant girls and the feminist potential of the liminal. Rowe's assertion of the unruliness of female visual spectacle, mocking laughter and disruptive, crude joke telling particularly inform Chaps. 5 and 6 of the book.

Across every teen screen text under analysis in this book, these moments of opposition create an alternative language of feminine adolescence that articulates girlhood as a powerful subject position. The liminal zone that each heroine enters provides a temporary escape route from the 'dilemma facing girls in a world where men hold the central if not the exclusive access to the position of subject' (Driscoll 2002, 31). Here, the girl deploys this language to oppose her place as object in patriarchal culture and claim the position of powerful subject. Turner argues that the liminal zone incorporates a 'liminal vocabulary' (1977, 37). This is a metalanguage, 'devised for the purpose of talking *about* the various languages of everyday, and in which mundane axioms become problematic, up for speculative grabs' (45 original emphasis). Turner suggests that the liminal can foster a language that not only questions the discourse of the dominant order, but also articulates a language that exceeds the boundaries of the status quo that can express alternative ways of being. Speaking from the place of the liminal, therefore, is a process of deconstruction where the 'various languages of everyday' are disarticulated and remade in 'speculative grabs' for new meanings, new ways of speaking. Redeploying Turner's concept of this vocabulary from a feminist perspective, this book theorises a screen language of teen girlhood that is expressed in liminal narrative moments. In these moments, the girl heroines articulate their opposition to the status quo. Therefore, liminal language is highly self-reflexive in that it talks back to the dominant power that is ordinarily 'accepted unthinkingly' (Turner 1967, 105), and also deeply transformative in that it finds ways to exceed the dominant order and express something entirely new. For example, the language of girl-as-subject is articulated visually, in the construction of the girl as the subject of a powerful and critical gaze in each text. By looking back at the male gaze that objectifies her, the heroine critically reflects on her position in patriarchal culture. She then opposes it by reversing the dominant terms of the gaze, which ordinarily serves masculine desires and fantasies, allowing these teen texts to generate new formal screen structures and aesthetics that articulate an active and authoritative feminine adolescent subject position. This liminal feminine adolescent language therefore carves out gaps within patriarchal visual culture to generate alternative images of femininity and spectatorial positions for women and girls to potentially occupy. The contemporary feminist stake in this new screen language of girlhood is clear: in its oppositional articulations it unsettles the structures that support patriarchal visual culture's objectification of girls and women to make way for alternative femininities on screen.

Writers such as Adrian Martin (1994), Driscoll (2002, 2011) have described the presence of liminality in teen film. For example, Martin writes that 'teen stories are about...the liminal experience: that intense, suspended moment between yesterday and tomorrow, between childhood and adulthood, between being a nobody and a somebody, when everything is in question, and anything is possible' (68). While Martin's description works well for identifying how rebellion and experimentation are represented on the teen screen, the political impact of this onscreen liminality has been undertheorised. In particular, I explicate what is at stake for feminism in teen screen liminality. A central inquiry for this book is: if narratives of girlhood-as-liminal give representational space to opposition, what kind of rupturing effect can this have on the way dominant regulatory discourses of girlhood limit and diminish the ways in which girls are represented on screen?

Foucauldian sociologist Nancy Lesko correctly points out that the adolescent is often regulated by a 'panoptical time' during which 'progress, precocity, arrest, or decline' are closely monitored by parents, teachers, medical professionals and so on (2001, 41). Mary Celeste Kearney calls this the 'colonisation of youth by adults; that is, the surveillance, regulation, and containment of their movements through time and space' (1998, 153). These feminist poststructuralist scholars have also shown that gendered discourses govern and shape the girl's rite of passage in limiting ways. The teen screen texts under analysis narrativise a liminal passage that temporarily relieves the heroines of these regulatory limits set out by patriarchal culture, carving out a space for exceeding or rupturing these constraints. The field of girlhood is therefore represented as more expansive and malleable during the liminal phase, and this in turn produces all kinds of new and alternative representations of the girl. In my redeployment of Turner's conceptualisation of liminality and Foucault's work on power and transgression, I consider the political potential of screen representations of girlhood as liminal. These heroines temporarily occupy a space and time characterised by a breakdown of conventional adult patriarchal hierarchy, authority and power, creating an aperture or gap in the status quo.

I am interested in charting the potential for girls' expressions of opposition, and the corrosive effects of these ruptures on patriarchal constructions of femininity. Close textual analysis comparing the literary tales and the film and television revisions provides the grounds for exploring how this rupture and transformation occurs in the contemporary texts. I argue that the formal elements of these teen screen texts are politically charged, as they destabilise and rework the gendered discourses embedded in the earlier fairy tale texts. I embrace a formal analysis of teen screen texts, and I argue for the political potency of the images and sounds under analysis as articulations of an alternative language of girlhood. My deployment of a feminist optic is similar to that of Projansky's, outlined earlier, but differs in relation to where I choose to focus it. While we are both interested in narratives about girlhood, I specifically redeploy Projansky's optic to read teen screen aesthetics and formal structures. Though Projansky's optic does not analyse this aspect of the teen screen, I argue that in the texts under analysis, feminist politics are discernible in their formal composition and structure. I look for moments of liminal rupture in their pretty, spectacular and excessive visual aesthetics, and map how the heroines use these elements to corrode adult, patriarchal rules and regulations. I believe that using the feminist optic in the new context of the study of liminal rupture will illuminate how contemporary representations of teen girlhood include instances of feminist communitas and solidarity; noncompliance and protest; and an expansion of the limits placed on feminine adolescence into new territories of empowerment. In short, I deploy a feminist optic to look for the ways in which the heroines of these texts subversively use these aesthetics to register their refusal to engage in some of the limiting, hegemonic rituals of girlhood, and replace them with more oppositional and disruptive liminal rituals.

Central to this book is a close formal analysis of the teen screen's prettiness, and its potential for articulating political content as a counterdiscourse that challenges the authority of the male gaze and masculine point of view. I investigate the formal elements of the pretty design of objects and spectacular *mise en scènes* (Chaps. 3, 4, 5 and 6), girls' voices and voice-overs (Chaps. 2 and 6) and fashion spectacle (Chaps. 5 and 6). Particularly inspired by Rosalind Galt's work on prettiness in art cinema (2011), I theorise instances of a pretty teen screen aesthetic that is a site of subversion which enacts an unsettling of patriarchal visual culture. Most of the major studies on teen film and television have not addressed the matter of pretty aesthetics, and when it has been it is often regarded with suspicion (see de Vaney 2002; Fox-Kales 2011). Indeed, this aspect of teen film and television is often considered antifeminist, with its supposed exclusive focus on the cosmetic, the fashionable and the glamorous (Fox-Kales 2011). This certainly may be the case in some instances of teen film and television, and a feminist deconstruction of how sexism and patriarchal power operate in these images is vitally important. However, wholesale rejection of this aesthetic devalues girl culture's feminine objects of choice, thus serving to perpetuate the conventional binary of 'good' masculine texts and tastes versus 'bad' feminine texts and tastes.

Furthermore, such a wholesale rejection of the pretty fails to perceive its potential to trouble the very power structure that, at first glance, it may appear to rely upon or support. Galt writes that the pretty cinematic image occupies a 'consistent space of exclusion' (2011, 8). She writes that:

> the modern history of anti-pretty aesthetics associates noble beauty and value with the male Western subject, inscribing a devalued feminine, queer, and foreign subject into the language of the decorative image. Discourses of primitivism, effeminacy, and orientalism work, often in combination, to map out a geopolitics of aesthetic disdain...to understand how the terrain of the excluded pretty offers rich soil for a radical aesthetics. Filmmakers

attuned to the political and aesthetic languages of exclusion turn to pretty styles to speak otherwise about their own place in the world. (300)

Derided and undervalued in cultural discourse and film theory, Galt illuminates how the pretty is frequently framed by 'a suspicion of the image per se' and how 'this debate allows all orientations except that of being political *in* the image. My account of the feminist pretty seeks to fill this gap by proposing a politics not based in feminine positionality, but in a perverse counteraesthetics of the desirable image' (256 original emphasis). Arguing for a feminist 'recuperative valuation' of this aesthetic (257), Galt reveals how 'the elements of mise-en-scene can work on embedded histories of gendered and raced representations *at the formal level*' (141 original emphasis). Throughout this book, I consider how the heroines of the texts under analysis deploy oppositional strategies of excess and prettiness that pervert and unsettle patriarchal visual culture's constructions of desirable femininity. The pretty becomes a counter-discourse from its 'space of exclusion', redeployed by the heroines to create images that disrupt the gendered terms of patriarchal imagery of girlhood, subverting the discourse from within. Through the pretty's capacity to unsettle this dominant imagery and structures of the gaze, a new visual language of feminine adolescent subjectivity, resistance and empowerment can be articulated.

My theorisation of the political potential of these filmic and televisual elements draws on the work of Jean-Luc Comolli and Jean Narboni, who argued that some films are able to 'throw up obstacles in the way of the ideology, causing it to swerve and get off course' ([1969] 2004, 817). They listed seven categories of film's relation to ideology, dubbing these more politically progressive films as examples of 'category "e"' (817). These films, 'which seem at first sight to belong firmly within the ideology and to be completely under its sway', create gaps and fissures that corrode ideology and 'end up by partially dismantling the system from within' (817). The films and television series that I analyse offer glimpses or moments of opposition through visual and aural excesses. Dominant structures need to maintain an illusion of naturalness, of being self-evident, in order to maintain their power and avoid opposition; indeed, as Kearney so succinctly states, this power 'organises and maintains itself through our complicity in systems of normalisation and regulation' (2010, 6). The visual and aural strategies of excess deployed by the heroines of these texts therefore momentarily disrupt conventional constructions of girlhood by showing them up, exposing and rupturing their artifice through spectacular performances of excess and prettiness. In so doing, the heroines all take the opportunity to oppose the power of the dominant.

THE CHAPTERS

Each textual analysis chapter analyses a particular traditional fairy tale and a contemporary teen screen counterpart, exploring how traditional fairy tale gender roles and narratives are demythologised and disenchanted in these contemporary teen screen revisions, and how this work of deconstruction opens the fairy tale up to new feminist narrative paths. Chapter 2's analysis of Catherine Hardwicke's *Red Riding Hood* explores the liminal zone as a narrow margin of feminine adolescent opposition. I argue that the film's audiovisual language creates a revisionary female subjective gaze and voice through the deployment of point-of-view shots and omniscient voice-over narration, and that these interventions into both sound and image reconfigure the 'Little Red Riding Hood' narrative to resignify the girl as subject, not object, of the narrative. My theorisation of voice-over and the girl's subjective point-of-view shot argues that the film disrupts the traditional demarcations of masculine authority over cinematic image and sound, carving out space for an audiovisual language of feminine adolescent subjectivity and authority to dominate the text. Perrault and Grimm's patriarchal narratives of female victimisation are altered as a result of Valerie's escape from conventional culture, transforming herself into a hunter who slays the wolf, and an errant traveller who occupies the 'ultraliminal' space of the forest as she protests against and breaks free of the confines of the domestic. This restores agency to the heroine and revalues straying from the path as a positive, liberating move.

Chapter 3 continues to explore the margin of liminality through an analysis of fantasy and dream sequences in another Hardwicke film, *Twilight*. I consider the passage between liminality and postliminality, and what kind of impact the former can have on the latter in the teen film rite-of-passage narrative. By examining Bella's slow-motion 'Sleeping Beauty' fantasy constructions with Edward cast as Beauty, I argue that the heroine of this contemporary text crafts a temporary unsettled zone that ruptures the narrative of feminine acculturation. In this liminal interval, Bella is able to adopt an alternative girlhood identity as author of the fantasies, active desiring gazer and protestor against her subordinate position within dominant culture. While Perrault's Beauty was represented as a passive figure trapped by time and secured as an eroticised object for the Prince's desiring gaze, Bella generates fantasy sequences that revise the gendered terms of this earlier text through her alterations to both time and image. Bella's construction of languorous temporality in her fantasy sequences opposes the panoptical time of adult patriarchal culture, which closely monitors and regulates 'normal' or 'acceptable' progress in the feminine rite of passage.

I also argue that in liminality, Bella's creation of prettified fantasy images of Edward as Beauty, which align his figure with sparkles, lace, porcelain skin and perfectly coiffed hair, allows her to temporarily refuse the male gaze and patriarchal culture's objectification of girls, and to ascend into the role of subject and holder of the desiring gaze. To explicate the importance of this imagery, I begin theorising a teen screen pretty capable of articulating political content. Through an analysis of these points of excess in the temporality and imagery of Bella's liminal fantasies, I identify instances of an alternative, oppositional, agentic, girlhood subjectivity in *Twilight*. Furthermore, I argue that the empowerment that Bella finds in these fantasy moments continued to create an impact beyond the fantasy realm: in the passage from liminality to her postliminal reality as wife and mother, Bella retains a measure of this agency in her transformation into a powerful vampire. The liminal margin is a time and space that not only provides an opportunity for the expression of an oppositional feminine adolescent subjectivity, but also allows these expressions of power to impact and create positive change within conventional culture in the passage to postliminality.

In Chap. 4, I further my argument about the political potential of theorising liminality for a feminist agenda with an analysis of communitas in the ABC Family television series *Pretty Little Liars*. The series revises Perrault's 'Bluebeard' narrative by depicting a communitas of teen sleuths who investigate multiple Bluebeard figures. I theorise a collective, scrutinising girls' gaze that interrogates the systemic violence and exploitation committed against girls and women within patriarchal culture. This gaze is intensely deconstructive, breaking the crime scene down and isolating each piece of evidence for close collaborative inspection. Through a deconstruction of the evidence in Bluebeard's forbidden chamber, the heroines are prompted to intervene into instances of patriarchal abuses of power, and to construct a counter-discourse to the official narrative about their friend's disappearance. This discourse is transmitted covertly amongst members of the communitas via pretty girl culture objects. Through their subversive deployment of the pretty, the contemporary 'Bluebeard' heroines are prompted to take collective action against perpetrators of violence against girls and women. As an aesthetic that not only exposes misogyny, but also provokes a response of female solidarity and action against it, the pretty becomes political, and a site of feminist intervention into patriarchal culture. The power of this language of feminine adolescent communication is clear: it continues to impact dominant culture beyond the liminal zone when the identity of each Bluebeard is revealed and held accountable for his crimes against girls and women.

Chapter 5 continues to explore the theme of liminal communitas, shifting the emphasis to representations of girls who collectively produce multiple alternative feminine adolescent identities. While *Pretty Little Liars* provides a representation of girls confronting and interrogating patriarchal power, *Gossip Girl* depicts its heroines attempting to fashion alternatives to this dominant power structure. I analyse *Gossip Girl's* revision of the 'Cinderella' tale, with a particular focus on the heroines' collective and spectacular displays of public liminality and rituals of status elevation through their use of masquerade and unauthorised deployments of DIY dress. The revision of the heroine's relation to the sartorial intervenes into the sexist politics of Perrault's fairy tale; in the contemporary revision, subversive uses of dress secure the heroine's access to the city streets and the economic marketplace, exceeding the confines of patriarchal power that define the heroine's journey in Perrault's tale. *Gossip Girl* presents a narrative in which girls can, at times, reject traditional and conservative configurations of femininity and instead expand the territory of girlhood into alternative zones. I examine how liminality provides an unsettled zone where girls can negotiate multiple, fluid and flexible girlhood identities that refuse to accommodate conventional feminine identities and reject the heterosexual romance as central to their fulfilment. The heroines become 'queens' or rulers of their social worlds, businesspeople, creators of all-girl street cultures and authors of creative online texts. I look for instances of liminal, performative excess in the text that unsettle the patriarchal politics of emphasised femininity, and open up a space for girlhood identities to emerge.

In Chap. 6, I return full circle to Chap. 2's theorisation of the fantasy of permanent or ultraliminality. While Valerie's escape to the ultraliminal realm of the forest in *Red Riding Hood* allows her to escape conventional culture and embrace an unconventional girlhood identity, the mermaids of *Aquamarine* enter into the ultraliminal zone of the ocean, which comes to represent a fluid field of expansive possibilities in which the heroines explore alternative ways of doing girlhood. Furthermore, because the heroines enter this space as a communitas, the opportunities for articulations of noncompliance are even greater. The film's revision of Andersen's 'The Little Mermaid' creates a liminal language of feminine adolescent protest against the feminine passivity and compulsory investment in heterosexual romance that the earlier text inscribed. The film restores the agency of voice to the mermaid, and in this restoration of agency the contemporary mermaids articulate their opposition to the patriarchal power that silenced their literary predecessor. This language of protest is expressed through shouting, singing and explosive laughter at the rituals and codes of hegemonic girlhood. I theorise this feminine adolescent language as an unruly expression, a way of talking back to the way girls are spoken into existence in patriarchal culture. These expressions created an important distance between patriarchal language and the girls, and that this distance constitutes a resistant space for the girls to critically reflect on and resist the modes of femininity it encodes. In each text under analysis, fairy tale narratives and conventions are deconstructed and then transformed to tell innovative stories about feminine adolescence on the teen screen, expanding the terrain of girlhood into new territories of agency, power and resistance.

NOTES

1. *Sabrina the Teenage Witch* moved from the ABC network to The CW in the year 2000.
2. *Buffy the Vampire Slayer* moved from the WB network to UPN in 2001.
3. See Jack Zipes (2011) for an example of this. In his book *The Enchanted Screen*, he tends to read 'mainstream' of the fairy tale as conventional, and more independent productions having the potential to offer a progressive rewriting of the tales.
4. Turner refers to liminality as both interstructural and antistructural throughout his many works on the subject. His earlier work, for example *The Forest of Symbols* (1967), referred to liminality exclusively as 'interstructural', while later works such as *The Ritual Process* (1969) and *Dramas, Fields and Metaphors* (1974) use both terms to describe liminality. As Turner began to adopt this new position on instances of liminality

as potentially both interstructural and antistructural, his work was able to explore the more disruptive, subversive and potentially transformative capacity of the liminal, allowing his theorisation to take on a political dimension.

5. Rowe's use of the term 'carnivalesque', in conjunction with Turner's definition of liminality, is derived from Mikhail Bakhtin's work on carnival, and its attendant elements of laughter, rites, festivals and play in the literary work of Rabelais. Bakhtin emphasised that these elements were 'outside officialdom' (1984, 6) and allowed for 'the suspension of all hierarchical precedence' which 'created…a special type of communication impossible in everyday life' (10). However, I focus primarily on Turner's construction of liminality and the play and experimentation made available in this zone because it relates more clearly to the transitory adolescent rite of passage. Meanwhile, carnivalesque is used in reference to experiences of festivals and calendrical rituals.

BIBLIOGRAPHY

Andersen, Hans Christian. [1837] 2008. The Little Mermaid. In *The Annotated Hans Christian Andersen,* trans. Maria Tatar and ed. Maria Tatar and Julie K. Allen, 119–155. New York and London: W.W. Norton and Co.

———. [1845] 2008. The Snow Queen. In *The Annotated Hans Christian Andersen,* trans. Maria Tatar and ed. Maria Tatar and Julie K. Allen, 17–69. New York and London: W.W. Norton and Co.

Atwood, Margaret. [1983] 1986. Bluebeard's Egg. In *Don't Bet on the Prince: Contemporary Fairy Tales in North America and England,* ed. Jack Zipes, 160–182. New York: Routledge.

Bacchilega, Cristina. 1997. *Postmodern Fairy Tales: Gender and Narrative Strategies.* Philadelphia: University of Pennsylvania Press.

———. 2008. Extrapolation from Nalo Hopkinson's *Skin Folk*: Reflections on Transformation and Recent English-Language Fairy-Tale Fiction by Women. In *Contemporary Fiction and the Fairy Tale,* ed. Stephen Benson, 178–203. Detroit, MI: Wayne State University Press.

———. 2013. *Fairy Tales Transformed? Twenty-First-Century Adaptations and the Politics of Wonder.* Detroit, MI: Wayne State University Press.

Bakhtin, Mikhail. 1984. *Rabelais and His World,* trans. Hélène Iswolsky. Bloomington: Indiana University Press.

Bavidge, Jenny. 2004. Chosen Ones: Reading the Contemporary Teen Heroine. In *Teen TV: Genre, Consumption, Identity,* ed. Glyn Davis and Kay Dickinson, 41–53. London: BFI Publishing.

Black, Rebecca W. 2008. *Adolescents and Online Fan Fiction.* New York: Peter Lang.

Brickman, Barbara Jane. 2007. Coming of Age in the 1970s: Revision, Fantasy, and Rage in the Teen-Girl Badlands. *Camera Obscura* 22 (3): 25–59. doi:10.1215/02705346-2007-014.

Burwell, Catherine. 2010. Rewriting the Script: Toward a Politics of Young People's Digital Media Participation. *The Review of Education, Pedagogy, and Cultural Studies* 32: 382–402. doi:10.1080/10714413.2010.510354.

Butler, Judith. 1999. *Gender Trouble: Feminism and the Subversion of Identity.* New York: Routledge.

Byers, Michelle. 2007. Gender/Sexuality/Desire: Subversion of Difference and Construction of Loss in the Adolescent Drama of *My So-Called Life.* In *Dear Angela: Remembering My So-Called Life,* ed. Michelle Byers and David Lavery, 13–34. London: Lexington Books.

Carter, Angela. 1979. *The Bloody Chamber and Other Stories.* London: Gollancz.

Comolli, Jean-Louis and Jean Narboni. [1969] 2004. Cinema/Ideology/Criticism. In *Film Theory and Criticism: Introductory Readings,* ed. Leo Braudy and Marshall Cohen, 812–819. New York: Oxford University Press.

Currie, Dawn H., Deirdre M. Kelly, and Shauna Pomerantz. 2009. *'Girl Power': Girls Reinventing Girlhood.* New York: Peter Lang.

De Vaney, Ann. 2002. Pretty in Pink? John Hughes Reinscribes Daddy's Girl in Homes and Schools. In *Sugar, Spice and Everything Nice: Cinemas of Girlhood,* ed. Murray Pomerance and Frances Gateward, 201–215. Detroit, MI: Wayne State University Press.

Donoghue, Emma. 1997. *Kissing the Witch: Old Tales in New Skins,* 1–10. New York: Harper Collins.

Driscoll, Catherine. 2002. *Girls: Feminine Adolescence in Popular Culture and Cultural Theory.* New York: Columbia University Press.

———. 2011. *Teen Film: A Critical Introduction.* Oxford and New York: Berg.

Faludi, Susan. 1991. *Backlash: The Undeclared War Against American Women.* New York: Crown.

Foucault, Michel. 1980. *The History of Sexuality,* vol. One. London: Penguin.

Fox-Kales, Emily. 2011. *Body Shots: Hollywood and the Culture of Eating Disorders.* Albany: State University of New York Press.

Galt, Rosalind. 2011. *Pretty: Film and the Decorative Image.* New York and Chichester: Columbia University Press.

Garcia, Maria. 2011. Rewriting Fairy Tales, Revisiting Female Identity: An Interview with Catherine Breillat. *Cineaste* 36 (3): 32–35.

Gateward, Frances, and Murray Pomerance. 2002. Introduction. In *Sugar, Spice and Everything Nice: Cinemas of Girlhood,* ed. Frances Gateward and Murray Pomerance, 13–21. Detroit, MI: Wayne State University Press.

Gennep, Arnold van. 1960. *The Rites of Passage.* trans. Monika B. Vizedom and Gabrielle L. Caffee. London and Henley: Routledge and Kegan Paul.

Genz, Stéphanie. 2009. *Postfemininities in Popular Culture*. Hampshire Basingstoke and New York: Palgrave Macmillan.

Gill, Rosalind. 2007. *Gender and the Media*. Cambridge: Polity Press.

Gonick, Marnina. 2006. Sugar and Spice and Something More Than Nice? Queer Girls and Transformations of Social Exclusion. In *Girlhood: Redefining the Limits*, ed. Yasmin Jiwani, Candis Steenbergen, and Claudia Mitchell, 122–137. Montreal, New York and London: Black Rose Books.

Greenhill, Pauline, and Jill Terry Rudy. 2014. Channelling Wonder: Fairy Tales, Television, and Intermediality. In *Channelling Wonder: Fairy Tales on Television*, ed. Pauline Greenhill and Jill Terry Rudy, 1–21. Detroit, MI: Wayne State University Press.

Greenhill, Pauline and Sidney Eve Matrix. 2010. Envisioning Ambiguity: Fairy Tale Films. In *Fairy Tale Films: Visions of Ambiguity*, ed. Pauline Greenhill and Sidney Eve Matrix, 1–22. Denver: University Press of Colorado.

Grimm, Jacob and Wilhelm Grimm. [1812] 2001. Rapunzel. In *The Great Fairy Tale Tradition: From Straparola and Basile to the Brothers Grimm*, trans. and ed. Jack Zipes, 489–491. New York and London: W.W. Norton and Co.

———. [1857] 2001. Little Red Cap. In *The Great Fairy Tale Tradition: From Straparola and Basile to the Brothers Grimm*, trans. and ed. Jack Zipes, 747–750. New York and London: W.W. Norton and Co.

Harris, Anita. 2003. gURL Scenes and Grrrl Zines: The Regulation and Resistance of Girls in Late Modernity. *Feminist Review* 75: 38–56. http://www.jstor.org/stable/1395861.

———. 2004. *Future Girl: Young Women in the Twenty-First Century*. New York: Routledge.

Heatwole, Alexandra. 2016. Disney Girlhood: Princess Generations and Once Upon a Time. *Studies in Humanities* 43 (1): 1–19.

Inness, Sherrie A. 1998. Introduction. In *Delinquents and Debutantes: Twentieth-Century American Girls' Cultures*, ed. Sherrie A. Inness, 1–15. New York and London: New York University Press.

Jones, Leisha. 2011. Contemporary Bildungsromans and the Prosumer Girl. *Criticism* 53 (3): 439–469.

Kaveney, Roz. 2006. *Teen Dreams: Reading Teen Film from Heathers to Veronica Mars*. London and New York: I.B. Tauris.

Kearney, Mary Celeste. 1998. Producing Girls: Rethinking the Study of Female Youth Culture. In *Delinquents and Debutantes: Twentieth-Century American Girls' Cultures*, ed. Sherrie A. Inness, 285–310. New York and London: New York University Press.

———. 2002. Girlfriends and Girl Power: Female Adolescence in Contemporary U.S. Cinema. In *Sugar, Spice, and Everything Nice: Cinemas of Girlhood*, ed. Frances Gateward and Murray Pomerance, 125–142. Detroit, MI: Wayne State University Press.

———. 2006. *Girls Make Media*. New York and London: Routledge.

———. 2010. Pink Technology: Mediamaking Gear for Girls. *Camera Obscura* 25 (2): 1–38. doi:10.1215/02705346-2010-001.

Kelly, Deirdre M. and Shauna Pomerantz. 2009. Mean, Wild, and Alienated: Girls and the State of Feminism in Popular Culture. *Girlhood Studies* 2 (1): 1–19. doi:10.3167/ghs.2009.020102.

Lesko, Nancy. 2001. Time Matters in Adolescence. In *Governing the Child in the New Millennium*, ed. Kenneth Hultqvist and Gunilla Dahlberg, 35–67. New York and London: RoutledgeFalmer.

Lewis, Lisa A. 1990. Consumer Girl Culture: How Music Video Appeals to Girls. In *Television and Women's Culture: The Politics of the Popular*, ed. Mary Ellen Brown, 89–113. London: Sage.

Luckett, Moya. 1997. Girl Watchers: Patty Duke and Teen TV. In *The Revolution Wasn't Televised: Sixties Television and Social Conflict*, ed. Lynn Spigel and Michael Curtin, 95–116. New York and London: Routledge.

Martin, Adrian. 1994. *Phantasms: The Dreams and Desires at the Heart of our Popular Culture*. Victoria: McPhee Gribble.

McRobbie, Angela. 2007. Postfeminism and Popular Culture: Bridget Jones and the New Gender Regime. In *Interrogating Postfeminism: Gender and the Politics of Popular Culture*, ed. Yvonne Tasker and Diane Negra, 27–39. Durham, NC: Duke University Press.

McRobbie, Angela. 2012. *The Aftermath of Feminism: Gender, Culture and Social Change*. London and Los Angeles, CA: Sage.

Morawski, Jill G. 1994. *Practicing Feminism, Reconstructing Psychology: Notes on a Liminal Science*. Ann Arbor: The University of Michigan Press.

Mulvey, Laura. 1989. Changes: Thoughts on Myth, Narrative, and Historical Experience. In *Visual and Other Pleasures*, 159–76. Bloomington and Indianapolis: Indiana University Press.

Nash, Ilana. 2015. The Princess and the Teen Witch: Fantasies of the Essential Self. In *Princess Cultures: Mediating Girls' Imaginations and Identities*, ed. Miriam Forman-Brunell and Rebecca C. Haines, 3–23. New York: Peter Lang.

Neumann, Iver B. 2012. Introduction to the Forum on Liminality. *Review of International Studies* 38: 473–479. doi:10.1017/S0260210511000817.

Perrault, Charles. [1697] 2001a. Little Red Riding Hood. In *The Great Fairy Tale Tradition: From Straparola and Basile to the Brothers Grimm*, 745–747. New York and London: W.W. Norton and Co.

———. [1697] 2001b. Bluebeard. In *The Great Fairy Tale Tradition: From Straparola and Basile to the Brothers Grimm*, trans. and ed. Jack Zipes, 732–735. New York and London: W.W. Norton & Company.

Polak, Michele. 2006. From the Curse to the Rag: Online gURLs Rewrite the Menstruation Narrative. In *Girlhood: Redefining the Limits*, ed. Yasmin Jiwani,

Candis Steenbergen, and Claudia Mitchell, 191–207. Montreal, New York and London: Black Rose Books.

Pomerantz, Shauna. 2007. 'Cleavage in a Tank Top: Bodily Prohibition and the Discourses of School Dress Codes.' *Alberta Journal of Educational Research* 53 (4): 373–386.

———. 2008. *Girls, Style, and School Identities: Dressing the Part*. New York and HampshireBasingstoke: Palgrave MacMillan.

Pomerantz, Shauna, Rebecca Raby, and Andrea Stefanik. 2013. Girls Run the World? Caught Between Sexism and Postfeminism in School. *Gender and Society* 27 (2): 185–207. doi:10.1177/0891243212473199.

Preston, Cathy Lynn. 2004. Disrupting the Boundaries of Genre and Gender: Postmodernism and the Fairy Tale. In *Fairy Tales and Feminism: New Approaches*, ed. Donald Haase, 197–212. Detroit, MI: Wayne State University Press.

Projansky, Sarah. 2014. *Spectacular Girls: Media Fascination and Celebrity Culture*. New York and London: New York University Press.

Purkiss, Diane. 2000. *Troublesome Things: A History of Fairies and Fairy Stories*. London: Penguin.

Renold, Emma and Jessica Ringrose. 2008. Regulation and Rupture: Mapping Tween and Teenage Girls' Resistance to the Heterosexual Matrix. *Feminist Theory* 9: 313–338. doi:10.1177/1464700108095854.

Ross, Sharon Marie. 2008. *Beyond the Box: Television and the Internet*. Malden, MA, Oxford and Victoria: Blackwell.

Rowe, Kathleen. 1995. *The Unruly Woman: Gender and the Genres of Laughter*. Austin: University of Texas Press.

Scheiner, Georganne. 2000. *Signifying Female Adolescence: Film Representations and Fans, 1920–1950*. Westport, CT: Praeger.

Sells, Laura. 1995. "Where Do the Mermaids Stand?" Voice and Body in *The Little Mermaid*. In *From Mouse to Mermaid: The Politics of Film, Gender and Culture*, ed. Elizabeth Bell, Lynda Haas, and Laura Sells, 175–192. Bloomington and Indianapolis: Indiana University Press.

Sexton, Ann. 1971. Cinderella. In *Transformations*, 53–58. Boston and New York: Mariner.

Short, Sue. 2006. *Misfit Sisters: Screen Horror as Female Rites of Passage*. New York: Palgrave MacMillan.

Stacey, Judith. 1990. Sexism by a Subtler Name? Poststructural Conditions and Postfeminist Consciousness in Silicon Valley. In *Women, Class, and the Feminist Imagination: A Socialist Feminist Reader*, ed. K.V. Hansen and I.J. Philipson. Philadelphia, PA: Temple University Press.

Tasker, Yvonne. 2012. *Enchanted* (2007) by Postfeminism: Gender, Irony, and the New Romantic Comedy. In *Feminism at the Movies: Understanding*

Gender in Contemporary Popular Cinema, ed. Hilary Radner and Rebecca Stringer, 67–79. Hoboken, NJ: Taylor and Francis.

Tatar, Maria. 2004. *Secrets Beyond the Door: The Story of Bluebeard and His Wives*. Princeton, NJ and Oxford: Princeton University Press.

Trites, Roberta. 1991. Disney's Sub/Version of Andersen's *The Little Mermaid*. *Journal of Popular Film and Television* 18 (4): 145–152.

Turner, Victor. 1967. *The Forest of Symbols: Aspects of Ndembu Ritual*. Ithaca, NY: Cornell University Press.

———. 1969. *The Ritual Process: Structure and Anti-Structure*. Chicago: Aldine Publishing Company.

———. 1974. *Dramas, Fields, and Metaphors*. Ithaca, NY and London: Cornell University Press.

———. 1977. Variations on a Theme of Liminality. In *Secular Ritual*, ed. Sally F. Moore and Barbara G. Myerhoff, 40–52. Assen: Van Gorcum.

Warner, Marina. 1995. *From the Beast to the Blonde: On Fairy Tales and their Tellers*. London: Vintage.

Waters, Melanie. 2011. Introduction: Screening Women and Women on Screen. In *Women on Screen: Feminism and Femininity in Visual Culture*, ed. Melanie Waters, 1–16. Basingstoke and New York: Palgrave Macmillan.

Zipes, Jack. 1994. *Fairy Tale as Myth/Myth as Fairy Tale*. Lexington: University Press of Kentucky.

———. 2011. *The Enchanted Screen: The Unknown History of Fairy-Tale Films*. New York and London: Routledge.

Filmography

Aquamarine. Dir. Elizabeth Allen. 2006.
Beastly. Dir. Daniel Barnz. 2011.
Beauty and the Beast. The CW. 2012–2016.
Beauty and the Beast. Dir. Bill Condon. 2017.
Brave. Dirs. Mark Andrews, Brenda Chapman, Steve Purcell. 2012.
Buffy the Vampire Slayer. The WB. 1997–2003.
Cinderella. Dir. Kenneth Branagh. 2015.
A Cinderella Story. Dir. Mark Rosman. 2004.
The Company of Wolves. Dir. Neil Jordan. 1984.
Edward Scissorhands. Dir. Tim Burton. 1990.
Ella Enchanted. Dir. Tommy O'Haver. 2004.
Enchanted. Dir. Kevin Lima. 2007.
Ever After: A Cinderella Story. Dir. Andy Tennant. 1998.
Freeway. Dir. Matthew Bright. 1996.
Frozen. Dirs. Chris Buck and Jennifer Lee. 2013.
Ginger Snaps. Dir. John Fawcett. 2000.

Gossip Girl. The CW. 2007–2012.

Into the Woods. Dir. Rob Marshall. 2014.

Maleficent. Dir. Robert Stromberg. 2014.

Penelope. Dir. Mark Palansky 2006.

Pretty Little Liars. ABC Family. 2010–.

Pretty in Pink. Dir. Howard Deutch. 1986.

Red Riding Hood. Dir. Catherine Hardwicke. 2011.

Sabrina the Teenage Witch. ABC. 1996–2003.

The Secret Circle. The CW. 2011–2012.

Snow White and the Huntsman. Dir. Rupert Sanders. 2012.

Sydney White. Dir. Joe Nussbaum. 2007.

Tangled. Dirs. Nathan Greno and Byron Howard. 2010.

Teen Wolf. MTV. 2011–.

Twilight. Dir. Catherine Hardwicke. 2008.

The Vampire Diaries. The CW. 2010–2017.

CHAPTER 2

An Escape to the Forest in Catherine Hardwicke's *Red Riding Hood* (2011)

Red Riding Hood: A Feminist Revision of the Fairy Tale?

The 'Red Riding Hood' tale is continually invoked in contemporary girls' visual culture, often to explore the space of transgression and freedom symbolised by straying from the straight path of hegemonic femininity, and the consequences of doing so. Werewolf stories in teen texts such as *Buffy the Vampire Slayer* (The WB 1997–2003), *Teen Wolf* (MTV 2011–), *The Vampire Diaries* (The CW 2009–2017), *The Boy Who Cried Werewolf* (Bross 2010), *When Animals Dream* (Arnby 2014), *Blood and Chocolate* (Garnier 2007), *Cursed* (Craven 2005) and *Ginger Snaps* (Fawcett 2000) demonstrate the enduring appeal of the liminal figure of the wolf in girlhood rite-of-passage narratives. In many instances, the tale is reconfigured with the girl as the wolf. In *Ginger Snaps*, for example, Ginger is bitten by a werewolf while walking through the woods at night and begins a beastly transformation. As she transforms over the weeks following the attack, she becomes violent, ravenous and destructive. While the film makes space for her unruly subversions, the threat she poses is nevertheless contained when her sister, Bridget, kills her. In other texts such as *Teen Wolf* and *The Vampire Diaries*, the girl wolves must regulate and contain their appetites and violent behaviour in order to avoid punishment. In both examples, the powerful girl wolf is to some degree characterised negatively and she must be confined in some way.

However, this is not always the case. For example, in Neil Jordan's 1984 film *The Company of Wolves*, based on Angela Carter's short story of

© The Author(s) 2017
A. Bellas, *Fairy Tales on the Teen Screen*,
DOI 10.1007/978-3-319-64973-3_2

the same name (1979), heroine Rosaleen undergoes a beastly transformation and, as Carter puts it, concludes her rite-of-passage journey 'between the paws of the tender wolf' ([1979] 1996, 220). *When Animals Dream* features a similar outcome, with werewolf Marie escaping persecution at the end of the film. So while we can still see the 'Little Red Riding Hood' tale being deployed as a kind of cautionary tale in teen screen texts in the tradition of Perrault and the Grimms, there are some that refuse this function, and open up the tale to more subversive readings of the errant, unruly girl. This space of subversion is where I locate my attention in this chapter, with an analysis of Catherine Hardwicke's film *Red Riding Hood*.

In addition to revisions that imagine the girl as a wolf, Red Riding Hood is also frequently figured as an avenging hunter or slayer, as in *Hard Candy* (Slade 2005), *Freeway* (Bright 1996), *Hanna* (Wright 2011) and episodes of *Buffy the Vampire Slayer* such as 'Fear Itself' (4.04) and 'Helpless' (3.12). In *Red Riding Hood*, the heroine is both hunter and witch. As Sue Short notes, Hardwicke appears to be influenced by Carter's 'Company of Wolves' and the film of the same name, 'revealing the extent to which contemporary fairy tale films are increasingly referencing one another' (2015, 149). While some critics have expressed disappointment about the film's romantic resolution—indeed, Short refers to it as a 'de-clawing' of the heroine (149)—I argue that the film undertakes a feminist revision of the tale by mapping the heroine's rite of passage as a liminal and flexible journey, and that this cannot be contained by the romance plot.

The film revises the gender relations represented in the Charles Perrault (1607) and Brothers Grimm (1857) versions of the 'Little Red Riding Hood' fairy tale through its reconfiguration of the heroine's journey through the forest as a liminal bid for freedom. This Gothicised fairy tale film maps heroine Valerie's resistance to patriarchal power and ideology through her escape from her oppressive father's home, where she has been imprisoned, and her entry into the liminal forest. By pursuing an errant journey into the otherworldly space of the woods, and adopting the alternative identities of the hunter and the witch, Valerie eschews the 'appropriate' domestic femininity that conventional culture requires her to adhere to, and constructs an alternative girl identity. Conducting a visual analysis of how this liberating geography is represented through Valerie's point of view, as well as an analysis of Valerie's omniscient voice-over narration that accompanies her traversal of this terrain, I theorise how liminality not only carves out a space for the girl's opposition to her position as subordinate object within patriarchal culture, but also allows an alternative, authoritative and powerful feminine adolescent subjectivity to emerge on the contemporary teen screen.

Feminist fairy tale revisions work to unsettle dominant patriarchal narratives and attempt to go beyond their confines to produce new representations of femininity in narrative. Cristina Bacchilega (1997) argues that this project is twofold: it firstly works to expose 'the rottenness of a social order that trades [on] (female) bodies' (96) to both the heroine and the reader/spectator, taking 'a gruesome fairy tale often deployed against women' and then transforming it into 'a story of successful, socially meaningful female initiation' (138). Bacchilega further emphasises the affirmative capacity of feminist revisionist fairy tale narratives: they foreground the heroine's 'self-discovery' of her voice and identity, which leads to her 'empowerment' (138). *Red Riding Hood* does just this: it exposes and critiques the sexist structures that hold the heroine's subordination to patriarchal authority in place, and represents the heroine's deployment of oppositional strategies that unsettle and subvert this masculine authority.

Teen fairy tale films often narrativise a liminal process through the depiction of adolescent descent or crossing over into an otherworld, like Little Red Riding Hood's journey into the strange, mysterious forest. Victor Turner (1982) writes that liminal rituals are 'frequently marked by the physical separation of the ritual subjects from the rest of society' (26), elaborating that 'the passage from one social status to another is often accompanied by a parallel passage in space, a geographical movement from one place to another...Sometimes this spatial symbolism may be the precursor of a real and permanent change' (25). This departure from conventional society symbolises a break with the status quo, and as Turner suggests, the liminal zone can be transformative. Because a journey into liminality is always a departure from the known, or the established order, it is a space that sometimes promotes a radical break with the structures, definitions and hierarchies associated with the dominant order. As Turner argues, liminal ritual subjects 'are at once dying from or dead to their former status and life, and being born and growing into new ones' (26). In other words, the escape into liminality is twofold: it is a refusal of, or turning one's back on, the structures, rules and definitions of dominant culture, and this refusal activates a 'being born' into a new identity that falls outside the bounds of status quo acceptability.

This oppositional and disruptive form of female heroism is evident in the rite-of-passage narrative in *Red Riding Hood*, mapping feminine adolescent resistance into the teen fairy tale. Valerie's journey into the forest is a defiant act, a moment that represents a refusal or repudiation of the gendered ideologies governing her domestic life. In this domestic space, she is urged to take up idealised feminine positions—wife, caretaker and 'good girl'—and her escape into the forest enacts a refusal of this ideology. By permanently escaping from the domestic, Valerie enacts a protest against dominant ideologies of femininity. Valerie's journey into the forest represents her desire to escape from patriarchal civilisation, and to enter a space of transgression where she can experience independence, autonomy and power as she takes up the alternative identities of a lone hunter, traveller and witch. When Valerie escapes into the forest, she decides to permanently occupy this space and refuses to return to conventional culture. This permanent escape into the liminal zone is what Turner (1969) calls 'ultraliminality', providing a fantasy of 'opting out' of conventional culture and the 'status-bound social order' (112). Like *The Company of Wolves*, *Red Riding Hood* charts a different path for the 'Little Red Riding Hood' heroine where the girl does not meet punishment at the end of her wayward journey but is instead rewarded, subverting the canonical endings prescribed by Perrault and the Grimms. The film draws a new map of the fairy tale forest and the heroine's journey through it; in doing so, the defiant, errant girl's rite of passage takes on new significances, and tells an alternative story of feminine adolescent unruliness.

The film's hybridisation of the fairy tale and girls' Gothic genres produces new outcomes for the 'Little Red Riding Hood' tale on the teen screen. Catherine Driscoll (2002) shows that 'feminine gothic [*sic*] texts are narratives of development that make gothic a genre of some significance to the formation of feminine adolescence' (231). The use of the feminine Gothic mode to revise the 'Little Red Riding Hood' tale allows Hardwicke to make salient the dark and disturbing implications of the Perrault and Grimm fairy tale, particularly in relation to their gendered dynamics. Because the feminine Gothic always 'shows women suffering from institutions they feel to be profoundly alien to them and their concerns' (DeLamotte 1990, 152), it holds the potential to critique those dominant institutions that foster the exploitation of women and girls. A central theme of the girl's Gothic, then, is an interrogation of 'the requirements of patriarchal culture for the young girl to give up active and agentic desire and accept her status as object of desire,' which are 'experienced by the girl as profoundly strange' (Martin 2013, 137). By Gothicising the fairy tale, Hardwicke exposes and critiques the patriarchal violence embedded in the Perrault and Grimm versions of the tale, through the emphasis on the Gothic themes of the girl's entrapment and imprisonment within a horrifying domestic realm presided over by a masculine authority figure, and narrativising the girl's intense dissatisfaction with her place within the domestic and other patriarchal institutions of power (Driscoll 2002, 231). Hardwicke's deployment of this Gothic trope—the girl's dissatisfaction with and desire to escape from her impending role as wife and mother—is explored in greater detail later in this chapter, with particular emphasis placed on how this contemporary teen screen revision narrativises the girl's pursuit of an escape route into an unruly realm.

This film not only interrogates the demands made of feminine adolescence in patriarchal culture, but to also represent resistance to those demands, showing that the girl's Gothic can provide fantasy narratives of escape from the demands of conventional femininity in patriarchal culture. The horrors that the heroine faces, and eventually conquers, create 'extraordinary experiences of self-revelation' (Driscoll 2002, 324). These narratives represent girls who, through their 'vigilance, resilience, and agency,' face, defeat and escape these domestic horrors (232). In her analysis of the Persephone myth in girl's fantasy and Gothic literature, Holly Virginia Blackford shows that the girl's escape from the dominant order is represented as a moment of disruptive liminality. She writes that 'the myth of Persephone [is] provocative of a girls' gothic, expressive of the dangers and inevitability of impending womanhood' (2012, 9). This Gothic Persephone myth articulates 'a deep ambivalence about growing up female; fantasy space enacts the ambivalence' (5). While this chapter does not focus on the Persephone myth, it nevertheless resonates with the contemporary Little Red Riding Hood's journey into the woods, because as Blackford asserts, 'as a uniquely indeterminate and homeless girl, fated forever to cycle between worlds, [Persephone] inspired paradoxical symbolism of growth and escape' (1). The theme of a fantasy escape into liminal, otherworldly space allows the girls' Gothic text to articulate their dissatisfaction and resistance towards these strictures, as well as offering a fantasy of alternatives to them.

Having established the theoretical background on space and liminality, this chapter goes on to survey feminist responses to the disempowerment of the girl in the Perrault and Grimm versions of the 'Little Red Riding Hood' fairy tale. I explore the shift from these earlier versions to Hardwicke's female-dominated revisionist production, arguing that the film presents a keen critical insight into the sexism embedded in the Perrault and Grimm texts. The chapter then explores how moments of opposition and rupture make way for alternative gender relations to emerge in the revision of the tale. I map Valerie's escape into the liminal realm of the forest in great detail. Chronicling her journey from the imprisoning Gothic domestic space and the tyrannical patriarchal figures who preside over it, and into the forbidden territory of the forest, I explore how liminal space offers a fantasy of a girl's noncompliance and escape from the oppressive demands of the status quo. I argue that this fantasy of escape and liminal transformation creates a powerful representation of teen girl agency for the teen screen, and how this provides an important space for representing an alternative language of girlhood on screen. In the third and final section of this chapter, I analyse the use of Valerie's authoritative voice-over narration and point-of-view shots from Valerie's perspective as she navigates this new space, positioning the girl as powerful storyteller who becomes an unruly figure in the liminal zone.

FEMINIST RESPONSES TO 'LITTLE RED RIDING HOOD'

Feminist analyses of the 'Little Red Riding Hood' tale, particularly those versions written by Perrault and the Grimms, have crucially examined the ways in which the figure of the girl is disempowered, violated and punished (Brownmiller 1975; Zipes 1986, 1989; Orenstein 2002). This section explores some of these important deconstructions of the 'Little Red Riding Hood' narrative in detail, particularly in relation to its function as a cautionary tale, as well as its representation of a punishing masculine gaze. I then provide close scene analyses of how Hardwicke's film actively critiques and challenges this patriarchal power as it exposes the extreme violence it engenders against women and girls.

Feminist critics have pointed out the tale's troubling gender dynamic of male violence and female shame in which the young girl is blamed for the violent encounter with the wolf. Susan Brownmiller famously argued that:

> Red Riding Hood is a parable of rape. There are frightening male figures abroad in the woods – we call them wolves, among other names – and

females are helpless before them. Better stick close to the path, better not be adventurous. If you are lucky, a *good*, *friendly* male may be able to save you from certain disaster. (1975, 310 original emphasis)

Jack Zipes concurred with Brownmiller's scathing assessment of the tale and has convincingly argued that both the Perrault and Grimm versions mobilised a story of 'male governance' (1989, 126) over feminine disobedience, unruliness and curiosity (123–124). Expanding on the discussion of violation and violence, Zipes discusses the dynamic of the gaze in the tale. He writes of the Perrault and Grimm versions:

the girl in the encounter with the wolf gazes but really does not gaze, for she is the image of male desire. She is projected by the authors Perrault and Grimm...as an object without a will of her own. The gaze of the wolf will consume her and is intended to dominate and eliminate her. The gaze of the wolf is a phallic mode of interpreting the world...Her identity will be violated and fully absorbed by male desire either as wolf or gamekeeper. (Zipes 1986, 248)

Zipes correctly points out the impossible position to which Little Red Riding Hood is relegated in the Perrault and Grimm versions of the tale. Because both the Perrault and Grimm versions of 'Little Red Riding Hood' function as cautionary tales that hinge on a transgression/violation binary (Tatar 2004, 1) in which the heroine's violation of transgression subsequently leads to the spectacle of her punishment, the story relies on a sexist dynamic of 'bad' feminine disobedience and unruliness that requires the discipline of masculine surveillance.

In Perrault's version of the 'Little Red Riding Hood' tale, there are two main gazes cast upon the young heroine: the predatory gaze of the wolf, and the gaze of surveillance and disapproval of the omniscient male narrator. The Grimms also added, in their later version of the tale, the gaze of the huntsman, the figure of 'law and order' (Zipes 1993, 78); and his surveying masculine gaze saves the day. As Catherine Orenstein (2002) has dryly commented on this development, Little Red Riding Hood, the naïve girl 'still foolish and prone to err, now...needed a man to save her', thus giving her 'a second chance to walk the straight path through life' (46). These two sets of masculine gazes work to control Little Red Riding Hood, creating a tale of 'male governance' over feminine unruliness (Zipes 1993, 81). The Perrault and Grimm versions of

'Little Red Riding Hood', then, work to police the borders of 'appropriate' femininity and to condemn expressions of femininity that fall beyond
that border. While the heroine certainly exercises agency by straying
from the path in this tale, the canonical versions of the tale narrativise
this moment of agency only to punish her for this transgression at the
conclusion of the story. The masculine gazes of the wolf, hunter and
omniscient male narrator work as disciplinary forces in these versions of
the tale, conspiring to contain the threat of feminine unruliness represented by Red Riding Hood's desire to 'stray from the straight path'.
Indeed, children's literature scholar Elizabeth Marshall (2004) has
shown how the 'Little Red Riding Hood' tale, particularly in its Perrault
and Grimm versions, is framed by the 'often contradictory discourses of
femininity that attempt to school the girl into a (hetero)sexual body...
[and these versions of the tale] map a subtle, yet no less coercive attempt
to contain and regulate the feminine body' (262).

The lesson that the tale is intended to instil in young readers and lis-
teners is clear when the Grimms' Little Red Cap tells herself: 'never again
will you stray from the path by yourself and go into the forest when your
mother has forbidden it' ([1857] 2001, 750). In Perrault's moral that
concludes the tale, he writes:

> One sees here that young children,
> Especially pretty girls,
> Polite, well-taught, and pure as pearls,
> Should stay on guard against all sorts of men.
> For if one fails to stay alert, it won't be strange
> To see one eaten by a wolf enraged. ([1607] 2001, 747)

Both Perrault and the Grimms create a very specific idealised image of
youthful femininity: to always obey, to be pure, polite and to resist that
which is 'forbidden'. While these narratives certainly provide representations of an agentic young girl pursuing a forbidden path, they contain
that agency through punishment—the threat of death in the Grimm version and an actual death in Perrault's. The tale therefore creates a space
for a girl's transgressive journey but ultimately cannot allow the girl to
continue on her unruly path; she has been taught her 'lesson' by the
tale's authoritative male figures.

Hardwicke's *Red Riding Hood* actively critiques this punishing masculine gaze by clearly exposing how it is bound up in the exploitation of
women, and then documenting Valerie's opposition and resistance to it,
particularly in the second half of the film. Mulvey's ([1975] 1989) semi-
nal work on the male gaze in classical narrative cinema interrogated the
ways in which male protagonists in film have traditionally 'articulate[d]
the look and create[d] the action', a role that entails power and omnipo-
tence, while female characters occupy the passive space of spectacle, or
to-be-looked-at-ness (19–20). She argued that this gendered imbalance
in film representations 'reflects, reveals, and even plays on the straight,
socially established interpretation of sexual difference which controls
images, erotic ways of looking, and spectacle' (14). Furthermore, 'the
female form displayed for [male] enjoyment' fulfils and sustains 'male
fantasy' and the continued classification of woman as an object for male
pleasure (21). The male character who comes to 'possess' the female
character in the narrative is identified with by the male spectator who,
by extension, also comes to possess the looked-at woman (21). The
structure of the gaze is conceived of as a patriarchal visual language of
control, domination and ownership of women, bound up in the culture's subordination and oppression of women. Woman connotes lack
within the psychoanalytic framework deployed by Mulvey, the 'bearer
of the bleeding wound; she can only exist in relation to castration and
cannot transcend it' (14), representative of 'a threat of castration and
hence unpleasure' (21). The male gaze can alleviate the fear evoked by
this threat either through investigating the woman with sadistic voyeur-
ism or turning her into a beautiful, eroticised object through fetishistic
scopophilia, which conceals and disavows her lack (22). Within this formulation, the woman onscreen can either be 'subjugat[ed]...through
punishment or forgiveness' (22), or fetishised into 'a perfect product'
by the male protagonist (22). Either way, she is subjected to a gaze that
possesses and controls her.

In the wake of Mulvey's hugely influential essay, feminist screen scholars began to suggest that while this theorisation of the male gaze provided
an important structure for identifying how patriarchal visual culture often
frames woman as image, it was so totalising and monolithic that it was difficult to formulate responses to alternative narratives. Challenges to Mulvey's
theoretical paradigm particularly emerged in the work of feminists who

sought to conceptualise a female or feminine spectatorial position or gaze (see Kuhn 1984; Williams 1984; Cowie 1990; Stacey 1994), and to identify instances in which female characters subverted sexist visual and narrative economies (see Rich and Williams 1981; Modleski 1988). For example, Teresa de Lauretis began looking for 'resistance or contradiction' to 'the language of the masters' (1984, 3). Furthermore, she argued that the psychoanalytic methodology was limiting because it 'depend[ed] on ... positing woman as the functional opposite of subject (man), which logically excludes the possibility ... of women ever being subjects and producers of culture' (20). Instead of relying on the grand narrative provided by psychoanalysis, de Lauretis suggested that 'reading between the signs' or 'rereading a text against the grain' (6) could reveal 'positionalities of identification available [to women] in narrative cinema' (107). In an article co-authored with Michelle Citron, Julia Lesage, Judith Mayne and Anna Marie Taylor, B. Ruby Rich similarly argued that while Mulvey's work allows for the analysis 'of the status quo, which is patriarchal', feminist theory worked to now 'go *beyond* [the status quo] rather than just analysing it' (1978, 87 original emphasis). Furthermore, a psychoanalytic account of cinema's gendered relations, which can only conceive of woman as lack and as other to the male, is inadequate if we are to analyse female subjectivity on screen.

So while Mulvey's paradigm provides a compelling foundation for deconstructing gendered relations on screen, it is only part of the story. For example, Hardwicke's film appears to be keenly aware of the dominant male gaze, and renders its mechanisms so explicitly and excessively that its violence becomes painfully obvious. *Red Riding Hood* does not simply reproduce the male gaze; it ruptures its normalisation. This visual representation of male characters attempting to violently control and possess Valerie serves a critical function in the film. The narrative chronicles the heroine's resistance and protest against these acts of masculine violence, and her final oppositional act of noncompliance when she escapes to the forest. The first half of the film chronicles a range of men who have their 'eyes on' Valerie, revealing the male gaze as control over the female as object. At the beginning of the film, Valerie is betrothed to a wealthy man named Henry. A townsperson remarks to Valerie: 'Henry's always had his eye on you. You're the pretty one.' Valerie recoils from this statement, which places her in the position of a mere pretty object; indeed Valerie explicitly describes her betrothal as 'being sold', drawing attention to the way in which she has been cast as object. In one scene set in the front garden of Valerie's home, her father—who

Fig. 2.1   Valerie's image captured in the gaze of the father/wolf

is also the wolf—attacks the heroine. As illustrated in Fig. 2.1, Valerie's image is reflected in an extreme close-up of one of the wolf's enormous eyes. Transfixed and unable to move, she is quite literally captured and controlled by his gaze. Creating an image that quite literally depicts the dynamics of the gaze—the wolf/male as possessor, the female figure as captured object—Hardwicke explicitly brings Perrault and the Grimms' male gaze to the surface of the film.

The Gothicised domestic, ruled by the tyrannical father/wolf, is a space of confinement, imprisonment and claustrophobia for heroine Valerie. Hardwicke's use of the Gothic mode allows her to present the horrors that underlie the domestic, and the subjugated, diminished position that women have often occupied within the patriarchal construction of this space. The patriarchs of the film enforce girlhood as a diminished position that requires absolute compliance to the male figure and the performance of 'good girl' femininity. Juliann E. Fleenor comments that this structure of horror in the home is typical of the female Gothic, writing that 'the Gothic world is one of nightmare, and that nightmare is created by the individual in conflict with the values of her society and her prescribed role' (1983, 10). Thus, the 'heroines...flight from male tyrants across fantastical landscapes' have been interpreted as 'politically subversive...articulating women's dissatisfactions with patriarchal structures and offering a coded expression of their fears of entrapment within the domestic and the female body' (Wallace and Smith 2009, 2). The home as horror comes to represent, in amplified form, the difficulties of complying with the demands of patriarchal culture. Hardwicke's explicit representation of patriarchal oppression and the male gaze in the first half of the film is serves a political function: Valerie opposes this oppressive patriarchal rule, and the narrative chronicles her liberation from its confines. The narrative therefore presents a fantasy of female victory in the face of masculine abuses of power.

The film's exposure of the mechanisms of violence and oppression that support patriarchal power is an essential aspect of how this female-dominated production launches its critique against the sexism embedded in the Perrault and Grimm versions of the tale. Natalie Hayton argues that the film produces a powerful critique of patriarchal power through this exposure of the tale's sexist dynamics: Valerie must make a choice 'between tradition and conformity... [and] making her own decisions instead of fulfilling a prescribed narrative destiny' (2011, 126–127). Valerie discovers that the wolf is her tyrannical father, exposing the true monstrosity of this Gothic patriarch, and she slays him in an act of bravery and strength. Once this patriarchal abuse of power is exposed in the first half of the film, Hardwicke unsettles the canonised tale's gender dynamics.

An Escape to the Woods: Straying from the Straight Path

Feminist analyses of the female role in myths and fairy tales have theorised the possibility of the heroine as an agentic and active subject. While many previous studies of the mythical rite-of-passage journey had been preoccupied with charting a male or masculine journey, as in the important work on the 'monomyth' by Joseph Campbell (1949),[1] feminist analyses set out to theorise a feminine equivalent that can represent the female protagonist's rite of passage in myth and fairy tale. De Lauretis powerfully comments that traditionally,

> the hero, the mythical subject, is constructed as human being and as male; he is the active principle of culture, the establisher of distinction, the creator of differences. Female is what is not susceptible to transformation, to life or death; she (it) is an element of plot-space, a topos, a resistance, matrix and matter. (1984, 119)

The female or the feminine in the tale, therefore, often acts as an object or space to be either conquered and vanquished, or staked out and claimed. As de Lauretis elaborates, 'the end of the girl's journey, if successful will bring her to the place where the boy will find her, like Sleeping Beauty, awaiting him, Prince Charming. For the boy has been promised…that he will find woman waiting at the end of *his* journey' (133 original emphasis). For de Lauretis, then, the project for feminism is 'to make a place for woman in myth—to imagine woman as subject in culture, to understand female subjectivity…to tell *her* story, the story of femininity' (125 original emphasis). Zipes argues that the project of the feminist fairy tale was 'created out of dissatisfaction with the dominant male discourse of traditional fairy tales and with those social values and institutions which have provided the framework for sexist prescriptions', working to not only expose these 'illusions' but to also present 'a different view of the world and spea[k] in a voice that has been customarily silenced' (1986, xi). The project of feminist fairy tale writing and criticism has therefore been to expand the position of the feminine in narrative.

De Lauretis' work asserts the importance of not only analysing how women and girls have been rendered as passive objects within narrative, but to also go beyond these limits to look for instances in which feminine subjectivity is centred in stories of female quests, journeys and rites of passage. This allows us to perceive the potential for fairy tale rewritings and variants to trouble the smooth patriarchal ideological surface of the canonised literary fairy tale texts by Perrault, the Grimms and Andersen. Indeed, they can rupture this surface, opening the fairy tale up to feminist appropriation and new, powerful stories about female journeys. These journeys often elide the patriarchal logic of closure through heterosexual romance, marriage and motherhood, creating new narrative structures for the fairy tale heroine to occupy. The screen texts analysed in this book participate in this form of rewriting the fairy tale, providing space for the fairy tale heroine to invade domains of male power and privilege, to resist the status quo of the heterosexual romantic rite of passage, and to seize alternative opportunities for fulfilment, agency and power.

Like de Lauretis, who worked to identify mythical narratives that could include powerful feminine identities and voices, Barbara Creed offers a feminine alternative to Campbell's 'monomyth' with a theorisation of a 'neomyth' or new myth capable of 'describ[ing] the structure of the heroine's journey' (2007, 19). The difference between the two forms of heroism are striking, for Creed argues that:

while male heroism is defined in relation to preservation of the male symbolic order, female heroism is...oppositional. In many contexts, the male hero signifies fixity, the female fluidity. Unlike the classic male hero, she rejects the phallocentric, fixed nature of the world, preferring instead to question the meaning of patriarchal civilisation and its values. (23)

Creed provides a wide variety of examples of this female hero in film, such as the women of *Thelma and Louise* (Scott 1991) and Joan from *The Passion of Joan of Arc* (Dreyer 1928). Creed's formulation of the female quest not only identifies how women can be figured as central authoritative drivers of narrative; it also points out that the female heroic narrative frequently involves the disruption of the 'male symbolic order', and an opposition to its foundational structures.

In *Red Riding Hood*, the heroine straying from the path is represented as an important assertion of resistance to the straight path and all that it represents. Bacchilega notes that contemporary feminist revisions of 'Little Red Riding Hood' reformulate the tale to emphasise the heroine's errant journey as positive, for 'straying from the path is necessary to acquire knowledge but what that leads to cannot already be known' (1997, 68). This emphasis on errant escapes from the 'known', the expected or the conventional opens up a fantasy space for the heroine to challenge and unsettle the boundaries of hegemonic femininity in patriarchal culture. This section of the chapter provides a visual analysis that contrasts the Gothic domestic space, presided over by Valerie's controlling father, and the geography of the forest, which represents a liminal and flexible zone. Valerie's escape from conventional culture is a gesture of noncompliance, and the liminal space acts as an otherworldly field of possibilities upon which Valerie can map an alternative version of doing girlhood.

In the first half of the film, Valerie is imprisoned in a dark and claustrophobic jail cell, chained and handcuffed, while in the second half of the film, she finds a way to escape this domestic horror. Valerie is expected to remain in the domestic sphere and marry Henry, thus being initiated into a traditional and idealised category of adult heterosexual femininity—becoming a housewife and mother. When Valerie first attempts to escape this fate, she is punished by being literally imprisoned within the domestic realm, trapped behind the bars of a wooden cage and shrouded in oppressive darkness. The ultra-tight framing around

Valerie's figure when she is enclosed in this domestic prison, and the static placement of the camera, similarly reflect this oppressive constriction. Valerie's subjugated position within the home could not be made clearer in this scene's representation of constricted and imprisoning spaces, the prison bar motif in the *mise en scène*, extreme low light and tight framing around the heroine's figure. Furthermore, Valerie's position within the home/prison allows the film's patriarchs to keep her under constant surveillance in the first half of the film, creating a space governed by a panoptic gaze—Valerie is unable to see her captors but they are able to monitor her closely. Michel Foucault describes this disciplinary apparatus through the example of Jeremy Bentham's 1791 architectural design for a Panopticon prison, which is designed so that the prisoner 'is seen, but he does not see; he is the object of information, never a subject of communication' ([1975] 1995, 200). Because the prisoners cannot see the guard, they can never know whether or not they are being watched and are therefore conditioned to internalise the prison's disciplinary power, 'even if it is discontinuous in its action; [so] that the perfection of power should tend to render its actual exercise unnecessary' (201). Foucault does not consider this structure of surveillance and discipline as unique to the prison; indeed, he argues that any time 'a task or particular form of behaviour must be imposed, the panoptic schema may be used' (205). In other words, Foucault argues that panopticism has become 'a generalised function' of the social body (207). However, Foucault also acknowledges the capacity for this disciplinary mechanism of the panoptic gaze to be contested or transgressed. He analyses the subject's capacity to move between power's threads (1980, 98), and how moving between these threads can create a space of opposition in which the subject discovers a 'narrow zone' in which transgression can occur (1977, 33), outside the time and space of 'mastery' ([1975] 1995, 159). I am particularly interested in exploring how the heroine contests the power of the adult, masculine gaze that surveils her for her 'correct' development into hegemonic adult femininity. The contestation of this power in narrative could be significant because if ruptures and contestations do arise in response to the politics of the male panoptic gaze, then an alternative optic could arise in the space of that rupture, one that offers a different paradigm of image-making and spectatorship.

Fig. 2.2   Panoramic framing and mobile camera movement in *Red Riding Hood*

Valerie's imprisonment at the hands of patriarchal authority figures shows the heroine caught in the disciplinary mechanism of the panoptic gaze. But Valerie is able to 'resist the grip' of this power (Foucault [1975] 1995, 27) by discovering the narrow zone of opposition between power's threads that Foucault theorises, and this zone is the liminal landscape of the fairy tale forest. The forest, located at the edge of the village, is a marginal space that exceeds the boundaries of the dominant order. When Valerie escapes to the forest in the second half of the film, the cinematography, *mise en scène* and lighting all shift dramatically. The forest scenes are represented in extreme contrast to the *mise en scène*, lighting, framing and static camera deployed in the domestic scenes, which evoke oppressive claustrophobia. In the forest, the fantasy realm of freedom and independence, bright light is highlighted through sunshine and brilliant white snow. The cinematographic framing is wide, giving an impression of Valerie's figure freely and fluidly moving in the frame. The camera movement is always mobile, moving across the landscape with fluent ease. The flexibility and fluidity of the figure's movement through the liminal landscape is further emphasised by the billowing undulations of Valerie's red cloak, as shown in Fig. 2.2.

The construction of free-flowing movement through the *mise en scène*, bright lighting, wide panoramic framing and itinerant camerawork create a forest geography defined by a sense of independence, freedom and mobility. Valerie's fluid, free-flowing movement within the liminal zone is a clearly oppositional move—she wilfully pursues an errant path that exceeds the limits imposed upon her within conventional culture. Walker's wide, panoramic framing emphasises the long, billowing, floating fabric of Valerie's cloak, and the heroine's confident strides across a vast expanse of open space, contributing to Hardwicke's feminist revision of the tale, in which the heroine is liberated from the masculine surveillance and discipline represented by the wolf and the disapproving male narrator. Hardwicke reconfigures the geography of the forest from a space of the girl's confinement and discipline to a landscape that represents possibilities for the heroine's unruliness: through this new lens, the forest becomes the location where the heroine is able to enact an opposition to the dominant order.

When Valerie enters the forest, she arms herself with a dagger and hunts down the wolf, her father, who has terrorised her. This liminal landscape is therefore coded as a space where Valerie can articulate her opposition to patriarchal authority. Turner writes that when the ritual subject enters the liminal otherworld, 'signs of their preliminal status are destroyed', and this leads to 'a special kind of freedom' that allows them to move 'beyond the normative social structure...[and] liberates them from structural obligations' (1982, 26–27). The film creates a fantasy world in which she can resist the dominant order and clearly articulate her opposition to the way in which she has been subjugated—she slays the wolf, and adopts the castigated identities of lone hunter and witch. Entry into a liminal otherworld stands for a fantasy of rebellion against the patriarchal culture from which Valerie flees. The escape to the otherworld represents a resistant practice against unsatisfactory gendered demands and strictures of the dominant culture. The theme of errant flight is cultivated not only as an expression of dissatisfaction with or ambivalence about the feminine role that the heroine is required to take up; it also allows for iterations of a girl's autonomy, independence and resistance to those cultural structures.

Through this enactment of unruliness, Valerie is able to discover and adopt an alternative and complex feminine adolescent identity. When the townspeople accuse her of being a witch, she does not struggle against this outsider identity; rather, she uses it to her advantage as a measure of resistance to the conventional feminine role she has been urged to adopt. Short, in her analysis of fairy tales and teen horror cinema, writes that the genre is preoccupied with 'the transgression of existing laws and boundaries' (2006, viii). She notes that the castigated outsider identities of wolf and witch are often adopted by teen horror heroines 'as an alternative to existing norms, adopting them as a measure of dissatis-faction and refusal' (105) and as a way to access and express 'forbidden emotions such as power, lust, and rage' (36–37). Embracing the outsider identities of the witch and hunter allows Valerie to confront the limits of the hegemonic femininity that she was compelled to internalise and perform in her preliminal life. The 'special kind of freedom' that Turner identifies within liminality allows Valerie to adopt an alternative identity that does not conform to hegemonic girlhood. She enacts aggression, opposition, lust and anger, traits ordinarily not deemed 'acceptable' for teen girls to express. These moments of disobedience represent a vari-ety of challenging and resistant girlhoods, allowing us to contemplate girl identities that go beyond the limits of the status quo. Furthermore, because feminine adolescent unruliness is represented as a necessary and positive trait—after all, Valerie's actions allow her to emerge triumphant and happy at the end of the rite of passage—the film encourages a posi-tive revaluation of modes of doing girlhood that are most often repre-sented negatively in mainstream media. In the context of a girls' media culture in which the fairy tale heroine is predominantly valued for her beauty and her experiences of romance (Haines 2014, 177), revisionist teen texts such as *Red Riding Hood* provide an alternative vision for the possibilities of girlhood through the fairy tale narrative.

Because the forest is an experimental space for the heroine in this film, it gives her the opportunity to design new ways of doing girlhood. Valerie finds ways to express forbidden emotions and actions such as anger and aggression in the space of the forest. Valerie also chooses to incorporate her love interest Peter, who is transformed into a 'good' wolf at the end of the film, into this space. Hayton expresses disappointment at this development, calling it a 'conventional romance…which over-shadows and blurs the feminist discourse' of the film as a whole (2011, 127), but the film complicates conventional heteronormative romantic resolution in ways that Hayton does not acknowledge. In fact, Valerie and Peter enter the forest together knowing that they will live apart, coming together at times when the moon does not affect Peter too strongly. Valerie insists upon her independence as she lives alone in the heart of the forest, because she has fought hard to gain this separation from conventional culture. Towards the end of the film Valerie declares in her voice-over narration that 'I could no longer live [in the town]. I felt more freedom in the shadows of the forest. To live apart carries its own dangers, but of those I am less afraid.' Valerie is engaging in a romance script, but in an alternative way: she is living independently, yet enjoying her relationship with Peter when it suits them both. This subverts the heterosexual romantic discourse of giving oneself over completely to the male lover, and the obliteration of female independence that such a coupling implies. Valerie creatively constructs and negotiates a romantic union in the forest that allows her to retain her freedom. This subversion of the norm of the romantic script, and Valerie's retention of her independence, signals the heroine's capacity to do girlhood differently through resistance practices.

LITTLE RED RIDING HOOD'S OMNISCIENCE: THE POINT-OF-VIEW SHOT AND THE VOICE-OVER

In this field of possibilities, Valerie opposes her position as subordinate object within the adult, masculine-dominated domain of her hometown. As she steps into the position of powerful subject within the forest space, she gains great narrative authority as storyteller and author of her own journey of empowerment. This is particularly evident in the film's representation of the heroine's point-of-view gaze and authoritative voice-over. The film carves out a representational space for a 'girl's gaze' (Kearney 2006) as a revisionary force, rupturing the dominance of adult masculine narrative authority. This revision of the gendered dynamics of image, gaze and voice in film narrative presents an opportunity to unsettle conventional representations of feminine adolescence, and to represent a girl's subjective position. Red Riding Hood becomes the storyteller and the authoritative point of view in the film. She uses her voice to articulate her resistance to what she calls the 'good girl' identity she is required to adopt, speaking back to and challenging this discourse. Pairing the teen heroine's authoritative voice-over with point-of-view shots provides a representation of Valerie's omniscience, authorial control and power over her rite-of-passage narrative. This shifts the authority from the disapproving gaze of the Perrault and Grimm narrators, revealing a significant transformation in the structures of power as the tale shifts from the early literary texts to the contemporary teen screen.

Mary Ann Doane's work on the female Gothic genre in classical Hollywood cinema analysed these two cinematic devices, the female voice-over and point-of-view shot, but was sceptical about the potential for the genre to offer its heroines sustained access to the agency of an authoritative point of view (1987, 150–151). Commenting on the structure of the gaze within the genre, Doane shows that it fruitfully offers a 'sustained investigation of the woman's relation to the gaze' (125). The genre attempts to present a female gaze by 'obsessively centring and recentring a female protagonist, placing her in a position of agency. It thus offers some resistances to an analysis which stresses the "to-be-looked-at-ness" of the woman, her objectification as spectacle according to the masculine structure of the gaze' (129). According to Doane, the genre also offers the potential for a female perspective to be expressed through voice-over narration. However,

> when the [female] voice over is introduced in the beginning of a film as the possession of the female protagonist who purportedly controls the narration of her own past, it is rarely sustained…Instead, voices-over are more frequently detached from the female protagonist and mobilised as moments of aggression or attack exercised against her. (150)

The disappearance of the heroine's authoritative gaze and narration as the film progresses undermines her access to agency. Furthermore, Doane points out that both the authoritative gaze and voice-over narration are not only taken from the heroine, they are taken over and replaced by a male character (151). For Doane, then, the female Gothic is a genre which offers a small measure of feminine agency through a short-lived access to an authoritative gaze, only to take it away. Doane's formal analysis of the female gaze and voice-over informs my own examination of these formal elements in *Red Riding Hood*. In particular, Doane's analysis suggests that the representation of woman as subject is possible, and that this representation provides an image of female agency on screen. This is a particularly important foundation for my analysis of instances where girls are represented as subjects and agents. However, I also expand upon Doane's theorisation by analysing how the heroines can maintain this agency, power and subjectivity on the contemporary teen screen.

Karen Hollinger elaborates on Doane's assertion that the heroine's perspective is obliterated in the female Gothic film:

> the female narrator's story can be finished, interpreted, or interrupted by a male character, exposed as a lie, or revealed as a misinterpretation of events…[Therefore] female narrational power is shut down in some way by a final decisive male intervention that implicates the spectator strongly in this masculine point of view. (1992, 35)

According to both Doane and Hollinger, this restoration of narrational power and agency to the masculine point of view undermines the potential for feminine agency to emerge as a significant force in the text. While Doane and Hollinger's analyses are a useful starting point for considering female point of view through the gaze and voice-over narration in the female Gothic, they lack a method for considering a text such as *Red Riding Hood* that *does* consistently sustain the heroine's perspective through voice-over narration and point-of-view shots. This is a contemporary Gothic fairy tale text that reinstates the heroine's agency as definitive and authoritative, and therefore a new way of considering the Gothic's narrational devices is required in the context of this chapter.

Hardwicke provides an important revision: Little Red Riding Hood is the omniscient storyteller and authoritative overseer of the narrative. Through this revision, Hardwicke subverts the all-too-familiar Perrault and Grimm narration that cautions girls about the perils of straying from the straight path. Instead, the story is told from the girl's perspective. Her voice-over narration is presented as retrospective as she looks back on her rite-of-passage journey. Valerie narrates the entire tale from her position in the ultraliminal forest, a space in which she feels powerful. This is important to note because, as I have elaborated, the first half of the film chronicles the heroine's terrible abuse at the hands of patriarchal power figures, including imprisonment and handcuffing. These images are presented along with Valerie's retrospective voice-over which describes how she escaped the grip of this oppression and became victorious in her independent journey into the fringe of the forest. Therefore, while the voice-over is presented in some scenes that depict Valerie's disempowerment early in the narrative, the retrospective, victorious nature of her telling of the tale suggests that she has reclaimed her voice. The activation of the girl's gaze and voice-over as central and authoritative in *Red Riding Hood* undermines the sexist structures that work to suppress and marginalise Valerie's power and point of view. With her agency restored, the Red Riding Hood heroine is shown to not only speak back to the male authorities in her world, but also articulate her demands beyond their strictures.

The film's deployment of a 'girl's gaze' and voice-over is central to its construction of feminine agency, power and resistance. Scholars such as Mary Celeste Kearney and Barbara Jane Brickman (2007) have theorised the possibility of an oppositional teen girl perspective and position in the cinema. Brickman asserts that the presentation of a teen girl point of view through point-of-view shots and voice-over narration may contain 'revisionary powers' (26). Because the teen girl point of view is traditionally a marginalised perspective, its privileging necessarily presents a challenge to the adult, straight male gaze that has dominated the cinema. Brickman writes that placing the marginalised female adolescent 'viewpoint and...consciousness' (26) at the centre of a film text has this capacity to be oppositional and challenging—a point of destabilisation and revision in the dynamic of the look and the voice. Kearney similarly calls for the critical development of the concept of the 'girl's gaze', which she suggests may counter the persistent 'privileging [of] male content, male spectators, and male directors' (2006, 196). While her work focuses predominantly on the need for girls to create their own film texts, it also provides a framework for considering how the girl's gaze might be theorised in relation to diegetic representations of teen girls, and for teen spectatorial positions. Kearney argues that a girl's gaze has the capacity to mobilise a 'relocating and reconfiguring' of familiar cinematic elements 'in order to tell [a girl's] own story' (190). For Kearney, this has the potential to undermine sexist paradigms 'related not only to the gendered practice of looking, but also to the broader gendering of action and productivity as male-specific qualities' (200). Because girls have frequently been framed by a focus on 'feminine appearance' and 'the goal of attracting heterosexual male attention' (215), this shift from object to subject of the gaze and active point of view has significant implications for destabilising dominant image-making and spectatorial practices. This unsettling of patriarchal visual culture carves out a space for multiple girls' stories to be included in the field of cinematic representation, therefore providing an opportunity to expand the boundaries of girlhood on screen in its capacity of including expressions of agency, resistance and empowerment.

While surprisingly little in-depth work has been done on the significance of female point-of-view narration and point-of-view shots in teen screen media,[2] Brickman provides a particularly insightful starting point. In her work on voice-over narration and female adolescent point of view shots in the teen film *Badlands* (Malick 1973), she asserts that the omniscient female adolescent in teen cinema can 'contradict the traditional use of male, authoritative voice-over in Hollywood film and speak from both diegetic and extradiegetic positions' (27). Brickman therefore contends that the agency of 'omniscient voice-over and controlling vision...

show[s] that female authority and authorship are possible' in the teen genre (49). When the teen girl narrator presides over the spectator's access to information, events and even other characters' interiority, these elements are made 'available to us through her agency' (35). Brickman's work provides a starting point for considering how the presentation of the teen girl's point of view gaze and authoritative voice-over functions not only as an expression of feminine agency within the text, but also as a challenge to the traditional authority of the masculine gaze and voice-over in screen media. By 'speaking back to how [girls] have been spoken into existence' (Pomerantz 2007, 383), *Red Riding Hood*'s Valerie challenges the way in which 'official' and institutionalised norms have constructed and regulated the boundaries of her adolescent girlhood.

The film establishes Valerie's point of view and gaze as authoritative from the opening shots. During the film's opening credits, Valerie's omniscient voice-over narrates the story of her journey into the forest. Her narration includes descriptions of the private thoughts and feelings of other characters, as well as events at which she was not present, confirming her point of view as omniscient, with the capacity to access privileged information. Hardwicke couples this voice-over narration with sweeping bird's-eye aerial views of the forest space, linking Valerie's voice with a sense of liberation, agency and power. Valerie is represented as in control of the narrative in her access to privileged information in her voice-over, and in the image track, which presents her point-of-view gaze as seemingly limitless in scope and powerfully mobile. The presentation of a girl's gaze challenges the visual tradition in which girls are objectified, scrutinised and denied a position of control or authority over the image, and the presentation of the girl's voice-over interjects into mainstream media's exclusion of girl's voices and stories. Therefore, the mobility of Valerie's perspective as she travels through this space represents more than just physical mobility; it represents the agency embedded in such movement and the capacity for that perspective to challenge the strictures of girlhood. Furthermore, this weaves the girl's voice into the imagery of the fairy tale landscape, mapping her story and journey into this liminal space. This provides a significant challenge to the domineering paternalistic gazes of the patriarchal authority figures who seek to control her and undermine her access to the gaze, and also challenges the authority of the disapproving, punishing male narrator that dominates the Perrault and Grimm versions of the 'Little Red Riding Hood' tale.

The focus on Valerie's perspective through her gaze and voice-over narration allows the film to challenge and revise one of the major themes of Perrault and the Grimms' tales: the paternal surveillance and coercion of the girl into a position of acquiescence and obedience. As Brickman suggests, the authoritative teen girl voice-over can provide a critique of 'the patriarchal order that keeps trying to silence her' (2007, 52). Valerie's point-of-view voice-over narration repeatedly critiques and repudiates the idealised 'good girl' discourse that she is required to take up. Valerie's identification of this discourse, and her ability to challenge and oppose it, is central to her capacity for agency. Jessica Ringrose suggests that girlhood agency lies in girls' critical awareness of (2013, 111) and capacity to 'manoeuvre [the] discourses' that seek to define, socially position, and discipline them (57). Throughout her voice-over narration, Valerie reiterates at several points (I count five) in the film her inability, or even her lack of desire to, conform to this identity of the 'good girl.' In her opening voice-over remarks at the beginning of the film, Valerie articulates her rebellion against the tale's stricture, 'don't stray from the path', stating that she could not and would not adhere to it: 'I tried to be a good girl. But I could not do it any longer.' Girlhood scholar Marnina Gonick writes that 'to be good within normative discourses of femininity usually means that a girl's desire is left unspoken or spoken only in whispers', silencing 'what has traditionally been socially and culturally forbidden to girls: anger, desire for power, and control over one's life' (2003, 64 and 65). Valerie Hey similarly writes that in order to belong and be accepted within dominant culture, girls must perform 'appropriate forms of femininity' (1997, 130). Hey asserts that feminine 'positions [are] coordinated through dominant gender narratives', creating a 'powerful coalition between dominant gender "scripts" and girls' own desire to be "normal"' (131). These idealised forms of good girl femininity include 'practicing caretaking and nurturing roles' and avoiding 'conflict and expressions of direct aggression' (Currie and Kelly 2006, 157). The removal of the male narrator's disapproving and punishing interdictions against Little Red Riding Hood straying from the path, and the addition of the heroine's authoritative perspective and voice-over which actively refutes the original message of the Perrault and Grimm warnings against female rebellion, creates a significant space in which discourses of idealised 'good girl' femininity can be contested and revised. This contestation allows Valerie to challenge the aspect of the 'good girl' discourse that forbids the expression of desire, and this opens up space for the introduction of the heroine's desiring gaze.

The second manifestation of Valerie's gaze as agency occurs in desiring point-of-view shots in the liminal forest. In the forest, beyond the restrictions of everyday culture, she finds a subjective desiring position. Kimberley McMahon-Coleman and Roslyn Weaver write that *Red Riding Hood* works to 'subvert the original message' of the Perrault and Grimm tales by celebrating Valerie's 'assertive sexuality', thereby undermining 'the original meaning of the tale and its warnings against young girls acting foolishly around men who might compromise their reputation and chastity' (2012, 60). This shift in point of view revises the dynamic between the wolf and the girl, so that the girl is no longer a simple victim of the predatory creature but instead actively engaged with it. This desiring gaze is displayed throughout the film, in shot–reverse shot sequences. In the first shot, Valerie's eyes are focused on in close-up and in the reverse shot, Peter, the 'good' wolf, is revealed as the object of her gaze. During this reverse shot, the camera, aligned with Valerie's gaze, zooms in slowly on Peter's figure. This zoom further emphasises the assertiveness and authority of Valerie's gaze, framing it as a gaze of considerable power and intensity. Valerie's desiring gaze always initiates this shot–reverse shot sequence, which is repeated throughout the film. This repeated cinematographic structure emphasises the forcefulness of the girl's desiring look, disrupting dominant ideals about feminine display for a heterosexual male gaze.

This is another point of commonality between Hardwicke's film and *The Company of Wolves*. As Marina Warner writes, Carter's text 'lifts the covers from the body of carnal knowledge usually more modestly draped in fairy tales...to conjure young girls' sexual hunger' (1995, 309). While Perrault warns young girls against seduction, providing a cautionary message in his final moral of the tale, Carter and Jordan, and in turn Hardwicke, do away with this message, instead foregrounding the girl's wayward gaze at the wolf, her object of desire. Many girlhood theorists such as Driscoll, Ringrose and Gonick have pointed out that contemporary Western culture requires the silencing of the girl's active desire and the initiation into the status of object of desire—the girl's desiring point of view and gaze are marginalised. Deborah Martin succinctly describes this structure of desire: 'the requirements of patriarchal culture for the young girl to give up active and agentic desire and accept her status as object of desire' (2013, 137). However, as with any gendered power structure, there is always the potential for a challenge, rupture and difference to be articulated. *Red Riding Hood*'s shot–reverse shot sequences that allow teen girl desire to be articulated attest to this space of difference. This challenge is significant because it contests the rigid boundaries that hold conventional gendered structures of looking in place and opening up a space for new and perhaps unexpected representations of the gaze in teen cinema.

The shot–reverse shot sequence that closes the film reveals Peter in his new wolf form. Valerie sees the wolf before her in the woods. His bright, yellow eyes and sharp teeth do not frighten her. In fact, she gazes intensely at Peter in his wolf form, and smiles with confidence and assurance. This privileging of her desire and desiring point of view through both the narrative and the shot–reverse shot sequences revises the dynamic of fear, violence and violation between girl and wolf. Instead, Hardwicke's Little Red Riding Hood heroine meets the wolf in the forest of her own design, and on her own terms. This claiming of an authoritative and central point of view undermines the dominating masculine gazes embedded in Perrault and the Grimms' literary versions of the tale, particularly those of the disapproving narrator, the brave huntsman and the predatory wolf. The heroine's perspective is restored to a central position, allowing her to rupture the 'good girl' discourse imposed upon her by the paternalistic figures in the film, as well as allowing her a desiring gaze that is often denied teen girls. Such a challenge and rupture to the cinematic system presents a revaluation of a feminine adolescent perspective. By deciding to permanently map herself into the ultraliminal landscape, and articulating her oppositional and challenging point of view, Valerie creates a space in which she can redraw the map of girlhood.

Conclusions: Representing Agency and Resistance in Teen Girl Media

Red Riding Hood provides us with a fairy tale heroine who is neither in need of rescue nor reprimand. While a number of contemporary teen 'Red Riding Hood' screen texts conclude with the girl's rescue or punishment, Hardwicke's text follows in the footsteps of feminist revisions such as Carter's 'Company of Wolves', allowing the heroine to determine her own fate. This allows the text to go beyond the limiting stereotypes of the helpless damsel who must be saved and the abject monster that must be destroyed. Both agency and resistance can be expressed through the teen–fairy tale hybrid text, including through formal elements such as the structure of the cinematic gaze and its visual representation of liminal spaces and mobilities. Representations of agency and resistance in the teen genre are important, because they offer an opportunity to engage with a version of feminine adolescence that is active, agentic, rebellious and innovative. In this chapter, I have explored how the teen heroine of *Red Riding Hood* navigates the significant constraints, prescriptions and limitations placed upon feminine adolescence, looking for the moments in which she is able to enact noncompliance in the face of those limiting structures.

While the text certainly ends with the romantic coupling, which Short complains enacts a 'de-clawing' of the heroine (2015, 149), I suggest that this does not necessarily undermine Valerie's earlier rebellions against the patriarchal status quo. Indeed, she independently negotiates a place for herself within the liminal space of the forest, and harnesses the power of the outsider identities of hunter, traveller and witch. While dominant iterations of the fairy tale romance often foreground the girls' 'dependency and helplessness', and reliance on male characters for help and care (Haines 2014, 161), *Red Riding Hood* provides a much more complex image of desire and agency. The girl actively initiates and pursues her relationship with the wolf and negotiates it on her own terms. So while the romance is present in the text, Hardwicke eschews dominant fairy tale conventions in favour of an alternative representation of feminine adolescent appetite and desire. These revisions and additions of what has been 'left unexploited' (Bacchilega 1997, 50) in the tale significantly alter the gendered dynamic of the Perrault and Grimm tellings of 'Little Red Riding Hood', and revalue the girl's waywardness as a positive trait.

In the first half of the film, Hardwicke presents the constraints, prescriptions and limitations of hegemonic femininity, demonstrating an acute awareness of the 'Little Red Riding Hood' tale's sexist dynamics, particularly in the Perrault and Grimm tellings, that render the girl powerless, both a victim and a temptress who 'deserves' the punishment of the wolf's violence and violation. The film shows how Valerie is subjected to the rule of the tyrannical patriarchs of her hometown, and it is here that she is subjected to such horrifying discipline as handcuffing, chaining and imprisonment. These punishments for her so-called transgressions prevent her access to a clear viewing position and freedom of movement, enforcing a masculine, panoptic gaze that places the girl under extreme surveillance. The film sets about exposing these violations as violent and oppressive, rather than necessary and even desirable, as the Perrault and Grimm tales would have it. Once the film exposes and unsettles these sexist narrative and representational structures, it then actively engages in a feminist revision of them, seeing Valerie reclaim her power from the men who seek to control her. She escapes into the other-worldly space of the forest and refuses to return to conventional society.

By entering the liminal margin of the forest, Valerie is able to enact a measure of resistance to the conventional femininity she is required to take up. This resistance is expressed through her move from the oppressive realm of the Gothic domestic, a space she is being urged to occupy as wife to a stranger. I have read Valerie's permanent or 'ultraliminal' escape into the forest as a key gesture of defiance against and dissatisfaction with a culture that demands limiting ways of doing girlhood and femininity. The representation of this highly flexible and mobile geography offers a new optic through which to view girlhood. In this zone of non-compliance, Valerie constructs an alternative feminine identity by occupying the subject positions of traveller, hunter and witch, eschewing the 'good girl' identity of obedience to paternal authority.

I have argued that *Red Riding Hood's* formal elements of the girl's voice-over and the presentation of the girl's gaze are central to an exploration of feminine agency in the text. This revision occurs not only at the level of the 'Little Red Riding Hood' narrative, and the oppressive male gazes embedded in its Perrault and Grimm literary tradition; it also ruptures the cinematic codes that fix the feminine figure in the position of passive object and the privileging of the straight white male gaze and voice, making room for new iterations of girlhood on the screen. My reading of liminal space in *Red Riding Hood* as a margin where the heroine could escape from the strictures of dominant culture argued for the potential for empowerment that this escape holds for the heroine. In the next chapter, I analyse another Hardwicke film, *Twilight* (2008), turning my attention from liminal space to liminal time. I explore the feminine rite of passage in more detail, and consider whether liminality can create a rupture that allows the girl's articulations of opposition to seep into and impact the postliminal world that she reintegrates into. I am particularly interested in exploring Bella's 'Sleeping Beauty' fantasy and dream sequences as liminal moments in time that temporarily suspend and disrupt her progression towards feminine acculturation, and her induction into adult womanhood. Furthermore, I consider how these disruptions impact upon her passage into the postliminal, and how they may, to some extent, create change in Bella's return to the status quo.

NOTES

1. Campbell's writing on the 'monomyth' focused on ancient heroic myths and primarily male hero figures (though he did include a small number of female heroes in his analysis). In his analysis of these myths, he identified an archetypal journey comprised of three stages: departure, initiation and return (1949).

2. One notable exception is Michelle Byers's (2007) essay on Angela Chase's voice-over narration in the teen television series *My So-Called Life* (ABC 1994–1995). Byers is extremely sceptical about the potential for agency to emerge from an authoritative teen point of view because the essay's theorisation of voice and the gaze is rooted in a discourse of girls-at-risk and media-effects methodology. She argues that Angela is grounded in the text as a passive feminine body to-be-looked-at, which undermines any sense of resistant voice-over (16). As a result, the essay does not consider the teen figure or the teen voice beyond a place of lack, powerlessness and objectification.

BIBLIOGRAPHY

Bacchilega, Cristina. 1997. *Postmodern Fairy Tales: Gender and Narrative Strategies*. Philadelphia: University of Pennsylvania Press.

Blackford, Holly Virginia. 2012. *The Myth of Persephone in Girls' Fantasy Literature*. New York and London: Routledge.

Brickman, Barbara Jane. 2007. Coming of Age in the 1970s: Revision, Fantasy, and Rage in the Teen-Girl Badlands. *Camera Obscura* 22 (3): 25–59. doi:10.1215/02705346-2007-014.

Brownmiller, Susan. 1975. *Against Our Will: Men, Women and Rape*. London: Secker and Warburg.

Byers, Michelle. 2007. Gender/Sexuality/Desire: Subversion of Difference and Construction of Loss in the Adolescent Drama of *My So-Called Life*. In *Dear Angela: Remembering My So-Called Life*, ed. Michelle Byers and David Lavery, 13–34. London: Lexington Books.

Campbell, Joseph. 1949. *The Hero with a Thousand Faces*. New York: Pantheon Books.

Carter, Angela. [1979] 1996. The Company of Wolves. In *Burning Your Boats: Collected Short Stories*, 212–220. London: Vintage.

Cowie, Elizabeth. 1990. Fantasia. In *The Woman in Question*, ed. Parveen Adams and Elizabeth Cowie, 149–196. Cambridge, MA: MIT Press.

Creed, Barbara. 2007. The Neomyth in Film: The Woman Warrior From Joan of Arc to Ellen Ripley. In *Women Willing to Fight: The Fighting Woman in*

Film, ed. Silke Andris and Ursula Frederick, 15–37. Cambridge Scholars Publishing: Newcastle.

Currie, Dawn H., and Deirdre M. Kelly. 2006. "I'm Going to Crush You Like a Bug": Understanding Girls' Agency and Empowerment. In *Girlhood: Redefining the Limits*, ed. Yasmin Jiwani, Candis Steenbergen, and Claudia Mitchell, 155–172. Montreal, New York and London: Black Rose Books.

de Lauretis, Teresa. 1984. *Alice Doesn't: Feminism, Semiotics, Cinema*. Bloomington: Indiana University Press.

DeLamotte, Eugenia C. 1990. *Perils of the Night: A Feminist Study of Nineteenth-Century Gothic*. New York: Oxford University Press.

Doane, Mary Ann. 1987. *The Desire to Desire: The Woman's Film of the 1940s*. Bloomington and Indianapolis: Indiana University Press.

Driscoll, Catherine. 2002. *Girls: Feminine Adolescence in Popular Culture and Cultural Theory*. New York: Columbia University Press.

Fleenor, Juliann E. 1983. Introduction: The Female Gothic. In *The Female Gothic*, ed. Juliann E. Fleenor, 3–30. Montreal: Eden Press.

Foucault, Michel. [1975] 1995. *Discipline and Punish: The Birth of the Prison*, trans. Alan Sheridan. New York: Vintage Books.

———. 1977. *Language, Counter-Memory, Practice: Selected Essays and Interviews*, trans. Donald F. Bouchard and Sherry Simon and ed. Donald F. Bouchard. Ithaca, NY: Cornell University Press.

———. 1980. *The History of Sexuality: Volume One*. London: Penguin.

Gonick, Marnina. 2003. *Between Femininities: Ambivalence, Identity, and the Education of Girls*. Albany: State University of New York Press.

Grimm, Jacob, and Wilhelm Grimm. [1857] 2001. Little Red Cap. In *The Great Fairy Tale Tradition: From Straparola and Basile to the Brothers Grimm*, trans. and ed. Jack Zipes, 747–750. New York and London: W.W. Norton and Co.

Haines, Rebecca C. 2014. *The Princess Problem: Guiding Our Girls Through the Princess-Obsessed Years*. Naperville, IL: Sourcebooks.

Hayton, Natalie. 2011. Cloaked Conspiracies: Catherine Hardwicke's *Red Riding Hood* (2011). *Adaptation* 5 (1): 124–128. doi:10.1093/adaptation/apr022.

Hey, Valerie. 1997. *The Company She Keeps: An Ethnography of Girls' Friendships*. Buckingham and Philadelphia, PA: Open University Press.

Hollinger, Karen. 1992. Listening to the Female Voice in the Woman's Film. *Film Criticism* 16 (3): 34–52.

Kearney, Mary Celeste. 2006. *Girls Make Media*. New York and London: Routledge.

Kuhn, Annette. 1984. Women's Genres. *Screen* 25 (1): 18–28.

Marshall, Elizabeth. 2004. Stripping for the Wolf: Rethinking Representations of Gender in Children's Literature. *Reading Research Quarterly* 39 (3): 256–270. doi:10.1598/RRQ.39.3.1.

Martin, Deborah. 2013. Feminine Adolescence as Uncanny: Masculinity, Haunting and Self-Estrangement. *Forum for Modern Language Studies* 49 (2): 135–144. doi:10.1093/fmls/cqs067.

McMahon-Coleman, Kimberley, and Roslyn Weaver. 2012. *Werewolves and Other Shapeshifters in Popular Culture: A Thematic Analysis of Recent Depictions.* Jefferson, NC and London: McFarland and Company.

Modleski, Tania. 1988. *The Women Who Knew Too Much: Hitchcock and Feminist Theory.* New York: Routledge.

Mulvey, Laura. [1975] 1989. Visual Pleasure and Narrative Cinema. In *Visual and Other Pleasures*, 14–26. Bloomington and Indianapolis: Indiana University Press.

Orenstein, Catherine. 2002. *Little Red Riding Hood Uncloaked: Sex, Morality, and the Evolution of a Fairy Tale.* New York: Basic Books.

Perrault, Charles. [1607] 2001. Little Red Riding Hood. In *The Great Fairy Tale Tradition: From Straparola and Basile to the Brothers Grimm*, 745–747. New York and London: W.W. Norton and Co.

Pomerantz, Shauna. 2007. Cleavage in a Tank Top: Bodily Prohibition and the Discourses of School Dress Codes. *Alberta Journal of Educational Research* 53 (4): 373–386. http://www.education.ualberta.ca/educ/journals/ ajer/53%20files/53(4)files/53(4).html.

Rich, B. Ruby, Michelle Citron, Julia Lesage, Judith Mayne and Anna Marie Taylor. 1978. Women and Film: A Discussion of Feminist Aesthetics. *New German Critique* 13: 82–107.

Rich, B. Ruby, and Linda Williams. 1981. The Right of Re-vision: Michelle Citron's *Daughter Rite. Film Quarterly* 35 (1): 17–22. http://www.jstor.org/stable/1212076.

Ringrose, Jessica. 2013. *Postfeminist Education? Girls and the Sexual Politics of Schooling.* London and New York: Routledge.

Short, Sue. 2006. *Misfit Sisters: Screen Horror as Female Rites of Passage.* New York: Palgrave Macmillan.

———. 2015. *Fairy Tale and Film: Old Tales with a New Spin.* Basingstoke and New York: Palgrave Macmillan.

Stacey, Jackie. 1994. *Star Gazing: Hollywood Cinema and Female Spectatorship.* New York: Routledge.

Tatar, Maria. 2004. *Secrets Beyond the Door: The Story of Bluebeard and His Wives.* Princeton, NJ and Oxford: Princeton University Press.

Turner, Victor. 1969. *The Ritual Process: Structure and Anti-structure.* Chicago: Aldine Publishing Company.

———. 1982. *From Ritual to Theatre: The Human Seriousness of Play.* New York: Performing Arts Journal Publications.

Wallace, Diana, and Andrew Smith. 2009. Introduction: Defining the Female Gothic. In *The Female Gothic: New Directions*, ed. Diana Wallace and Andrew Smith, 1–12. Basingstoke and New York: Palgrave Macmillan.

Warner, Marina. 1995. *From the Beast to the Blonde: On Fairy Tales and their Tellers*. London: Vintage.

Williams, Linda. 1984. "Something Else Besides a Mother": *Stella Dallas* and the Maternal Melodrama. *Cinema Journal* 24 (1): 2–27. http://www.jstor.org/stable/1225306.

Zipes, Jack. 1986. A Second Gaze at Little Red Riding Hood's Trials and Tribulations. In *Don't Bet on the Prince: Contemporary Fairy Tales in North America and England*, ed. Jack Zipes, 227–260. New York: Routledge.

———. 1989. "Little Red Riding Hood" as Male Creation and Projection. In *Little Red Riding Hood: A Casebook*, ed. Alan Dundes, 121–128. Madison: University of Wisconsin Press.

——— (ed.). 1993. *The Trials and Tribulations of Little Red Riding Hood* (2nd ed.). New York and London: Routledge.

FILMOGRAPHY

Badlands. Dir. Terrence Malick. 1973.

Blood and Chocolate. Dir. Katja von Garnier. 2007.

Boy who Cried Werewolf. Dir. Eric Bross. 2010.

Buffy the Vampire Slayer. The WB. 1997–2003.

The Company of Wolves. Dir. Neil Jordan. 1984.

Cursed. Dir. Wes Craven. 2005.

Freeway. Dir. Matthew Bright. 1996.

Ginger Snaps. Dir. John Fawcett. 2000.

Hanna. Dir. Joe Wright. 2011.

Hard Candy. Dir. David Slade. 2005.

My So-Called Life. ABC. 1994–1995.

The Passion of Joan of Arc. Dir. Carl Theodor Dreyer. 1928.

Red Riding Hood. Dir. Catherine Hardwicke. 2011.

Teen Wolf. MTV. 2011–.

Thelma and Louise. Dir. Ridley Scott. 1991.

The Vampire Diaries. The CW. 2010–2017.

Twilight. Dir. Catherine Hardwicke. 2008.

When Animals Dream. Dir. Jonas Alexander Arnby. 2014.

CHAPTER 3

When Sleeping Beauty Wakes: The *Twilight* Film Series, Liminal Time and Fantasy Images

INTRODUCTION: FANTASIES OF REBELLION ON THE TEEN SCREEN

Teen sleeping beauties abound in contemporary screen texts. Some of these representations reproduce familiar images of a glamorous and completely passive girl. For example, Nicolas Winding Refn's *The Neon Demon* (2016) creates a series of spectacular tableaux in which adolescent models are posed to appear dead, while male photographers look at them with desire. In the opening scene, protagonist Jessie, clad in a latex mini dress, lies deathly still on a couch, her legs provocatively thrown open, her vacant face made up with ornate sparkles and jewels, and thick garnet-red blood dripping from her 'gashed' neck. The film compulsively, fetishistically returns to imagery of catatonic teen girls who are beautiful but docile, captured by the gaze of the male characters. *The Neon Demon* is one example among many, including countless episodes of popular series such as *CSI* (CBS 2000–2015) and *Criminal Minds* (CBS 2005–) that centre on investigating crimes committed against comatose and paralysed young women, reminding us that images of feminine passivity remain a potent source of fascination in contemporary visual culture.

This repeated invocation of the unconscious girl as a source of visual pleasure reaffirms and normalises the gendered binary of passive female versus active male. As Maria Tatar writes, 'myths naturalise ideology' (2014, 154), and the above texts are certainly examples of this.

© The Author(s) 2017
A. Bellas, *Fairy Tales on the Teen Screen*,
DOI 10.1007/978-3-319-64973-3_3

However, as Tatar goes on to point out, fairy tale revisions also have the capacity to 'denaturalis[e] myth and refram[e] old stories in new terms' (154). Feminist literary revisions of the 'Sleeping Beauty' tale include Angela Carter's short story 'The Lady of the House of Love' (1979), Jane Yolen's novel *Briar Rose* (1992) and Anne Sexton's poem 'Briar Rose (Sleeping Beauty)' (1971). On the screen, Catherine Breillat's TV movie *La Belle Endormie* (2010) and Julia Leigh's Australian film *Sleeping Beauty* (2011) interrogate and subvert the passive position of the sleeping girl by 'signal[ling] the possible activity of an inner life, a hidden subjectivity kept from the viewer', as critic Genevieve Yue argues (2012, 35). Some filmic revisions are particularly preoccupied with subverting Disney's influential 1959 version of the tale. For example, Jamie Babbit's surreal short film *Sleeping Beauties* (1999) reimagines the tale as a queer love story between two young women, Clea and 'Princess Charming'. Juxtaposing images of the lesbian romance with a range of familiar features from classic Disney princess texts, including songs and the iconic jewelled storybook that frames the beginning and end of the films, disrupts the heteronormative ideology embedded in the earlier texts and opens the narrative up to new possibilities. More recently, Disney's *Maleficent* (Stromberg 2014) displaced the romance narrative and the figure of the male rescuer displaced the romance narrative, instead imagining a loving relationship between Sleeping Beauty and her 'fairy godmother', Maleficent. These subversive teen 'Sleeping Beauty' screen texts enact the demythologising function mentioned above and restoring agency to the girl. *Twilight* is particularly unusual in this context of 'Sleeping Beauty' films because it enacts a gender reversal in which the male character, Edward, is cast as Beauty. While the previous chapter showed that contemporary visual culture features a number of gendered transformations in which Red Riding Hood becomes the traditionally male role of the wolf or hunter, such reversals are far less common in retellings of the 'Sleeping Beauty' tale. As Tatar notes, 'our culture has worked hard to privilege sleeping beauties over handsome slumberers' (2014, 144). I am interested in moments in *Twilight* that disrupt this privileging, and the outcomes that this produces in the way the tale is told on the teen screen.

Echoes of the 'Sleeping Beauty' fairy tale run throughout the *Twilight* film series. Bella's fantasy and dream sequences are structured around the tale's symbols and imagery of enchanted slumbers; the magical suspension of time; images of a reclining Beauty and an active, desiring gaze at the reclining figure. However, these fantasy sequences shift the gendered terms of this tale: Edward is cast as Beauty, and he is constructed as a luminous, sparkling spectacle for Bella's active, desiring gaze. Therefore, Charles Perrault's characterisation of the feminine figure as a passive spectacle to be scrutinised and surveilled by a male gaze is challenged in Bella's fantasy sequences. In this fantasy revision, Bella reverses the terms of the gaze by positioning vampire Edward as her object of desire. His image is spectacularised and prettified, associated with the excesses of pattern, lace and sparkles, and this perversion of gendered categories of the image allows for a new set of relations to emerge in which the girl is able to claim a desiring gaze. Through my redeployment of Sarah Projansky's methodology of the feminist optic, which searches for instances of girl's empowerment and alternative ways of doing girlhood on the teen screen (2014, 10–11), I locate Bella's fantasy, pretty images of Edward as sites of feminine adolescent power. The tale's theme of 'correct' development, feminine acculturation and timely progress towards an idealised womanhood is also challenged by the languorous delays that Bella engineers in her fantasy sequences. In revising these elements of the Perrault (1697) and Brothers Grimm (1857) versions of 'Sleeping Beauty', Bella claims her fantasy space as a rebellion, creating the potential to include other possible modes of doing girlhood, including the capacity for authorship, protest, dissatisfaction and the clear articulation of desire and a desiring gaze.

The 'Sleeping Beauty' tale is frequently read through a Bettelheimian (1978) psychoanalytic lens as a metaphor for the adolescent girl's maturation into feminine adulthood, signalled by the happy ending resolution of heterosexual romance, marriage and, in some versions, motherhood (see Kolbenschlag 1983; Lieberman 1986; Zipes 2002). Stephenie Meyer's *Twilight* novels, and the blockbuster films based on the novels,[1] certainly follow this conservative heteronormative 'Sleeping Beauty' resolution in some respects. Teen protagonist Bella is 'awakened' by her Prince Charming, vampire Edward, they marry, have a baby and go on to spend eternity together as a family. Several scholars have written about this heteronormative narrative movement as a retrograde and conservative postfeminist fantasy (Seifert 2009; Platt 2010; Veldman-Genz 2011). However, I challenge the simplicity of this reading of *Twilight*. It is clear that Bella's journey into feminine adulthood is, in many ways, structured according to a very narrow definition of feminine identity. However, the scholarship on *Twilight* to date has not adequately accounted for the film series' significant focus on liminality, with its repeated references to the 'Sleeping Beauty' tale and Bella's sleeping, fantasising and dreaming process that occurs before her induction into the strictures of womanhood. These liminal intervals are important to address, because it is here that *Twilight's* most subversive, rebellious and challenging moments of doing girlhood arise. By theorising Bella's rite of passage through Turner's conceptualisation of the passage from liminality to postliminality, I chart the ways in which these fissures impact upon the status quo, arguing that liminality can instigate change and embolden the heroine to contest the boundaries of her feminine identity.

At points in the *Twilight* series, postfeminist cultural ideals about femininity seem to dominate the text, particularly through the paradigm of 'active hero/passive heroine' (Taylor 2012, 34), a return to domesticity via the glorification of marriage and motherhood (Renold and Ringrose 2008, 329; Negra 2009, 47), and the obliteration of personal independence in favour of romantic connection (Gill 2007, 218; McRobbie 2008, 543). It is clear that *Twilight* contributes to postfeminist media culture's celebration of 'conservative gender paths' (Tasker 2012, 70). However, I argue that this postfeminist ideal of girlhood and feminine acculturation is also challenged, interrupted and even rejected at times during Bella's fantasy and dream sequences. To be sure, these challenges do not *undo* the postfeminist discourse that runs throughout the film series, but I do think that they *unsettle* it. With a particular focus on the fantasy and dream sequences that proliferate throughout *Twilight* (Hardwicke 2008) and *New Moon* (Weitz 2010), I argue that Bella temporarily rejects two important discourses that delimit the girl as an object in contemporary patriarchal culture. The first discourse to be challenged is that of feminine beauty and desirability, which requires girls to silence their own desire whilst simultaneously presenting a desirable image for a heterosexual male gaze. The second discourse to be contested is the strict monitoring of 'normal' or timely linear development and progress towards ideal womanhood and its attendant theme of fulfilment through heterosexual romance and motherhood.

Twilight's unruly fantasy elements, which disrupt these gendered boundaries, include an articulation of gender rebellion. Moments of gender rebellion are significant to note, because they work 'against emphasised femininity, a discourse that reinforces women's subordination to men' (Kelly et al. 2006, 22). These moments are, as Jessica Laureltree Willis points out, ones in which girls can 'invent and invert notions of gender' (2009, 101). She further writes that using 'imagination as a resource' is one way in which girls exercise agency because it is here that they can find 'spaces for manoeuvring within cultural possibilities for re-conceptualising notions of gender' (109). In fantasy, Bella exercises agency, both challenging and rewriting some of the strictures that define girlhood. Bella's rejection of these objectifying discourses defies the paradigm of feminine passivity and submission that pervade the Perrault and Grimm versions of the 'Sleeping Beauty' tale. These fantasy sequences not only revise the gender dynamics of the fairy tale; they also provide an expansive imaginative space through which Bella can explore alternative desires, identities and subjective positions. I therefore consider these unruly fantasy elements, which challenge and rupture discourses that govern girlhood through sexist power structures, central to a feminist reading of the text.

Elizabeth Cowie's theorisation of fantasy informs my reading of *Twilight*. In her psychoanalytic account of cinematic fantasy,[2] Cowie argues that it 'involves, is characterised by, not the achievement of desired objects, but the arranging of, a setting out of, desire; a veritable *mise-en-scène* of desire ... The fantasy depends not on particular objects, but on their setting out and the pleasure of fantasy lies in the setting out, not in the having of objects' (1990, 159). She goes on to suggest that in such a setting out, the spectator is presented with 'a varying of subject positions so that the subject takes up more than one position and thus is not fixed' (160). In *Twilight*, Bella designs fantasy sequences in which possible modes of femininity that fall outside the definitional boundaries of 'good' girlhood can be engaged. This reconfigures gendered relations in fantasy, affording the heroine a position from which to articulate her desire and enact a desiring gaze. In this way, Bella's fantasy sequences are a setting out, an invitation to spectatorial identification with a female gaze and desire.

Therefore, fantasy provides a significant challenge and rupture to cultural discourses that seek to fix, stabilise, normalise and restrict girlhood, for it is a practice of setting out and exploring multiple possibilities for being in the world. Furthermore, it provides a method for theorising girls and girlhood (both onscreen and as spectators) as active and in flux rather than as fixed and static categories. This variability of objects, positions and 'settings out' provides an invitation to explore multiple, contradictory and perhaps challenging ways of doing girlhood. Bella's alternative fantasy universe, which she constructs in the privacy of her own bedroom, includes the breaking of several normative rules that govern girlhood and replacing them with more agentic possibilities for girlhood. Bella creates a fantasy space that she has authored and designed, and this fantasy space challenges the notion that girls have little or no control over the processes of their rite of passage (Lesko 2001, 51). It is through this authorship that Bella is able to break down the visual economy that places girls in a position of emphasised femininity and reconfigure the gendered categories of the image and the gaze. Furthermore, the fantasy sequences manipulate temporality and frustrate linearity, undermining the progression towards feminine acculturation and adult womanhood that the wider narrative of *Twilight* pushes her towards. In this chapter, I undertake an against the grain analysis of *Twilight* to explore the contradictions and spectacular excesses embedded in the fantasy sequences, and the unsettling effect they have on the remainder of the narrative of feminine acculturation.

The next section following this introduction surveys feminist responses to the literary tradition of the 'Sleeping Beauty' tale, particularly in its popular Perrault and Grimm versions. This work revealed the deeply problematic and sexist nature of the tale's glorification of Beauty's passivity and powerlessness. Some of this work, particularly that of Madonna Kolbenschlag (1983), Marcia K. Lieberman (1986) and Karen Rowe (1986), saw the glorified ideals of femininity in the tale at work within the wider culture and the acculturation of teenage girls, particularly through romantic ideology. While these 'Sleeping Beauty' ideals are certainly at work within the *Twilight* texts, they are also challenged, particularly in Bella's fantasy and bedroom sequences, to include an agentic expression of girlhood. The next two sections explore how Bella's fantasy scenes revise the 'Sleeping Beauty' tale, creating ruptures in its patriarchal narrative of feminine acculturation and rite of passage. Through the feminist poststructuralist theory of Nancy Lesko and Valerie Walkerdine (1990), I analyse moments in the text where Bella challenges the discourse of feminine development and 'normal' progress towards womanhood. Arguing that the fantasy sequences create an interjection into this discourse by halting its progression through a focus on languorous sleep states and slow motion, I theorise liminal time as an interval that suspends the progress towards idealised womanhood and provides an opening for the exploration of alternatives. In this opening or fissure, Bella's opposition to her subordinate position within patriarchal culture is articulated, and she experiments with the subject positions of author, desiring subject and protestor. I then explore Bella's deployment of spectacle and pretty aesthetics in her 'Sleeping Beauty' fantasy sequences, revealing that her excessive, decorative designs and fabrications of Edward reconfigure the gendered dynamics of the earlier text's representation of spectacle and the gaze. Redeploying Rosalind Galt's (2011) concept of the cinematic pretty, I analyse how Bella casts Edward in the role of Beauty in these sequences through associating his figure with materials such as lace and glitter, providing an image that allows the heroine to escape her conventional role as object. This not only challenges existing dynamics of the gaze, but also creates a new visual language in which an active and desiring teen girl gaze is possible. These excesses of spectacle and temporality are rebellious elements of Bella's fantasy world, creating fissures in the existing structures that contain and govern expressions of girlhood.

'Sleeping Beauty': Feminine Passivity in the Tradition of the Tale

The 'Sleeping Beauty' fairy tale has been vigorously critiqued by feminist scholars, who point out the sexist dynamic of feminine adolescent passivity and masculine dominance that the tale represents and even promotes. The tale links feminine glamour and patient waiting create a troubling association between feminine beauty, passivity and desirability. Indeed, feminist scholars such as Karen Rowe, Marcia K. Lieberman and Madonna Kolbenschlag (1983) found that this privileging of feminine glamour and passivity reflected the expectations and restrictions placed on girls and women in contemporary culture. This research revealed how the tale upholds the patriarchal script of feminine passivity and subservience to masculine authority, and furthermore, that the tale shrouds this disturbing script in the guise of romantic love between the Prince and Princess. I argue that *Twilight* both participates in and also contains elements that disrupt this tradition of fairy tale femininity.

Feminine passivity is central to the 'Sleeping Beauty' tale, as the girl unwillingly submits to her rite of passage into womanhood. In the anonymous fourteenth-century telling of the tale entitled *Perceforest* (Bryant 2013) and Giambattista Basile's version of the tale, 'Sun, Moon and Talia' ([1634]2001), the Prince rapes and impregnates the Princess as she lies in her enchanted comatose state, inducting her (unwillingly) into the role of mother. While Perrault and the Grimms removed this extreme violation in their canonical versions of the tale, the sexist paradigm of feminine passivity versus masculine dominance is preserved in the narrative of the helpless maiden and the brave, active Prince. When the heroine awakes from her slumber and completes her rite of passage into adult femininity, she is promptly installed in the roles of wife and mother. Feminine beauty is, as Lieberman writes, represented in the tale as 'a girl's most valuable asset, perhaps her only valuable asset' (1986, 188). She elaborates, 'since the heroines are chosen for their beauty ... not for anything they do ... they seem to exist passively until they are seen by the hero, or described to him. They wait, are chosen, and are rewarded' with marriage (189). The figure of Sleeping Beauty, in both the Perrault and Grimm versions, is described as pure spectacle. For example, Perrault describes the scene of the Prince's discovery in terms that highlight and spectacularise passive feminine beauty:

> he entered a chamber completely covered with gold and saw the most lovely sight he had ever looked upon – there on a bed with the curtains open on each side was a princess who seemed to be about fifteen or sixteen and whose radiant charms gave her an appearance that was luminous and supernatural. ([1697] 2001, 691)

The scene is described as opulently extravagant, with the girl's figure set in a room studded with gold, laying on a bed with the curtains suggestively thrown open. Fixed in her comatose state, the girl functions here as passive spectacle, 'the most lovely sight', for the Prince's pleasure. The tale is structured according to patriarchal ideals of feminine passivity and masculine dominance, and that these ideals become particularly evident in the description of the Prince's masculine gaze at his object of erotic desire.

Feminist theory involves a critique of patriarchal imagery and its representation of women in order to deconstruct and unsettle the structures that maintain its authority and pervasiveness within visual culture. Feminist film and cultural criticism has also been centrally concerned with the sexist dynamics that construct woman as passive spectacle for a determining male gaze, and the ways in which they are played out and reproduced in the cinema. Mulvey writes that 'the beauty of the woman as object and the screen space coalesce; she is no longer the bearer of guilt but a perfect product, whose body, stylised and fragmented by close-ups, is the content of the film and the direct recipient of the spectator's look' ([1975] 1989, 22). In her role as 'perfect product', the female figure on screen is fixed in a position of stylised spectacle-to-be-looked-at. She is placed in this position of spectacle, dissected by the camera and the gaze of the male figure on screen (as well as the male spectator), in order to be placed under visual scrutiny. Cultural theorist Sandra Lee Bartky further elaborates that the scrutiny of the gaze functions as a disciplinary force which ensures that 'normative femininity [comes] more and more to be centred on woman's body ... its presumed heterosexuality and its appearance' (1990, 80). This gaze becomes so culturally pervasive that 'the disciplinary power that inscribes femininity in the female body is everywhere and nowhere; the disciplinarian is everyone and yet no one in particular' (74). Significantly, the girl is not only compelled to make herself available as spectacle for this gaze; she is also compelled to internalise it so that she may style herself appropriately as an object of desire. This gaze therefore works as a profound disciplinary force, involved in the maintenance of gendered power relations in which girls and women not only present themselves as objects of the gaze, but also view and therefore define themselves through it.

In addition to the economy of the gaze in the 'Sleeping Beauty' tale, the girl is also reduced to an even further measure of passivity in her status of helplessness and waiting for rescue. The tale's obsession with time and waiting is evinced in its attention to detail in accounting for it: the marking out of the child's birth, her sixteenth birthday, the enchanted one hundred year's slumber and the marriage that takes place on the brink of the girl's entry into womanhood. This is especially evident in the Grimm version, 'Briar Rose' which even employs a visualisation of the passing one hundred years with the image of the 'briar hedge' which 'began to grow all around the castle, and it grew higher each year. Eventually, it surrounded and covered the entire castle, causing it to become invisible' ([1857] 2001, 697). This meticulous effort to carefully document, circumscribe and categorise each stage of the girl's life suggests a regulative impulse in the tale, in that it sets out a timeline of 'appropriate' feminine development. As Carolyn Fay comments, the moral of the tale appears to be 'women, marry without delay, a message that is consistent with the narrative's theme. Isolating oneself from the world is [represented as] destructive' (2008, 272). Feminist fairy tale scholars have also pointed out that the tale creates a sexist dynamic in which the adolescent girl helplessly waits for a painstaking length of time for the brave Prince to rescue her from enchanted slumber. Rowe argues that fairy tales such as 'Sleeping

Beauty', in their 'portrayals of adolescent waiting and dreaming, patterns of double enchantment, and romanticisations of marriage' which 'gloss' the pernicious aspects of 'the heroine's inability to act self-assertively, [her] total reliance on external rescues [and] willing bondage to father and Prince' work to 'perpetuate the patriarchal *status quo* by making female subordination seem romantically desirable, indeed an inescapable fate' (1986, 209 original emphasis).

Kolbenschlag concurs with Rowe's theorisation of 'adolescent waiting and dreaming'. She considers the 'Sleeping Beauty' tale a metaphor for the process of female adolescent acculturation, a process she refers to as women's 'paralysis' (1983, 17). Kolbenschlag further argues that in adolescence, the girl:

> sees herself as someone that things will happen to, not as one who will make them happen. She has no conception of 'autonomy' as a life-goal; she seeks only the state of 'belonging-to.' From this, she will draw her identity and sustenance – the expected 'kiss' of one who will awaken her from her dormant 'sleep.' (17)

Jack Zipes concurs in his characterisation of Sleeping Beauty as 'a housewife in-training', arguing that the tale feeds into the patriarchal myth that 'women are indeed helpless without men, and without men they are generally catatonic or comatose, eternally waiting for the right man, always in a prone, death-like position, dreaming of a glorious marriage' (2002, 214). Kolbenschlag and Zipes draw attention to Beauty's passive progress through her rite of passage; they show how the theme of patient waiting, of being helplessly caught in time, works to secure Beauty as a submissive figure. All three theorists consider Beauty's period of waiting to be a stultifying, damaging time during which she is indoctrinated into the belief that her eventual 'glorious marriage' will save her. Kolbenschlag and Zipes' wider characterisation of marriage as a sort of false consciousness, and the bride as a duped victim of that false consciousness, is not necessarily constructive because it unwittingly reinscribes the sexist conceptualisation of feminine subjectivity as vulnerable and non-agentic, but they nevertheless helpfully draw attention to the theme of waiting and the passing of time in the feminine rite of passage. This time period of waiting, argues Ann Duggan, is one which requires Beauty to relinquish all that she desires: 'we might view Sleeping Beauty's hundred-year sleep as another supreme example of female patience (she waits a hundred years for a husband), which could also be read in terms of *the erasure of all desire*. To wait a hundred years is practically not to desire at all' (2008, 223–224 original emphasis). Waiting for the Prince, and then becoming his wife as soon as he has saved her, positions Beauty as not only a passive inductee into her rite of passage into adult womanhood; she is also divested of an opportunity to express and actively pursue her desires on her own terms.

TWILIGHT AND TIME: THE ANTISOCIAL PROTEST OF BELLA'S FANTASY SEQUENCES

In *Twilight*, Bella reconceptualises both the elements of spectacle and time in her fantasy 'Sleeping Beauty' sequences in ways that are resistant to the tale's construction of girlhood as passivity. Bella's fantasy scenarios are centrally concerned with the suspension of time, which provide moments of disruption that challenge the narrative's linear and conservative progression that demands feminine acculturation into hegemonic womanhood. Like Sleeping Beauty, Bella's rite of passage or 'awakening' works towards inducting her into the roles of wife and mother. However, Bella actively engineers these disruptive intervals of liminal time that challenge and resist this progress, unlike her fairy tale predecessor whose suspended hypnotic state represented an extreme loss of agency and power. Both the seriality of the *Twilight* texts and the deployment of filmic techniques such as slow motion and the slow dissolve in the fantasy sequences work to disrupt linearity, defer progress and challenge narrative cohesion. Bella's 'Sleeping Beauty' fantasy sequences not only challenge but also unravel these forces that seek to govern, define and delimit 'acceptable' or 'normal' girlhood. The temporary unravelling of these borders allows the fantasy sequences to include other, potentially disruptive ways of doing girlhood. In these fantasy moments, Bella is temporarily relieved of this construction of time that works to contain and control the progression of girlhood. These intervals or fissures in the narrative are therefore oppositional and also generative, because they provide a space in which Bella creates an alternative and empowering feminine adolescent identity. Furthermore, I argue that these liminal fissures are porous, and allow for Bella's fantasy construction of an agentic mode of doing girlhood to seep into her postliminal reality.

Much of the literature on *Twilight* points out the conservative and retrograde narrative, which chronicles Bella's ascension to the traditional feminine roles of wife and mother (Seifert 2009; Platt 2010; Wilson 2011). However, little has been made of the significant labouring of this final resolution over several books and films, and the effect that this delay has on the rite-of-passage narrative. As Maria Leavenworth points out, 'the *Twilight* saga is not an extended series in the same sense [as a television serial], but it similarly resists closure, and specifically *romantic* closure, in the first three texts' (2011, 78 original emphasis). Indeed, in her work on serialised texts, Jennifer Hayward argues that serialisation necessarily engages 'the trope of refusal of closure' (1997, 141). In addition to the delay and resistance of closure inherent in the serial format of the text, *Twilight's* 'Sleeping Beauty' scenes, which focus on Bella's dreaming and fantasy states, in particular, dramatically slow narrative development, and become points of temporal excess that frustrate and challenge the progression to idealised womanhood. The preoccupation with time, timeliness, schedules and progress is reflected throughout the teen screen genre, which frequently focuses on ritual milestone events that mark out maturation and the postliminal conclusion of the rite of passage—teen films about the prom, graduation day and the loss of virginity are examples of this.

The *Twilight* series participates in this preoccupation with progression towards adulthood, including events such as going to the prom, graduating from high school, loss of virginity, moving out of the family home, marriage and motherhood. As Kathleen Rowe Karlyn comments, teen films that follow this conventional rite-of-passage resolution work towards 'domesticating their young protagonists,' seeing them 'gracefully acquiescing to a social order still largely defined by patriarchy and capitalism' (2011, 79–80). However, the serialisation of a teen text such as *Twilight*, as well as its frequent deployment of techniques such as slow motion and the slow dissolve, necessarily defers and frustrates this resolution of maturity, entering into adult femininity and the responsibilities and expectations that come with it. Such a deferral and frustration, I argue, registers a measure of the heroine's dissatisfaction and ambivalence about these acculturating processes that seek to secure her into adult femininity.

Bella constructs these 'Sleeping Beauty' sequences in her bedroom, which is represented as her own private and independent space where she can exercise mastery and control over her fantasy scenarios. Since Angela

McRobbie and Jenny Garber's pivotal study 'Girls and Subcultures' (1976), girlhood studies scholars have brought attention to the creative capacity of girls' bedroom culture, theorising its subversive and potentially empowering aspects (Harris 2001; Kearney 2007). Anita Harris suggests that bedroom culture can function as a kind of 'retreat', which can be read as 'an active choice on the part of young women refusing to participate in particular constructions of girlhood' (2001, 133). She elaborates, 'the scrutiny of young women remains ... and it is this scrutiny that forces them into private places to reflect and resist' (133). The bedroom culture that Bella authors and designs in the fantasy realm is indeed a resistant space, where the construction of girlhood as desirability without desire is thoroughly refused and undermined. It is in this enabling bedroom culture that Bella situates and authors fantasy 'Sleeping Beauty' scenes. Instead of accepting her role as passive object for the scrutiny that Harris describes, she chooses to author fantasy scenarios in which she authors a resistant protest, revealing the potential for this 'retreat' space as one that enables oppositional and alternative girlhood identities to be expressed.

In the Perrault and Grimm versions of the 'Sleeping Beauty' tale, Beauty's slumber and suspension in time represents a time over which she has no control, power or agency. One of the primary shifts in the fairy tale between these earlier texts and Bella's revisionist fantasy is that the heroine's authorial control over the fantasy sequences' suspension of time is made clear, injecting the tale with a new measure of feminine authority, agency and power. As shown in Fig. 3.1, at the beginning of one fantasy sequence in Hardwicke's *Twilight* a black and white filmstrip moves slowly across the screen. The soundtrack features the clicking and whirring of the film running through a projection machine, further emphasising themes of production and projection.

This establishes Bella's fantasy as a kind of film within the film, a scene that she has constructed, written, directed and projected. The scene is of Bella's artful and purposeful design, the careful setting out, and the creative production of the fantasy *mise en scène* of desire, to borrow Cowie's phrase. Bella authors scenarios and images of her own design, not only subverting the scrutiny girls are placed under, but creating in its stead a clear position from which to enact a desiring gaze and to articulate her desire. In this liminal fantasy, Bella asserts herself as a subject who temporarily takes control of the narrative, bringing her defiance of normative feminine adolescent progress and development to the surface of the film.

Fig. 3.1 Bella's 'Sleeping Beauty' fantasy is visualised on a black and white filmstrip, emphasising her role as 'director' and creator of the fantasy sequence

It is during this liminal, oppositional interval in the narrative that Bella can articulate her protest.

Time, timeliness, temporality and ideologies of 'normal' physiological and psychological development work to define and regulate the borders around what constitutes 'appropriate' or acceptable feminine adolescence within postfeminist culture. They define, for example, the 'acceptable' or 'normal' age at which girls should begin to explore their sexuality, have sex for the first time and so on (Driscoll 2002; Carpenter 2009) . These temporalities work to contain and manage girlhood. Foucault writes that 'time penetrates the body and with it all the meticulous controls of power' ([1977] 1995, 152), citing the timetable and the military march as examples of how power can be exercised through the regulation of how subjects should progress and evolve over time, as well as defining the desirable end product of this progression. Foucault elaborates that 'power is articulated directly onto time; it assumes its control and guarantees its use. The disciplinary methods reveal a linear time whose moments are integrated, one upon another, and which is oriented towards a terminal, stable point; in short, an "evolutive" time' (160). Power and time become inextricably interlaced in regulatory discourses because time provides another mode of surveillance where productivity, progress and 'appropriate' development can be measured. It also defines and enforces an acceptable end point that the subject must reach, orienting them towards achieving a predetermined resolution or goal. Through a Foucauldian analysis of adolescence and time, Lesko crucially elucidates how time can be a panoptical 'totalised mode of surveillance', and 'linear, historical time moving toward "progress" [can] be examined for how it disciplines subjectivities and objective knowledge' (40). Lesko elaborates:

> a dominant aspect of the discourse of adolescence is its location within panoptical time, within a time framework that compels us ... to attend to progress, precocity, arrest, or decline. Adolescence both makes and marks time. The developmental framework is simultaneously colonial (with privileged, invisible viewers and hypervisible, temporalised, and embodied others) and administrative (ranking, judging, making efficient and productive). (41)

Lesko's work reveals that this time framework enforces progress and development in order to regulate and discipline adolescence. The monitoring of girls' progress towards womanhood is inextricably linked to this panoptical time that Lesko describes—the scrutinising and standardising of 'normal' feminine development enforced and perpetuated by dominant adult structures such as the school system, and medical and psychological discourses.

Bella's anxiety about the regulation of her development and progress towards womanhood is most clearly expressed in the dream sequence that opens *New Moon*, the second film of the series. In the dream, Bella sees a large clock tower with enormous, slowly ticking, gold hands. It is later revealed that this image of the clock is a premonition about the location from which Bella must save Edward. However, at the beginning of the film, Bella's dream image of the ticking clock immediately fades into another dream sequence. In this sequence, Bella introduces Edward to her grandmother, only to discover that she has magically turned into the older woman. The grandmother vanishes and is replaced by a mirror, which reflects Bella's aged transformation. Bella awakes from this temporal nightmare to find that it is her eighteenth birthday. Bella's fear of growing older and desire to become a vampire manifests in this dream. Catherine Driscoll suggests that 'Bella's desire to stop aging ... is a rejection of maturity as a transformative process and dedication instead to replicating tableaux of teenage beauty' (2011, 100). Driscoll's analysis of *Twilight*'s construction of time provides a good platform for the development of my argument about Bella's challenge to adolescent progress and her temporary rejection of maturity as potentially subversive and disruptive. This halting of progress represents a moment where Bella protests against and rejects many of the normalised and naturalised markers of acceptable feminine girlhood. The very fact that Bella's fantasies work to forestall progress is significant to a feminist reading of the text, for it not only undermines conservative narrative logic but also affords Bella a period of time during which she can defy the normative fulfilment of feminine acculturation. Lesko refers to the framework of adolescence as 'expectant time' (51). She writes that:

> youth are positioned [as] ... waiting passively for the future ... The dominant concepts regarding youth's position in the Western societies, 'development' and 'socialisation,' make it impossible for youth to exercise power over life events or to represent themselves, since they are not fully developed or socialised ... 'expectant time' pushes us to consider the experiences of being caught in age and time. (51)

Expectant time frames adolescence as a rite of passage in which teens are 'caught' and a period during which they are unable to shape the course of their acculturation. Walkerdine elaborates the specificity of expectant time for feminine adolescence. She writes that girlhood is represented as a period of 'preparation for the prince' in both fairy tales and girls' literature (1990, 97). The point of resolution, the Prince's arrival, is 'attractive precisely because it is the getting and keeping of the man which in a very basic and crucial way establishes that the girl is "good enough" ... It is because getting a man is identified as a central resolution to problems of female desire that it acts so powerfully' (99). This temporality constructs passive progress towards idealised feminine adulthood, which continues to be at least in part defined by romantic ideologies, heterosexual partnership and motherhood. Interestingly, though the *Twilight* series' narrative works towards this resolution that Walkerdine describes, its forestalling techniques of editing, spiralling camerawork and slow motion consistently frustrate, refuse and defy its fulfilment.

Janice Hawes has examined the *Twilight* novels' use of the 'Sleeping Beauty' fairy tale motif and their repetition of the theme of 'sleep and sleep-like states' (2010, 163). She argues that:

when [Bella] is not passively awaiting her prince Edward, she is actively
avoiding the dancing, dating, shopping, and bickering of the social whirl
that is high school. Her sleep is symbolic of her own avoidance of the everyday rituals associated with adolescence and of a desire to escape, rather
than confront, her insecurities. (163)

Hawes reads Bella's sleep differently from the usual interpretation of the
'Sleeping Beauty' tale: rather than representing 'a waking into adolescence ... Bella's sleep represents an avoidance of adolescence, with all of
its awkwardness and challenges' (166). For Hawes, this avoidance and
delay of feminine development into the roles and rituals of womanhood
is negative. She writes, 'for Bella, facing these fears is not the answer.
Instead, she wants to be transformed into what for her is an image of
perfection and invulnerability: a vampire' (169). Hawes does not consider the potentially empowering aspect of avoidance and delay—temporarily resisting the acculturating processes of feminine development
that work to produce stable, heteronormative versions of girlhood and
womanhood. In this temporary interval of resistance, other versions
of girlhood identities are articulated, providing an opportunity for the
expansion the terrain of feminine adolescence into alternative expressions
and performances.

In many of *Twilight*'s 'Sleeping Beauty' fantasy and bedroom scenes,
there is an intense focus on sleep and dreaming, and a heavy-handed
deployment of filmic techniques such as slow motion, ultra-slow dissolves and slowly spiralling camera movements. At the beginning of one
of these scenes, Edward and Bella move towards one another and kiss
at a painstakingly slow place. This lingering on the incremental, and
almost barely perceptible, movement stops the narrative in its tracks.
The soundtrack punctuates this languor with the couple's slow, rhythmic
inhalations and exhalations. In the next sequence, there is a transition of
shots between a medium and close-up shot of Edward and Bella asleep.
As shown in Fig. 3.2, the ultraslow dissolve settles on the scene like a
fine mist.

As this dissolve occurs, the transition between shots creates a decorative image in which the figures are adorned with superimposed golden
firefly fairy lights and the embellished floral design of Bella's bedspread.
The camera spirals in on the two figures very slowly as this transition
between shots occurs, creating a dreamy, hypnotic slowing down and
reduction of time. This scene of Bella and Edward sleeping is extended

Fig. 3.2   The ultraslow dissolve and spiralling camera movement in *Twilight*

through the use of the ultraslow dissolve and the dreamy spiralling movement of the camera. As opposed to the determining forces of logic, linearity and progress, delay provides indeterminate time. Bella's purposeful slowing down of time in her fantasy sequences refuses to accommodate the roles and responsibilities of impending womanhood. Instead, this languorous time is ruled by her expressions of desire, her enjoyment of Edward—and the defiantly intense focus of her attention on these pleasures.

Bella's 'Sleeping Beauty' fantasy sequences engineer a liminal, suspended time that ruptures narrative progression towards the heroine's ascension into idealised adult femininity. Scholars such as Carolyn Fay (2008) and Martine Hennard Dutheil de la Rochère (2010) have suggested that the 'Sleeping Beauty' fairy tale's suspension of time can represent the heroine's defiance against the demands placed upon her as she enters adult femininity, making this tale ideal for feminist appropriation and revision. Fay argues that in Perrault's telling of the tale, 'while the hundred years' sleep represents a narrative period of withdrawal and focus on the self, there is also an antisocial aspect to it … When she falls asleep, the rest of the world ceases to exist for her' (268). However, this antisocial defiance is tempered when she is woken up, because she is swiftly brought back to her 'proper' feminine place: 'the awakened princess is quickly recuperated and transformed into a wife, a mother, a queen—a woman defined by societal and familial roles' (271). I suggest that this antisocial defiance is made more powerful in *Twilight*'s revision of the tale because it represents the sustained effects of Bella's entry into liminal time, even after she has completed the passage into the postliminal. This also suggests that liminal time can provide an opportunity to invent or fantasise about new social relations, and then to act on them.

Bella's construction of liminal time is particularly important because it provides her with an interval in which she can temporarily suspend the progress of her rite of passage and explore alternative subject positions and desires. In liminal time, or what Turner calls 'leisure time', the ritual subject experiences '*freedom from* a whole heap of institutional obligations prescribed by the basic forms of social, particularly technological and bureaucratic, organisation ... For each individual, it means a *freedom from* the forced, chronologically regulated rhythms' (1982, 36 original emphases). It also provides a '*freedom to* enter, even to generate new symbolic worlds ... It is, furthermore ... *freedom to* transcend social structural limitations, freedom to play ... with ideas, with fantasies, with words ... and with social relationships' (37 original emphases). Turner's description of liminal time as outside the 'institutional obligations' of everyday social structures suggests that it provides an interval where regulatory and panoptic time is suspended for the ritual subject. As Turner emphasises, in this suspended liminal time the rules of regulatory time temporarily give way to a time of experimentation, engagement with fantasy and alternative social relations. This is the time that Bella engineers for herself in her fantasy sequences. In *Twilight*, delay and ultra-slow motion become points of excess, rupturing the narrative logic of progress and the acculturating processes that work to induct Bella into an idealised feminine adulthood. Bella actively constructs these points of temporal excess through her fantasies, creating a time that is not ruled by these regulatory pressures. This withdrawal from the narrative of progress and feminine acculturation not only troubles its seemingly 'natural' smooth development; it provides a significant interjection of the heroine's ambivalence and dissatisfaction towards these processes of maturation and growing up girl.

It would be difficult to argue that the *Twilight* books and film series promote a consistent, progressive feminist message about gender and sexuality. However, I suggest that there are important moments in the film texts where Bella is able to exercise a measure of power that ruptures the smooth veneer of this narrative about feminine acculturation. These ruptures allow the power and agency found in the liminal phase to seep into and impact upon her passage into postliminality. Bella does fulfil her feminine rite of passage, reintegrating into the status quo by becoming a wife and mother. However, she also insists on becoming a powerful vampire in her own right, sustaining the agency and empowerment that she discovered in her liminal fantasy explorations of an alternative mode of doing girlhood. When Bella becomes a vampire in *Breaking Dawn— Part One* (Condon 2011), she acquires new supernatural gifts and strengths that allow her to reverse the terms of power between herself and Edward in her postliminal life, as she becomes the stronger, more powerful protector and fighter in the relationship. This shift in the narrative's positioning of Edward and Bella suggests that the hierarchical breakdown enacted during the liminal period unsettled and eroded the power dynamics in the postliminal phase, emboldening Bella to redefine her position within her rite of passage towards adult womanhood. In this way, Bella returns to the norm but also creates change within it, and this is, according to Turner, one of the most important potentials embedded in the passage from the liminal to the postliminal. As Turner writes, 'innovation ... occurs in interfaces and limina, then becomes *legitimated* in central sectors' (1982, 45 original emphasis). Bella's protest against her position as object within conventional culture, and her assertion of power in her liminal fantasies, seep into and, to borrow Turner's phrase, become legitimated to an extent when she returns to conventional culture at the end of her rite of passage.

TWILIGHT AND SPECTACLE: RECONFIGURING THE IMAGE AND THE GAZE

The Perrault and Grimm versions of the 'Sleeping Beauty' fairy tale hinges on an encounter between feminine beauty and passivity which is represented as essential to being desirable, and an active, dominating, male Prince. This encounter places the unmoving and unconscious girl at the centre of a scene of spectacle, upholding sexist structures of the gendered image and gaze. This section considers how Bella's pretty fantasy designs of Edward designate him as the Beauty in her revision of the 'Sleeping Beauty' narrative, challenging the tale's privileging of dominant masculine desire over a subservient feminine object. One of the primary oppositions across all of the texts under analysis in this book is the heroines' resistance to their subordinate position as objects within patriarchal visual culture. By unsettling and therefore creating a fissure in this dominant visual paradigm, the heroines find moments in which they can claim a new visual language of feminine adolescence. I theorise a teen screen pretty aesthetic as a site of intervention, a terrain where Bella articulates her opposition to hegemonic constructions of femininity that demand that girls present themselves as desirable objects for a determining masculine gaze, and creates an alternative visual language of feminine adolescent desire.

I argue for the disruptive potential of cinematic spectacle and prettiness, and that Bella's spectacular and pretty fantasy images of Edward reconfigure the gendered politics of the image and the gaze. Here I am reading spectacle and prettiness against the grain, acknowledging that while mainstream teen film and television texts are produced within the ideological system of a capitalist patriarchal power structure, they can also be riddled with elements that contradict and create ruptures in the very system to which they appear to belong. As film theorist Barbara Klinger writes in her article on cinema and ideology, there are films that may 'appear ideologically conservative' with smooth closure, but this 'veneer ... is not only unconvincing, but countered by a system of meaning produced stylistically ... A combination of "excessive" narrative problems encountered during the film, and the manner in which elements of the mise-en-scène undercut the affirmative ending, conspire to disturb the harmonising tendencies of closure' (1984, 38–39). I read *Twilight*'s spectacular elements as points of contradiction and excess that threaten the cohesion of the narrative's ideologically conservative resolution. My hope is that this reading draws attention to the complexities of Bella's girlhood rite of passage in ways that have not yet been considered.

Interestingly, it is the spectacular aesthetic of the *Twilight* films that some scholars have labelled as potentially harmful and seductive to a teen girl audience. Natalie Wilson, for example, writes that *Twilight* acts as a powerful 'drug' for unsuspecting female fans, who become 'prisoners to its allure' (2011, 6). Only those who maintain the 'critical distance' of 'mocking' and 'resisting' the films' spectacular visual excesses (6–7) can succeed in refusing the harmful 'seductive message' of fulfilment through true love and romance with a Prince Charming that *Twilight* narrativises (8). Margaret Kramar similarly laments, 'unfortunately, modern teenagers ... may not be able to extricate themselves from Bella's mind-set or question her underlying assumptions analytically' (2011, 26). This suspicion of *Twilight*'s visual spectacle, and their anxiety about girl spectators' apparent inability to critically engage with this imagery, reveals a profound investment in masculine aesthetics, characterised by the coolly distant visual style they invoke as the ideal image, and the detached, mocking, analytic gaze they prize as the ideal spectatorial position. In contrast, they characterise *Twilight*'s feminine aesthetic as a kind of alluring drug, a dangerous seduction that acts as a trap for vulnerable and naïve teen girl spectators who cannot resist or extricate themselves from the allure of the image.

These readings of *Twilight* are informed by the media-effects strand of girls' media studies, which is often concerned with the narrow and prescriptive nature of screen representations of feminine adolescence and the potential negative effects these representations could have on female adolescent viewers (see for example Gilligan 1982; Pipher 1994; Lamb and Brown 2006). Much of this theory is less concerned with a close analysis of the texts and more with the harmful effects they could inflict on girl viewers. Mary Pipher, in her bestselling book *Reviving Ophelia: Saving the Selves of Adolescent Girls* (1994), argued that these representations contributed to a 'girl poisoning culture' (28). She argued that contemporary culture's obsession with 'junk values' (23)—everything from eating disorders, pornography, casual sex, increased divorce rates and commercial advertising aimed at girls—was exerting 'social pressure' on girls 'to put aside their authentic selves' (22). This culture was considered deeply destructive; indeed, Pipher compared media culture to 'a sleazy, dangerous tinsel town with lots of liquor stores and few protected spaces' that girls were vulnerable to and could not escape without adult intervention (27). Insisting that there was a 'preadolescent authenticity' to be rescued and rediscovered within teenage girls (26), Pipher aligned contemporary culture and media with an inauthentic and dangerous representation of girlhood, and preadolescence as a kind of utopia, innocent of 'destructive' media, an uncomplicated and unmediated expression of a 'true' self. Sharon Lamb and Lyn Mikel Brown concurred in their book *Packaging Girlhood: Rescuing Our Daughters From Marketers' Schemes* (2006). They described media culture as a 'bright and shiny world' that 'gobbles up [our] interesting, feisty daughters and spits them out in pink satin Wonderbras and panties' (xi). While these studies draw attention to some of the ways in which restrictive images of femininity circulate within the culture and impact upon girl consumers, the feminist media effects methodology primarily reiterates girls as powerless in the experience of adolescence and the media, and struggles to account for any ruptures or shifts in representation that might take place. There is an assumption about the feminine image and the feminine spectator as necessarily devoid of any capacity for political or critical engagement, and an unwitting perpetuation of limiting stereotypes about girls as powerless dupes spellbound by an intoxicating yet inauthentic image.

Through their media effects approach to *Twilight's* spectacular excesses, Wilson and Kramar posit that the politics of the feminine image is corrupt, harmful and embedded with sexist messages. As noted above, these authors also claim that a productive reading of the text only emerges in the cold, distant manner that opposes and scorns the 'image in its imageness' (Galt 2011, 256), so that masculine austerity and distance is prized as a superior form of engagement with the moving image, while feminine 'overcloseness' is regarded with suspicion and disdain. Wilson and Kramar also miss the rich potential for the spectacular and pretty teen screen image to be politically potent and invested with details that significantly disrupt *Twilight's* conservative narrative flow. Such a reading is important for a feminist perspective on the cinematic text, for, as Galt writes, a consideration of the pretty considers 'how the image is gendered formally and how thematic iterations of gender in film can be read not just against women's historical conditions, but against the gendered aesthetics of cinema itself' (255). Redeploying Projansky's feminist optic, which seeks out and '*sees the presence*' of alternative images of girl-hood, even '*within the centre*' of contemporary visual culture (2014, 11 original emphases), inspires me to read against the grain and look for the potential for an oppositional politics within Bella's deployment of prettiness. Using this optic to look at Bella's engagement with spectacle and prettiness highlights how the excess of these elements not only undermine the conservative ideology of the narrative's progress; they also work to create a new set of gendered relations through the image and the gaze. In this new set of relations, Bella claims authorial control over the spectacular design of her fantasy image of Edward, providing her with an opportunity to enact a desiring gaze. This optic prompts me to identify the oppositional elements of these fantasy images, arguing for a reading of the pretty 'being political *in* the image' (Galt 2011, 256 original emphasis). I argue that these images of Edward encode a new set of gender relations at the formal level. By looking otherwise at the pretty, I

Fig. 3.3 Edward's figure is associated with the spectacular excess of moonlight, pattern and lace in Bella's dream image

argue for reading Bella's inventive teen screen aesthetics as an expressive surface that articulates an oppositional girl's subjective point of view.

The pretty excess of Bella's fabrication of Edward reconfigures the gendered norms of the gaze and desire. In her 'Sleeping Beauty' fantasy sequences, Bella is not coded as the 'Beauty'; Edward, the glittering, perfectly groomed, alabaster-skinned eternal teenager, is. In these scenes, and indeed throughout the film series, Edward's figure is repeatedly associated with sparkles, lace, shimmering light, soft skin and immaculately coiffed hair. In one 'Sleeping Beauty' fantasy scene in *Twilight*, Bella dreams that Edward is in her bedroom. Edward's face is framed in extreme close-up. He is bathed in a golden, shimmering moonlight that shines in through the window. This moonlight shines through a lace curtain, which creates a dramatic dappled frill pattern of glimmering light and shade across Edward's glowing skin, as illustrated in Fig. 3.3.

As I explored in the previous section, Perrault's account of the Prince gazing upon Beauty describes the feminine figure as 'the most lovely sight', 'radiant', 'luminous and supernatural'. In *Twilight*'s revised 'Sleeping Beauty' scene described above, these gendered terms of spectacle are reversed, with Edward's golden shimmering image appearing radiant, luminous and supernatural, providing Bella with 'the most lovely sight'. By reversing the gender roles inscribed in the earlier text, Bella is temporarily relieved of the conventional feminine position as object and claims the position of desiring subject. Bella's revision and restaging of the 'Sleeping Beauty' tale's representation of spectacle unsettles the sexist visual economy upon which it relies, and temporarily transforms the girl's position in relation to the image and gaze.

The fantasy moment described above associates Edward's figure with these elements of visual and decorative spectacle. At the formal level, this image expresses an important political intervention: by unsettling the traditional spectacularisation of the feminine figure and instead associating the masculine figure with sparkles, lace and pattern, the image represents an unsettling of the conventional dynamics of the gaze within patriarchal visual culture. Such an association is excessively spectacular, for as Galt argues, 'a patterned image is corrosive and unnecessary' (121). The supplemental nature of the decorative, its very gratuitousness, is troublesome, because it exceeds the requirements of the narrative and potentially disrupts its ideology. These spectacular textural details disrupt the gendered politics that govern girlhood and the gaze. Mulvey's famous argument that the male figure onscreen cannot 'bear the burden of objectification' ([1975] 1989, 20) is challenged in *Twilight*'s construction of Edward as an extravagantly shimmering spectacle. Klinger's against the grain analysis of Douglas Sirk's melodramas argues that the deployment of an excessive or unreal *mise en scène* can work to 'subvert the system [of representation] and its ideology from within' (1994, 14). Jane Gaines, in her work on the textural excesses of costume in classical Hollywood cinema, similarly argues that these elements have the capacity to become a 'dissonant detail' (2011, 150) in the text that is resistant to, in excess of and uncontained by the 'conservative' narrative flow.[3] The work of Klinger and Gaines builds on Jean-Louis Comolli and Jean Narboni's definition of the 'progressive text' ((([1969] 2004) by analysing previously unconsidered 'feminine' or frivolous' cinematic elements as sites of excess that perform a critical function. As Galt writes, Comolli and Narboni's work assumes that only 'modernist strategies of unpleasure' can generate political critique on screen (2011, 194), so feminist writers such as Klinger and Gaines contested this limitation in the theorisation of the progressive text by arguing that spectacular cinematic images can indeed hold political potential, because they have the capacity, in their excess, to rub up against and possibly erode the conservative ideology that the narrative works to hold in place. In her work on teen screen aesthetics, Kay Dickinson elaborates that one cinematic component may 'radically contradict' another, and that such a contradiction of a conservative narrative or image may defy, challenge and even overwhelm it (2003, 15). Dickinson sees this challenge at work in the text as potentially 'not only an intrinsic property, but also … a political tool at work within both the object of analysis itself and its audience's active perception' (19). Moments of disruptive visual spectacle, therefore, can be seen as having political potency and potential as it not only challenges the normative ideology of the narrative, but also prompts a similarly unruly response from the spectator.

The spectacular aesthetic created by Bella significantly challenges the immense scrutiny that girls and women are placed under—it enacts the 'radical contradiction' that Dickinson argues for. This is significant because, as Susan Bordo argues, the 'grip' of controlling surveillance and scrutiny is one of contemporary culture's ways of regulating, monitoring and manipulating the female body 'as an absolutely central strategy in the maintenance of power relations between the sexes' (1985, 76–77). Bella's fantasy sequences challenge the visual structures that hold this subordination in place by designing a visual economy in which she can evade this scrutiny and instead take up an active and subjective desiring position. This is an instance in which 'the female gaze could be seen to "interrupt" patriarchal discourse, to the extent of disrupting the objectifying erotic gaze at women' (Evans and Gamman 2005, 28). I read Bella's prettified, glittering, luminous fantasy images of Edward as her counter-discourse to the way patriarchal visual culture objectifies girls, as she temporarily relieves herself of the burden of sexual objectification and transfers this burden to Edward's figure. The pretty therefore provides a new way to theorise a visual language of feminine adolescence, which produces alternative subject positions for the heroine to occupy within visual culture.

The spectacle of Edward's glittering, luminous skin challenges the gendered politics of the image and the gaze. The first time Edward reveals his sparkling skin, these gendered politics of image and gaze are revised, creating a significant invitation for the heroine to enact a desiring look. Edward and Bella are in the forest, and Edward stands in the sunlight, revealing that it is the reaction of light and vampire skin that creates this glittering effect. Edward unbuttons his coat and shirt as he stands in this spotlight of sunshine, and his face and torso light up with the lustrous shimmer of thousands of tiny diamonds. The scene then cuts

Fig. 3.4 Bella's desiring gaze at Edward as he reveals his luminous, sparkling body to her

to Bella's face in close-up as she admires Edward's pretty sparkling display, as shown in Fig. 3.4.

Bella exclaims 'You're beautiful!' as the camera cuts to her point of view and slowly pans up his torso, lingering on this spectacle, as shown in Fig. 3.5.

This visual display of the male figure's prettiness for the heroine perverts the sexist structures of the gaze which fix the female figure in the role of passive spectacle and assert the control of the male figure. For it is Edward's figure that is aligned with spectacle and the over-the-top design of glamorous decoration, and it is Bella who actively enjoys this display—indeed, she calls him 'beautiful'. Such a perversion of gendered categories carves out a space for a new set of relations to emerge through the image.

In the suspended liminal time of fantasy, Bella is able to temporarily escape her position as object within contemporary patriarchal culture. The liminal intervals and gaps in the narrative provide Bella with an opportunity to take up the position of subject, finding that she can stage, author, design and explore fantasy scenarios in which her desires and demands are met. During these scenes, Bella experiments with an alternative girl identity as she claims this subjective, authoritative position

Fig. 3.5 The camera, aligned with Bella's desiring gaze, slowly pans up Edward's sparkling body in a close-up shot

within the text. By restaging the 'Sleeping Beauty' fairy tale and reversing its gender dynamic, Bella explores an alternative and oppositional subject position. Fantasy becomes the liminal forum for the setting out and experimentation with this new-found agency and power. As I have already suggested, the ruptures caused by these oppositional intervals in the narrative allow Bella's more expansive girlhood identity to seep into her postliminal life. Turner's description of the relationship between the liminal and postliminal as a porous 'intimate bond' (1969, 202), a 'process' in which both feed back into and transform one another (203), reveals that while these phases are certainly defined as distinct, the passage between them is fluid, allowing for breaks to be enacted in the status quo when the ritual subject returns to conventional society. Even as she occupies the conventional position of wife and mother at the end of her postfeminist rite-of-passage narrative, she also ascends to a higher-ranking position within her new vampire clan, and this allows her to claim a powerful subject position that extends beyond the liminal fantasy realm. The new set of gender relations that Bella imagines in her pretty fantasy images of Edward also continues to impact upon her postliminal life by claiming new supernatural powers and gifts that surpass Edward's, allowing her to shift into the powerful role of protector and warrior.

CONCLUSIONS: TRANSFORMATIVE LIMINALITY
ON THE TEEN SCREEN

Like other twenty-first-century teen screen revisions of the 'Sleeping Beauty' tale, *Twilight*'s fantasy and leisure times are represented as productive and transformative spaces in which the heroine can explore and act upon her own desires. Breillat's *La Belle Endormie* and Rosemary Myers' *Girl Asleep* (2015) feature girls who fall into deep slumbers and dream about possible modes of being beyond the strictures of the everyday. These films emphasise the imaginative potential of the tale's liminal phase, and restore agency to the girl who is navigating it on her rite-of-passage journey. *Twilight*'s depiction of liminal time goes even further, as a result of its seriality and extended duration across multiple films. Many teen 'Sleeping Beauty' screen texts revise the tale in fascinating and complex ways, but *Twilight* includes a very rare example of a reversal of its gendered dynamic. In a visual culture that continues to obsessively return to the mythical image of the helpless slumbering girl being acted upon by men, *Twilight*'s fantasy sequences offer an alternative configuration of this familiar scene. This serves a demythologising function in which the position of girl as passive, awaiting rescue and romance, is subverted and replaced with a more complex and agentic scene of the girl's desire.

This chapter has argued that through fantasy and liminal time, *Twilight*'s heroine Bella is afforded a space in which she can both protest against some of the strictures of girlhood and creatively innovate new positions to occupy, expanding the terrain of what is possible for girlhood to include. Liminal time not only provides an opportunity for rebellion against everyday strictures; it also holds creative potential for the valuable work of reconfiguring and reimagining gendered relations. I have argued for fantasy and liminality as ruptures in *Twilight*'s narrative of feminine acculturation, and how this interval of the unsettled zone allows the heroine to push against the boundaries of the teen girl rite of passage, and expand it into new territories of feminine agency and power.

While many scholarly explorations of the *Twilight* texts have thoroughly examined Bella's postfeminist journey into womanhood, few have adequately considered the resistant and unruly elements in the texts that unsettle this conservative closure. For as Gottschall et al. note, popular images, and the ways in which girls engage with them, can both 'rupture and reiterate ways of doing girlhood' (2013, 35), and that in this process 'multiple meanings of girlhood seem to be embodied and enacted' (39). They argue that in any particular media or 'real life' example, it is possible for 'markers of conventional girlhood [to be] enabled and constrained in complex ways' (40). *Twilight* is a deeply ambivalent text; while it does represent a conservative rite-of-passage narrative, unsettling contradictions also emerge that trouble the smooth veneer of this conservative ideology. Furthermore, the passage from liminality to postliminality is porous, allowing the agency that Bella harnesses in the liminal zone to seep into and impact upon her return to the status quo. This reading acknowledges that the postliminal is a return to conventional culture; however, it also suggests that the empowerment and authority gained in the liminal zone cannot be strictly contained because, as Turner demonstrates, the passage from liminality to postliminality is one of flow and change. Turner's definition of liminal time as 'an instant of pure potentiality where everything, as it were, trembles in the balance' (1982, 44) reveals its inventive potential, and its capacity to imagine or even enact new social relations.

I have framed this exploration of Bella's opposition to the conventional rite of passage into womanhood through an analysis of how her fantasies revise and intervene into the 'Sleeping Beauty' fairy tale's narrative of feminine acculturation. Rejecting the objectified position of the sleeping girl passively awaiting the Prince's brave rescue, Bella instead deploys these bedroom fantasies in ways that bring her authority and resistance to the fore. This emerges in her alterations and innovative designs in relation to both the image and temporality. Bella's suspension of regulatory panoptic time and entry into liminal time creates moments in the text that provide articulations of both feminine adolescent rebellion and innovation. During this time, Bella experiments with the identities of author, protestor and desiring subject, identities that rupture conventional constructions of girlhood and provide moments in which an alternative feminine adolescence is made possible. While the narrative marches forward towards Bella's ultimate postliminal passage into womanhood, Bella resists this closure by creating fantasy sequences in which time is magically suspended or elongated. Through the frequent use of cinematic techniques such as slow motion, spiralling camera movement and ultraslow dissolves, Bella's fantasy and bedroom sequences present a consistent impulse to halt and frustrate linear narrative progression. Bella's intense anxiety about, and resistance to, the fulfilment of her rite of passage into adult feminine roles reveals a measure of dissatisfaction with and ambivalence towards these processes. Bella is able not only to question this process, but also enact alterations upon it through her temporal interjections. Creating moments that are not ruled by the requirements of acculturation and the rules and responsibilities of maturation, Bella affords herself moments determined solely by her own desires and demands.

The film's visual representation of spectacle and pretty excess also provide Bella with an opportunity to oppose and unsettle the status quo. In Bella's designs of 'Sleeping Beauty' fantasy scenarios, Edward is cast in the role of Beauty. Her designs of these bedroom tableaux are spectacular, including elaborate and excessive displays of pattern, fabric and sparkles on Edward's figure. This not only provides Bella with an opportunity to take up an actively desiring gaze at Edward; it significantly challenges and reconfigures the gendered dynamics of the image, imbuing her fantasy designs with political potential. By redeploying Projansky's feminist optic to look at teen screen aesthetics in a new way, I have read the pretty as the site where Bella is able to break down the visual economy that places girls in a position of emphasised femininity, a scrutinised spectacle presented for a heterosexual male gaze, and reconfigure the gendered categories of the image and the gaze. Bella's deployment of pretty aesthetics articulates a new visual language of feminine adolescence: the heroine secures a subjective position as author and designer of the image, as a desiring subject, and as a resistant protestor against her subordinate, objectified position within contemporary patriarchal visual culture. The pretty therefore functions as a site where the heroine articulates her opposition to conventional culture, investing this formal aspect of the film with political and feminist meanings.

Through these fantasy alterations to both image and temporality, Bella is able to carve out a space for the expression of an alternative girlhood identity. As Cowie suggests, fantasy is a setting out of multiple possibilities, positions and objects. Bella's fantasies set out an alternative universe of new possibilities, positions and objects for her feminine rite of passage. These liminal intervals of time provide important instances where girlhood is not constrained by the everyday structures that govern and define it, providing a representation of feminine adolescence that goes beyond the conventional. Bella's fantasy 'Sleeping Beauty' scenarios, which move beyond the everyday structures that govern and contain girlhood, provide a representation in which those governing forces can be resisted and even ruptured.

Chapter 2 and this chapter have considered the presence of alternative and oppositional girls on the contemporary teen film screen. My readings of *Red Riding Hood* and *Twilight* have considered how their representations of feminine adolescent heroines included moments of opposition and resistance to the status quo, and how these moments impacted upon the dominant in the postliminal phase. In the next two chapters, I shift focus to the teen television screen with an analysis of *Pretty Little Liars* (Chap. 4) and *Gossip Girl* (Chap. 5). I examine the representation of oppositional girl groups as examples of liminal communitas and how they may create an even more powerful depiction of feminine adolescent resistance. The feminist optic of this book searches for alternative and challenging girl identities and subjectivities, and in looking at the representation of girl communitas I find moments of female solidarity in the face of patriarchal oppression. In *Pretty Little Liars*, this community provides a space for the representation of a collective critical girl's gaze back at how patriarchal culture fosters systemic exploitation and violence against girls and women. The series' revision of the 'Bluebeard' fairy tale interjects moments of girls' collective investigation of, and action against, masculine abuses of power. This new framing of the 'Bluebeard' tale through a lens of feminine adolescent solidarity is one of the most important revisions that *Pretty Little Liars* makes to the narrative, because it represents moments of united intervention into patriarchal power and the construction of alternative social relations.

NOTES

1. Meyer's novels in the book series were *Twilight* (2005), *New Moon* (2006), *Eclipse* (2007) and *Breaking Dawn* (2008). The films in the 'Twilight Saga' series were *Twilight*, *New Moon* (Weitz 2009), *Eclipse* (Slade 2010), *Breaking Dawn—Part One* (Condon 2011) and *Breaking Dawn—Part Two* (Condon 2012).
2. While there is not enough space in this chapter to fully elaborate the Freudian and Lacanian psychoanalytic background to Cowie's theorisation of fantasy, it is vital to explore her contention that fantasy is a setting out of possibilities, entry points, identifications and desires.
3. See also Stella Bruzzi's work on the excesses of the 'smashing' dress or costume in cinema, which she argues can operate as an 'interjection' that can be so disruptive as to undermine the 'normative reality' of the film's narrative progression (1997, 17).

BIBLIOGRAPHY

Bartky, Sandra Lee. 1990. *Femininity and Domination: Studies in the Phenomenology of Oppression*. New York and London: Routledge.

Basile, Giambattista. [1634] 2001. Sun, Moon, and Talia. In *The Great Fairy Tale Tradition: From Straparola and Basile to the Brothers Grimm*, trans. and ed. Jack Zipes, 685–688. New York and London: W.W. Norton and Co.

Bettelheim, Bruno. 1978. *The Uses of Enchantment: The Power and Importance of Fairy Tales*. Harmondsworth: Penguin.

Bordo, Susan. 1985. Anorexia Nervosa: Psychopathology as the Crystallisation of Culture. *The Philosophical Forum* 17 (2): 73–104.

Bruzzi, Stella. 1997. *Undressing Cinema: Clothing and Identity in the Movies*. London and New York: Routledge.

Bryant, Nigel (trans.). 2013. *A Perceforest Reader: Selected Episodes from Perceforest: The Prehistory of King Arthur's Britain*. New York: Boydell and Brewer.

Carpenter, Laura M. 2009. Virginity Loss in Reel/Real Life: Using Popular Movies to Navigate Sexual Initiation. *Sociological Forum* 24 (4): 804–827.

Carter, Angela. [1979] 1996. The Lady of the House of Love. In *Burning Your Boats: Collected Short Stories*, 195–209. London: Vintage.

Comolli, Jean-Louis, and Jean Narboni. [1969] 2004. Cinema/Ideology/ Criticism. In *Film Theory and Criticism: Introductory Readings*, ed. Leo Braudy and Marshall Cohen, 812–819. New York: Oxford University Press.

Cowie, Elizabeth. 1990. Fantasia. In *The Woman in Question*, ed. Parveen Adams and Elizabeth Cowie, 149–196. Cambridge, MA: MIT Press.

Dickinson, Kay. 2003. Pop, Speed, Teenagers and the "MTV Aesthetic". In *Movie Music, The Film Reader*, ed. Kay Dickinson, 143–151. London and New York: Routledge.

Driscoll, Catherine. 2002. *Girls: Feminine Adolescence in Popular Culture and Cultural Theory*. New York: Columbia University Press.

Duggan, Anne E. 2008. Women Subdued: The Abjectification and Purification of Female Characters in Perrault's Tales. *The Romantic Review* 99 (3–4): 211–226.

Evans, Caroline and Lorraine Gamman. 2005. The Gaze Revisited, or Reviewing Queer Viewing. In *A Queer Romance: Lesbians, Gay Men, and Popular Culture*, ed. Paul Burston and Colin Richardson, 12–61. London: Routledge.

Fay, Carolyn. 2008. Sleeping Beauty Must Die: The Plots of Perrault's "La belle au bois dormant". *Marvels and Tales* 22 (2): 259–276.

Foucault, Michel. [1977] 1995. In *Discipline and Punish: The Birth of the Prison*, trans. Alan Sheridan. New York: Vintage Books.

Galt, Rosalind. 2011. *Pretty: Film and the Decorative Image*. New York and Chichester: Columbia University Press.

Gaines, Jane. 2011. Wanting to Wear Seeing: Gilbert Adrian at MGM. In *Fashion in Film*, ed. Adrienne Munich, 135–159. Bloomington: Indiana University Press.

Gill, Rosalind. 2007. *Gender and the Media*. Cambridge: Polity Press.

Gilligan, Carol. 1982. In *A Different Voice: Psychological Theory and Women's Development*. Cambridge, MA, and London: Harvard University Press.

Gottschall, Kristina, Susanne Gannon, Jo Lampert, and Kelli McGraw. 2013. The Cyndi Lauper Affect: Bodies, Girlhood and Popular Culture. *Girlhood Studies* 6 (1): 30–45.

Grimm, Jacob and Wilhelm. [1857] 2001. Briar Rose. In *The Great Fairy Tale Tradition: From Straparola and Basile to the Brothers Grimm*, trans. and ed. Jack Zipes, 696–698. New York and London: W.W. Norton and Co.

Harris, Anita. 2001. Revisiting Bedroom Culture: New Spaces for Young Women's Politics. *Hecate* 27 (1): 128–138.

Hawes, Janice. 2010. Sleeping Beauty and the Idealized Undead: Avoiding Adolescence. In *The* Twilight *Mystique: Critical Essays on the Novels and Films*, ed. Amy M. Clarke and Marijane Osborn, 163–178. Jefferson, NC, and London: McFarland and Company.

Hayward, Jennifer. 1997. *Consuming Pleasures: Active Audiences and Serial Fictions from Dickens to Soap Opera*. Lexington: University Press of Kentucky.

Dutheil, Hennard, and Martine de la Rochère. 2010. "But Marriage itself is no Party": Angela Carter's Translation of Charles Perrault's "La Belle au bois Dormant"; or, Pitting the Politics of Experience against the Sleeping Beauty Myth. *Marvels and Tales* 24 (1): 131–151.

Kearney, Mary Celeste. 2007. Productive Spaces. *Journal of Children & Media* 1 (2): 126–141. doi:10.1080/17482790701339126.

Kelly, Deirdre M., Shauna Pomerantz, and Dawn H. Currie. 2006. "No Boundaries?" Girls' Interactive, Online Learning about Femininities. *Youth Society* 38 (3): 3–28. doi:10.1177/0044118X05283482.

Klinger, Barbara. 1984. "Cinema/Ideology/Criticism" Revisited: The Progressive Text. *Screen* 25 (1): 30–44.

———. 1994. *Melodrama and Meaning: History, Culture, and the Films of Douglas Sirk*. Bloomington and Indianapolis: Indiana University Press.

Kolbenschlag, Madonna. 1983. *Goodbye Sleeping Beauty: Breaking the Spell of Feminine Myths and Models*. Arlen House: Dublin.

Kramar, Margaret. 2011. The Wolf in the Woods: Representations of 'Little Red Riding Hood' in *Twilight*. In *Bringing Light to Twilight: Perspective on a Pop Culture Phenomenon*, ed. Giselle Liza Anatol, 15–30. New York: Palgrave Macmillan.

Lamb, Sharon, and Lyn Mikel Brown. 2006. *Packaging Girlhood: Rescuing our Daughters from Marketers' Schemes*. New York: St. Martin's Press.

Leavenworth, Maria Lindgren. 2011. Variations, Subversions, and Endless Love: Fan Fiction and the *Twilight* Saga. In *Bringing Light to Twilight: Perspectives on a Pop Culture Phenomenon*, ed. Giselle Liza Anatol, 69–81. New York: Palgrave Macmillan.

Lesko, Nancy. 2001. Time Matters in Adolescence. In *Governing the Child in the New Millennium*, ed. Kenneth Hultqvist and Gunilla Dahlberg, 35–67. New York and London: RoutledgeFalmer.

Lieberman, Marcia K. 1986. "Some Day My Prince Will Come": Female Acculturation through the Fairy Tale. In *Don't Bet on the Prince: Contemporary Feminist Fairy Tales in North America and England*, ed. Jack Zipes, 185–200. Aldershot and New York: Gower.

McRobbie, Angela. 2008. Young Women and Consumer Culture: An Intervention. *Cultural Studies* 22 (5): 531–550. doi:10.1080/09502380802245803.

McRobbie, Angela and Jenny Garber. [1976] 2000. Girls and Subcultures. In *Feminism and Youth Culture*, 2nd ed., ed. Angela McRobbie, 12–25. London: Macmillan Press.

Meyer, Stephenie. 2005. *Twilight*. London: Atom.

———. 2006. *New Moon*. New York: Little, Brown and Co.

———. 2007. *Eclipse*. New York: Little, Brown and Co.

———. 2008. *Breaking Dawn*. New York: Little, Brown and Co.

Mulvey, Laura. [1975] 1989. Visual Pleasure and Narrative Cinema. In *Visual and Other Pleasures*, 14–26. Bloomington and Indianapolis: Indiana University Press.

Negra, Diane. 2009. *What a Girl Wants: Fantasizing the Reclamation of Self in Postfeminism*. London: Routledge.

Perrault, Charles. [1697] 2001. Sleeping Beauty. In *The Great Fairy Tale Tradition: From Straparola and Basile to the Brothers Grimm*, trans. and ed. Jack Zipes, 688–695. New York and London: W.W. Norton and Co.

Pipher, Mary. 1994. *Reviving Ophelia: Saving the Selves of Adolescent Girls*. New York: Putnam.

Platt, Carrie Anne. 2010. Cullen Family Values: Gender and Sexual Politics in the *Twilight* Series. In *Bitten by Twilight: Youth, Media, and the Vampire Franchise*, ed. Melissa A. Click, Jennifer Stevens Aubrey, and Elizabeth Behm-Morawitz, 71–86. New York: Peter Lang.

Projansky, Sarah. 2014. *Spectacular Girls: Media Fascination and Celebrity Culture*. New York and London: New York University Press.

Renold, Emma, and Jessica Ringrose. 2008. Regulation and Rupture: Mapping Tween and Teenage Girls' Resistance to the Heterosexual Matrix. *Feminist Theory* 9: 313–338. doi:10.1177/1464700108095854.

Rowe, Karen E. 1986. Feminism and Fairy Tales. In *Don't Bet on the Prince: Contemporary Feminist Fairy Tales in North America and England*, ed. Jack Zipes, 209–226. Aldershot and New York: Gower.

Rowe Karlyn, Kathleen. 2011. *Unruly Girls, Unrepentant Mothers: Redefining Feminism on Screen*. Austin: University of Texas Press.

Seifert, Christine. 2009. Bite Me! (Or Don't). *Bitch* 42: 23–25.

Sexton, Ann. [1971] 1986. Briar Rose (Sleeping Beauty). In *Don't Bet on the Prince: Contemporary Feminist Fairy Tales in North America and England*, ed. Jack Zipes, 114–118. Aldershot and New York: Scholar Press.

Tasker, Yvonne. 2012. *Enchanted* (2007) by Postfeminism: Gender, Irony, and the New Romantic Comedy. In *Feminism at the Movies: Understanding Gender in Contemporary Popular Cinema*, edited by Hilary Radner and Rebecca Stringer, 67–79. Hoboken: Taylor and Francis.

Tatar, Maria. 2014. Show and Tell: Sleeping Beauty as Verbal Icon and Seductive Story. *Marvels & Tales* 28 (1): 142–158.

Taylor, Anthea. 2012. "The Urge Towards Love is an Urge Towards (Un)Death": Romance, Masochistic Desire and Postfeminism in the *Twilight* Novels. *International Journal of Cultural Studies* 15 (31): 31–46. doi:10.1177/1367877911399204.

Turner, Victor. 1969. *The Ritual Process: Structure and Anti-Structure*. Chicago: Aldine Publishing Company.

———. 1982. *From Ritual to Theatre: The Human Seriousness of Play*. New York: Performing Arts Journal Publications.

Walkerdine, Valerie. 1990. *Schoolgirl Fictions*. London and New York: Verso.

Willis, Jessica Laureltree. 2009. Girls Reconstructing Gender: Agency, Hybridity and Transformations of "Femininity". *Girlhood Studies* 2 (2): 96–118.

Wilson, Natalie. 2011. *Seduced by Twilight: The Allure and Contradictory Messages of the Popular Saga*. Jefferson, NC and London: McFarland and Company.

Yolen, Jane. 1992. *Briar Rose*. New York: T. Doherty Associates.

Yue, Genevieve. 2012. Two Sleeping Beauties. *Film Quarterly* 65 (3): 33–37.

Zipes, Jack. 2002. *The Brothers Grimm: From Enchanted Forests to the Modern World*. New York: Palgrave Macmillan.

FILMOGRAPHY

La Belle Endormie. Dir. Catherine Breillat. 2010.
Breaking Dawn (Part One). Dir. Sean Condon. 2011.
Breaking Dawn (Part Two). Dir. Sean Condon. 2012.
Criminal Minds. Distributed by CBS. 2005–.
CSI. Distributed by CBS. 2000–2015.
Eclipse. Dir. David Slade. 2010.

Gossip Girl. The CW. 2007–2012.
Maleficent. Dir. Robert Stromberg. 2014.
The Neon Demon. Dir. Nicolas Winding Refn. 2016.
New Moon. Dir. Chris Weitz. 2010.
Pretty Little Liars. ABC Family. 2010–.
Sleeping Beauties. Dir. Jamie Babbit. 1999.
Sleeping Beauty. Dir. Julia Leigh. 2011.
Twilight. Dir. Catherine Hardwicke. 2008.

CHAPTER 4

Liminal Communitas and Feminist Solidarity: Transforming 'Bluebeard' in *Pretty Little Liars* (ABC Family 2010–)

INTRODUCTION: MARGINALITY AND THE TEEN DETECTIVE'S GAZE

In Charles Perrault's 'Bluebeard', which is, according to Cristina Bacchilega the most culturally pervasive and well-known version of the tale (1997, 161), the primary focus is placed on the girl's curiosity as a feminine vice and punishable offence. Perrault details the ways in which Bluebeard tortures his wife for her 'offence', and this focus on feminine violations of prohibition (Tatar 2004, 1) allows the writer to deflect the blame from the murderer to the girl. The murderer is slain at the very end of the tale, but the heroine exercises little agency in this conclusion, as she must wait for her brothers to rescue her, and furthermore, she is promptly reinstated in the confines of marriage with a new husband. Feminist writers, filmmakers and artists have often revised the tale with a particular focus on revaluing the girl's curiosity as a brave and necessary trait, interrogating the patriarchal structure of marriage, and restoring blame to the murderous husband. Cristina Bacchilega writes that feminist literature such as the short stories 'Bluebeard's Egg' by Margaret Atwood ([1983] 1986) and 'The Bloody Chamber' by Angela Carter ([1979] 1996) above all foreground and prioritise a representation of the heroine's agency (1997, 113). Contemporary filmmakers have also offered important revisions. In Catherine Breillat's *Barbe Bleue* (2009) and Jane Campion's *The Piano* (1993) and *In the Cut* (2003), courageous heroines emerge victorious from Bluebeard's locked room. These

© The Author(s) 2017
A. Bellas, *Fairy Tales on the Teen Screen*,
DOI 10.1007/978-3-319-64973-3_4

feminist texts shift the position of the woman and the girl in the fairy tale, providing representations of heroines who overcome the oppression that they face.

A number of teen films include locked room mysteries, and stories of adolescent girls attempting to escape the clutches of a murderous man. Many of these are horror or thriller texts including classics such as *Halloween* (Carpenter 1978), *Slumber Party Massacre* (Holden Jones 1982) and *A Nightmare on Elm Street* (Craven 1984), as well as contemporary teen films such as *When a Stranger Calls* (West 2006), *The Glass House* (Sackheim 2001) and *The Uninvited* (The Guard Brothers 2009). After all, as Marina Warner posits, the 'Bluebeard' tale 'can be seen as one of the slasher film's progenitors' (1995, 270). The locked room mystery is also seen in other teen texts such as *Nancy Drew* (Fleming 2007), which tell the mystery story in a comedic tone, while the excellent television series *Veronica Mars* (UPN 2004–2007) frames the investigation within a neo-noir context. Many of these texts highlight the girl's bravery and intelligence, as well as her capacity to outwit the killer and save herself from harm. The texts often focus on a lone investigator, or a 'final girl' (Clover 1992) in the case of the horror texts, confining the representation of girlhood agency to an individual character. I am interested in the Bluebeard-inflected aspects of the teen mystery soap opera *Pretty Little Liars* because it shifts the tale from a representation of an isolated girl to a girl group, and therefore provides a revision that expands the representation of female agency into the realm of collective organised action and solidarity in the face of patriarchal oppression.[1]

In this series, four high school girls investigate the mysterious disappearance and possible murder of their friend, fifteen-year-old Alison. They unite to cooperatively uncover the secrets of Alison's disappearance and possible death, unlocking the secrets concealed within Bluebeard's locked chamber. This new focus upon the girl group in the tale unsettles Perrault's conservative marital conclusion: the central relationship is one of solidarity and cooperation between girls, exceeding the confines of dominant narratives of feminine fulfilment through heterosexual romance and domesticity. The emphasis on the girl group communitas unsettles adult masculine authority within the revisionist narrative, representing girls who enact socially meaningful action against the status quo. Therefore, I claim communitas as a feminist element of this contemporary televisual retelling of 'Bluebeard'.

As seen in the previous chapter, *Twilight* certainly includes some subversive liminal elements that resist the closure of the feminine rite of passage. Nevertheless, the end of the fourth film ensures this resolution, and Bella is neatly instated into the roles of wife and mother. This closure can be seen as a patriarchal strategy of containment, a delimiting of 'acceptable' femininity. In television's serial format, which the following two chapters explore, there is no such closure, or at least a greater resistance of closure, as each storyline unfolds over a sustained period of time. In resisting the normalising impulse of narrative closure, the television text has provided many examples of women's stories that are able to go beyond the restrictions of the 'happy ending' and into far more subversive, liminal territory. Martha Nochimson's (1992) work on the daytime soap opera points out that 'ordinary narrative process—defined by our culture as "realistic"—is a quest for male identity' (74), while the soap's lack of closure fails to 'support the hero's desire for control', therefore allowing the narrative to become 'a reflection of the heroine's desire to resist control' (118). Similarly, in her groundbreaking work on the soap opera, Ien Ang explored the instability and changeability of identification in television. Ang writes that soap operas 'are fundamentally anti-utopian: an ending, happy or unhappy, is unimaginable', and therefore becomes a field of endless negotiation and experimentation for heroine and spectator (1996, 90). For Ang, this makes the soap a 'secure space' for both the text and spectator to test out contradictory, ambivalent and possibly subversive performances and fantasies of femininity (95). In *Pretty Little Liars*, this subversion manifests in the form of feminine curiosity and a desire to know, and the heroines' multiple transgressions of male prohibitions as a result of this investigatory impulse.

Traces of the 'Bluebeard' tale are apparent in this television series' narrative of young female detectives investigating mysterious Bluebeard figures. One of the central symbols of Perrault's 'Bluebeard' tale, the forbidden chamber, is the space in which these young detectives scrutinise the abuse of women and girls. Like Perrault's Bluebeard, who abuses his masculine power over his very young wives, the multiple Bluebeard figures in this contemporary text are all adult male authority figures who have victimised and murdered multiple girls. I analyse this contemporary text's representation of the forbidden chamber, providing a comparison between Perrault's description of the room with the teen screen's depiction of it. Like Perrault's young bride, who was driven by curiosity to uncover her husband's horrific secret, the girl investigators are similarly driven by a desire to expose Bluebeard's crimes against Alison. The teen screen revision, like Perrault's earlier text, hinges on the girl's encounter with knowledge about masculine abuses of power and violence. However, in the revision, the result of attaining this knowledge has radically different outcomes: it leads to the heroines' empowerment, rather than the punishment detailed in Perrault's account of the tale. I am particularly interested in exploring the heroines' united investigation and response to a collective of Bluebeard figures including teachers, doctors, policemen, boyfriends and fathers. In these moments of critical investigation, the heroines collectively oppose instances of patriarchal oppression.

The legacy of the contemporary female detective narrative is embedded with a feminist agenda. Writers such as Bethe Schoenfeld (2008) and Priscilla Jones and Manina Walton (1999) have traced the link between the second-wave feminist movement and the emergence of contemporary women's detective fiction.[2] As Schoenfeld writes, 'in the past three decades, an entirely new subgenre of mystery fiction has evolved— women writing about women protagonists concerned with women's issues' (837). Jones and Walton write that the feminist movement of the 1970s 'created a second-wave "feminisation of crime writing"' (27). They remark that since this wave of feminist detective fiction written by women, the genre has become centrally concerned with 'questions of women's agency' and how they 'establish the distinctive voice of an empowered female subject, and this, clearly, is not just a formal but is also a political gesture' (4). The assertion of the woman's agency within the detective narrative challenges the position to which women have traditionally been relegated within the genre: as the femme fatale or the helpless damsel. It pursues new narrative paths in the detective genre, foregrounding a powerful and agentic female subject.

The female detective narrative and the 'Bluebeard' tale are closely linked. Several scholars have explored how female detective novels, films and television series rework and revise Perrault's 'Bluebeard' narrative (see Mulvey 1996; Tatar 2004; Cornelius 2012). Maria Tatar writes that many female detective films are 'modelled on the Bluebeard plot' (2009, 17), and often position the heroine as 'an expert detective...[with a] spirit of adventure, curiosity, and desire for knowledge' (22). However, Tatar points out that these filmic revisions, from Hitchcock to Campion, often 'stage a double movement between agency and victimisation, between a sense of adventure and timidity, between investigative curiosity and masochism, always within the confines of marriage' (23), and this tension between agency and victimisation in 'Bluebeard' films will be more thoroughly analysed in the second section of this chapter. I agree with Tatar's assessment of these 'Bluebeard' films, particularly in relation to their confinement of the female investigator's narrative to the domestic sphere, the mysteries of the husband's past and heterosexual romance. The heroine's investigative gaze offers an important measure of agency, but it is ultimately tempered by confining this gaze to the traditionally feminine realm of the home, and in the service of resolving the marriage plot.

In *Pretty Little Liars*, the interjection of a teen girl communitas into the 'Bluebeard' narrative shifts the tale in a new direction, beyond some of these limitations. Because the series provides representations of friendship and solidarity forged between girls in the face of masculine authority and oppression, the heterosexual romance is displaced from the centre of the narrative, and the investigation prompts the sleuths to venture out of the domestic realm to intrude upon masculine domains of power to solve the crime. The serialisation of the text also allows for an investigation of multiple Bluebeards and their crimes against Alison and other girls and women; there are many Bluebeards in *Pretty Little Liars* who have conspired to victimise Alison and other girls and women. Therefore, Bluebeard's crimes are represented not as single, strange, isolated incidents; instead, they are acknowledged as widespread problems. This representation of male violence as systemic, and the representation of repeated instances of girls' opposition and collective action against it, shifts the 'Bluebeard' narrative into new, and sometimes feminist, territories.

Communitas is a central concept that informs this chapter, and the remainder of the book. I am most interested in how the revision of the fairy tale through the addition of feminine adolescent communitas to the narrative produces moments of feminine adolescent solidarity and collective opposition to the status quo. Jones and Walton argue that the female detective narrative is able to explore 'women's ability to exercise individual and collective agency (the ability to act, to intervene)' (1999, 3). While Jones and Walton mention the potential for the representation of 'collective agency' in women's detective fiction, they primarily consider individual female agency in their analysis because, as Schoenfeld comments, the female detective figure in crime fiction usually works alone (2008, 850–851). I explore how *Pretty Little Liars'* focus on collective agency creates opportunities for the representation of feminine adolescent agency and resistance on the teen screen.

Victor Turner writes that communitas is a connection of solidarity forged between ritual subjects during liminality, allowing for 'fully, unmediated communication' (1977, 46). Turner never discussed feminism in his theorisation of communitas; however, I redeploy the concept for a feminist agenda to analyse how female solidarity, protest and organised action are made possible during this liminal period of coming together. He elaborates that it is a 'social antistructure, meaning by it a relation quality of full, unmediated communication, even communion… which arises spontaneously in all kinds of groups, situations, and circumstances [*sic*]' (145). The three elements that Turner argues prompts the formation of a communitas are 'liminality, outsiderhood, and structural inferiority' (1974, 231). From this position, ritual subjects are able to collectively 'call in question the whole normative order' (268). The heroines of *Pretty Little Liars* are outsiders in a number of ways: as girls, they are excluded from the dominant adult masculine field; and as sleuths, they are excluded from the official or authorised channels of investigation.

From this place of exclusion and marginality, communitas allows ritual subjects to create an innovative liminal language as a new mode of communicating knowledge between members of the group. Turner argues that in communitas, the group creates 'sensorily perceptible rituals and symbols which frame and consolidate their identity as a communitas' (1977, 48) by inventing modes of communication uniquely understood by those within the group. Turner writes that 'I would expect to find in liminal situations daring and innovation both in the modes of relating symbolic and mythic elements and in the choice of elements to be related. There might also be the introduction of new elements and their various combinations with old ones' (1974, 255). In *Pretty Little Liars*, the heroines develop these daring and innovative 'sensorily perceptible rituals and symbols' that Turner identifies as central to communitas by inventing covert modes of communication through their use of pretty objects as clues. As the sleuths conduct their investigation, they discover crucial evidence embedded in pretty objects, and use this evidence to solve the mysteries at hand. This evidence goes unnoticed in the official channels of the investigation, allowing the pretty objects to become a covert language of detection exclusively available to the sleuths. Importantly, this pretty visual language of feminine adolescent communication is coded as the most powerful mode of detection: it is where the most crucial clues are embedded, and these pretty clues reveal the complicity of adult male authority figures in the crimes against Alison and other girls and women. The pretty becomes a site of feminine adolescent resistance to patriarchal power, and provokes the heroines to take action against it by holding these men accountable for their actions. In my feminist reading of this text, I consider the pretty to be politically important.

Communitas is a connection forged between outsiders or marginals, and the language they share is similarly invisible to the dominant order. This marginal position of the teenage girl does not, however, as girlhood scholar Tuula Gordon points out, 'signify powerlessness in any simple sense' (1996, 35). Indeed, the margins, or what Turner calls 'antistructure', can become a space where the rigid structures of the dominant centre temporarily dissolve. In this momentary dissolution of the status quo, ruptures in the dominant order can take effect. The antistructural margin is resistant space, a fissure in the dominant order. *Pretty Little Liars* represents the marginal position of the female adolescent sleuth as a site of opposition. By pursuing their detective work from the margins, the sleuths are not only able to perceive and detect things that the police cannot; they are also able to resist the dictates of the centre, creating critical ways of seeing and engaging with the world from the subject position of 'girl'.

Several feminist scholars have interpreted the female sleuth's position as an outsider as a subversive place from which to look and act. For the sleuth 'represent[s] not just an eye that sees but a voice that speaks from the margins, a voice originating in a character who both talks and behaves in an insubordinate manner' (Jones and Walton 1999, 194). The female sleuth is insubordinate and disruptive to the male-defined order and authority that seeks to govern her. As Kimberly Dilley asserts in her work on contemporary women's mysteries, 'power and control can be accrued on the basis of economic wealth, perceived racial superiority, or masculine gender. These amateur sleuth mysteries...both illuminate these discrepancies and find solutions other than calling in the police' (1998, 125). As these theorists argue, the female sleuth narrative allows for a marginalised feminine voice of dissent to be articulated. At the margins of the official investigation, the sleuth observes and illuminates the exploitation of masculine power through her own unauthorised investigation. Her insubordination and noncompliance to the authority of the masculine-dominated official investigation allows her to read the crime against the grain, and also through this corrosive act to often create ruptures in the system of patriarchal exploitation. In this space of rupture, alternative feminine identities, voices and narratives can be represented. The liminal space of the margin can therefore destabilise the status quo that works to keep girls and women subordinate, creating a representation of social change that continues into the postliminal phase once the crime is solved. As I explicated in the previous chapter, the postliminal is the final stage in the tripartite rite-of-passage structure, where the ritual subject returns to conventional culture after their journey through liminality. In the passage between the liminal and postliminal, there is the potential for the transformation enacted during the former stage to seep into and create change in the latter stage. The sleuths' investigation in the liminal space of the margin can create social change in the passage towards the postliminal phase, when each Bluebeard figure is brought to justice.

Having established *Pretty Little Liars* within the 'Bluebeard' fairy tale and female detective narrative tradition, the next section of this chapter surveys the feminist literature on this tradition in greater detail. I analyse Perrault's 'Bluebeard' along with feminist readings of the tale such as Bacchilega (1997), Marina Warner (1989, 1995) and Tatar (2004, 2009), before going on to consider how Perrault's tale has been taken up and revised in female detective fiction and women's films. I then examine how *Pretty Little Liars* comments on this tradition through one of its key revisions: mobilising a group of female detectives. I analyse the representation of liminal communitas in *Pretty Little Liars*, and how this shift in the 'Bluebeard' tale creates a narrative that includes moments of feminist solidarity and support between girls as they collectively scrutinise the gendered politics of authority and exploitation. The fourth section of the chapter explores pretty aesthetics as a representational site where rupture, opposition and intervention into patriarchal power is depicted in this series. In the fifth and final section, I explore how the series extends an invitation for girl spectators to engage with the communitas and collective critical girls' gaze that is represented on screen, and how this may create opportunities for moments of deconstructive and possibly feminist spectatorship.

FEMINIST RESPONSES TO THE 'BLUEBEARD' TALE: THE DIFFICULTY OF THE FEMALE INVESTIGATORY GAZE

I am particularly interested in charting the changes made to the identity of the female detective, and her access to agency and the gaze, as she investigates the horrors of the masculine figure's secret chamber, in the passage from Perrault's text to the contemporary teen screen revision. Feminist analyses of the 'Bluebeard' fairy tale have investigated Perrault's emphasis on the extreme punishment of the wife for her quest for knowledge, examining the sexist dynamics that underlie this punishment, particularly in relation to the association the tale draws between women, curiosity, disobedience and sinfulness. These theorists have also charted the ways in which the tale has been transformed in contemporary culture, particularly by the feminist authors, artists and filmmakers discussed in the introduction, who have repositioned the feminine figure in the narrative, highlighting her bravery, agency and empowerment. I argue that *Pretty Little Liars* participates in this shift, particularly as it provides a visual language for the representation of a collective critical girls' gaze at a collective of Bluebeard figures.

Perrault's 'Bluebeard' frames feminine curiosity, and the wife's desire to see behind her husband's forbidden door, as the primary transgression perpetrated in the story. Commenting on this framing of feminine curiosity and transgression, Warner writes:

> one of the many peculiar aspects of the story 'Bluebeard'...is that the narrative focuses on Fatima's disobedience, not on Bluebeard's mass murders. The initial weight of the story swings the listener or reader's sympathies toward the husband who instructs his young wife, and presents his request for her obedience as reasonable, the terror she experiences when she realises her fate as a suitable punishment, a warning against trespass. (1989, 125)

Framing feminine curiosity as the central crime places the 'Bluebeard' tale 'in line with cautionary tales about women's innate wickedness: with Pandora, who opened the forbidden casket, as well as Eve, who ate of the forbidden fruit' (Warner 1989, 125. See also Tatar 2003, 163; Anderson 2009, 7). The opening of the door to the forbidden chamber in Perrault's 'Bluebeard', then, secures the weight of blame, sin and evil not on the murderer whose slain wives lay in the forbidden chamber, but on the new wife whose curiosity drove her to disobey his orders. While Perrault's tale certainly narrativises a 'drive for knowledge [which] turns the wife into an energetic investigator, determined to acquire knowledge of the secrets hidden behind the door of the mansion's forbidden chamber' (Tatar 2004, 60), it is ultimately a cautionary tale, insisting on this action as reprehensible, a wicked transgression that deserves punishment.

Perrault dedicates at least two-thirds of his tale to meticulously describing the wife's suffering and torture: he describes her as a 'poor distressed creature' ([1697] 2001, 734) who 'thought she would die from the fright' (733), 'dishevelled and in tears' (734). As Bluebeard tortures her with threats of death, she helplessly flings 'herself at her husband's feet, weeping and begging his pardon, with all the signs of true repentance for having disobeyed him' (734) before 'he seized her by the hair with one hand and raised his cutlass with the other' (734). Bluebeard's punishment for his crimes against women barely receives a mention, as his wife's brothers simply 'passed their swords through his body and left him dead on the spot' (735) in the final moments of the tale. This extraordinary focus on detailing the heroine's suffering at the hands of her husband frames the tale as 'a text that enunciates the dire consequences of curiosity and disobedience' (Tatar 2004, 7). The young bride's gaze at the horrifying scene is impossibly fated, and the authority of Bluebeard's gaze is absolute: he will always see the tell-tale mark of his wife's transgression, signified in Perrault's version by an indelible spot of blood on the key to the forbidden room, and he will always punish her for her 'crime'. The inescapability of this authoritative masculine gaze and its punishing effects on the young bride are fundamental to the representation of feminine curiosity in the narrative.

This gendered structure of the gaze becomes even more apparent in classical Hollywood retellings of the tale that attempt to provide the heroine's point of view, but that ultimately confine her agency to the domestic realm and the resolution of the marriage plot. Feminist theorists such as Mary Ann Doane (1987), Laura Mulvey (1996), Tatar (2004) have examined 'Bluebeard's' cinematic retellings, focusing especially on women's films of classical Hollywood cinema.[3] The female protagonist of the 'Bluebeard'-inflected film has proved particularly appealing for these feminist analyses, for she is an active investigator who seems to claim a subjective position. In her work on films of this kind, Doane's feminist psychoanalytic account argues that the films situate 'the woman as agent of the gaze, as investigator in charge of the epistemological trajectory of the text, as the one for whom the "secret beyond the door" is really at stake' (1987, 134). Instead of being subjected to the male character's investigation and his 'sadistic gaze', which 'assert[s] control and subject[s] the guilty person through punishment or forgiveness' (Mulvey [1975] 1989, 22), the heroine, at least momentarily, escapes her role as object and occupies a subjective point of view through her detective work.

However, Doane ultimately finds that in these films there is a constant tension between 'the heroine's active assumption of the position of subject of the gaze and her intense fear of being subjected to the [male] gaze', a tension that the heroine cannot ultimately overcome (127). The potential volatility and disruptiveness of this gaze must be contained through domestication and 'the delegation of the detecting gaze to another male figure who is on the side of the law' by the end of the film (135). This not only results in 'the passivisation of the female subject of the desire to know', but also secures the female detective in a position of impotence 'in terms of the actual ability to uncover the secret or attain the knowledge which she desires' (135). Doane explicates the difficulty that the female detective experiences in sustaining access to the gaze in these classical Hollywood 'Bluebeard' films. Her ability to attain and mobilise a secure subjective and authoritative position is ultimately stifled by the film's insistence on feminine domesticity and the female figure's subordination to the powers and authority of the male gaze. However, in the contemporary example of *Pretty Little Liars* there are moments that overcome and expand the limits of this tradition, particularly in relation to the heroines' access to agency and the gaze.

Pretty Little Liars similarly participates in visualising the 'Bluebeard' heroine's gaze, self-consciously reflecting on the tradition of the literary 'Bluebeard' tale, as well as its women's film descendants. Images of locked boxes and keys to forbidden rooms are repeated throughout the series. In a particularly interesting scene in episode five of season four, sleuth Hanna Marin searches for a way to enter a forbidden closet, which she suspects holds evidence related to a murder that the heroines are investigating. As illustrated in Fig. 4.1, the scene very knowingly reflects on 'Bluebeard's' theme of the 'woman at the keyhole' or the woman straining to see the 'secret beyond the door'. The scene is shot from inside the darkened space of the closet, framed by total darkness. Looming large and bright in the centre of the frame is the closet's

Fig. 4.1   Hanna peeps through the keyhole (4.05)

keyhole. Hanna squints intently through it, trying to discern the contents of the closet.

Combining the dramatic visual of the hyperbolically, almost surreally, large keyhole with Hanna's inquisitively squinting eye in the centre of the frame reveals the series' knowingness about the tale's intense focus on the female figure's visual curiosity, her powerful need to discover the secret behind the locked door and to encounter the knowledge forbidden to her. *Pretty Little Liars* also reveals its self-consciousness about the 'Bluebeard' tale's traditional narrative of the woman's punishment. In episode twenty-four of season two, the sleuths uncover a morbid 'Bluebeard'-inspired tableau behind the door of a locked cupboard. Within the cupboard, one of the culprits of Alison's disappearance has arranged a miniature bloody chamber adorned with a child's doll covered in bright red blood, and half-buried in dirt, as shown in Fig. 4.2.

This mechanised 'talking' doll has been programmed to repeat the phrase 'Follow me, end up like me.' This sinister and frightening display behind the locked door has been engineered as a warning, a threat to the sleuths who are growing ever closer to discovering the truth behind Alison's disappearance. The message of this Bluebeard figure's staged tableau is clear: if the sleuths follow their curiosity, violate his prohibition and continue to investigate his murderous plot, they will be brutally

Fig. 4.2   Bluebeard's miniaturised bloody chamber (2.24)

punished for their transgression. The female sleuth's uncovering of abuses committed against other girls in *Pretty Little Liars* echoes the detective work of the heroine in the 'Bluebeard' fairy tale, who violates her husband's ban and enters his forbidden chamber only to discover the mutilated bodies of his previous wives. However, unlike Perrault, the series does not narrativise the punishment of the sleuths for their violation of Bluebeard's prohibition: it represents resistant heroines who do not cower in the face of this threat but rather resolve to take organised action against it. Furthermore, unlike Perrault's representation of a single, vulnerable woman facing the abuse of her murderous husband, the series shifts the tale towards a representation of feminine empowerment through the group of girl detectives who support one another and collectively investigate the crimes committed against Alison. Rather than waiting for a male character to rescue them, as Bluebeard's wife had to, these heroines use their collective power to confront and oppose adult masculine authority.

Contemporary feminist texts that revise the 'Bluebeard' tale attempt to reclaim this investigative curiosity as a positive trait, and I locate *Pretty Little Liars* within this contemporary revisionist movement. As Tatar points out, 'while earlier ages denounced Bluebeard's wife for her "reckless curiosity" and her "uncontrolled appetite," our own culture has turned her into something of a heroine, a woman whose problem solving skills and psychological finesse make her a shrewd detective, capable of rescuing herself' (2004, 3–4). The heroine of the contemporary 'Bluebeard' tale must be both brave and daring, for as Tatar writes, she 'cannot rely on her brothers for rescue' and therefore 'take[s] on agency in startling new ways' (2009, 17). Bacchilega argues that a shift in focus in the tale allows for these new themes of agency, bravery, and initiation to emerge in the narrative:

> If the 'Forbidden Chamber' rather than the 'Bloody Key' is treated as the tale's central motif, then 'Bluebeard' is no longer primarily about the consequences of failing a test – will the heroine be able to control her curiosity? – but about a process of initiation which *requires* entering the forbidden chamber...The test is whether she can acquire this knowledge and then use it cleverly enough to triumph over death. (1997, 107 original emphasis)

This reconfigures the tale into a narrative about the heroine's transformative journey into the forbidden chamber, and the way she uses the knowledge gained there to overcome the story's murderous patriarch. While Perrault primarily focused on detailing the punishment of the young bride for her so-called crime of violating her husband's prohibition, contemporary texts such as *Pretty Little Liars* revise the narrative by representing the heroine's entry into this forbidden space as not only necessary but also transformative.

Pretty Little Liars participates in this shift in the 'Bluebeard' narrative, providing a representation of the heroines' sustained access to the gaze. As the heroines intrude upon Bluebeard's forbidden chamber, they use a forceful and agentic gaze, visualised by the extreme close-up shot. In the next section of this chapter, I explore communitas and the collective girls' gaze, theorising how deconstructive visual techniques provide representations of a new critical feminine adolescent language for the teen screen. The sleuths enter Bluebeard's forbidden chamber, using their collective critical gaze to deconstruct the power dynamic that this space represents. Through these moments of deconstruction and critical investigation of Bluebeard's abuses of adult masculine power, the heroines corrode and expose these patriarchal figures' complicity in the subordination and exploitation of girls.

COMMUNITAS: CRITICAL GIRLS' GAZES AND SOLIDARITY IN *PRETTY LITTLE LIARS*

The series' representation of a multiple, diverse, female adolescent gaze defies the monolithic structure of the male gaze. The shared and dynamic access to the gaze is particularly evident in the sleuths' use of technologies such as phones, cameras, laptops and tablets to send visual and audio clues to one another as they investigate Bluebeard's forbidden room, distributing this knowledge for shared access. This shared research enables a deconstruction of the evidence as the heroines select and break down each clue for closer scrutiny and analysis, and this technique of deconstruction is mirrored in this chapter's close visual analysis of these scenes set in Bluebeard's chamber. Additionally, through this collective act of deconstruction, the heroines fracture the official narrative of Alison's disappearance, which has been fabricated by the corrupt male-dominated police force, exposing the abuses of adult masculine power and the men responsible for the exploitation and violence committed against the girl. I locate moments of feminist intervention into patriarchal power in *Pretty Little Liars'* representation of communitas, highlighting the political potential of this representation of girls' solidarity on the teen screen.

Perrault's 'Bluebeard' features female protagonists—Bluebeard's collection of brutally murdered wives, and his two new victims, his bride and sister-in-law—who are all almost completely powerless and victimised. The young bride does exercises a measure of agency in her investigation of the forbidden chamber, but when she enters the chamber and discovers the bloody, decapitated bodies of Bluebeard's previous seven wives hanging from the ceiling like trophies, she helplessly realises that her fate will also be a gruesome death at the hands of her murderous husband. Her sister, Anne, can only signal for help from a remote window in the castle, waiting for their brothers for rescue. This group of women is subjected to extreme violence and disempowerment at the hands of patriarchal authority. The televisual revision of the tale transforms the narrative position and identity of the feminine figures: the representation of the group of victimised and tortured young women shifts into a representation of a group of girl investigators who forcefully expose Bluebeard's crimes against girls and women.

Communitas provides a way to theorise the power of the girl group of sleuths in *Pretty Little Liars*. Communitas is a coming together of liminal ritual subjects who, at least momentarily, enter into 'alternative social arrangements' (Turner 1974, 134). During this communal moment outside the status quo, the ritual subjects access a measure of clarity about the norm from which they are momentarily standing apart, and are able to deconstruct and critique it from their marginal position. As Turner writes, communitas is fundamentally 'a way both of being detached from the social structure—and hence potentially of periodically *evaluating* its performance—and also of a "distanced" or "marginal" person's being more attached to *other* disengaged persons—and hence, sometimes of evaluating a social structure's historical performance in common with them' (1982, 51 original emphases). Communitas fosters a collective effort to unsettle dominant power structures, to expose their inner workings, affecting a rupture in the system. In other words, communitas allows for an actively critical position where collectives of ritual subjects evaluate and resist the status quo, performing 'a scrutinisation of the central values and axioms of the culture in which it occurs' (1969, 167). In communitas, the heroines of *Pretty Little Liars* interrogate the status quo through their investigation of the male authority figures involved in Alison's disappearance, and enter into a new network of relationships with girls that produce moments of oppositional, critical and collective action against patriarchal oppression.

While very little academic research has been done to specifically address representations of communitas in teen girl screen media,[4] writers such as Mary Celeste Kearney and Yvonne Tasker have explored the feminist value of depictions of female friendships and solidarity on the teen screen. Kearney argues that in many films that focus on female adolescent friendships, girls 'develop a strong support system by communicating intimately with their girlfriends and standing up for themselves and each other in the face of adversity, especially misogyny' (2002, 135). Privileging this bond between girls therefore 'involves female characters acting in a space not defined by male characters or by a narrative progress towards heterosexuality' (Tasker 2002, 153), diversifying representations of girlhood and creating narratives of solidarity between girls, going beyond dominant scripts of compulsory heterosexual romance.[5] This representation of female solidarity and shared access to the gaze is also significant because it challenges dominant discourses about girls that frame and pathologise them as sexist stereotypes, such as 'mean girls', bitches and backstabbers.

One way in which the heroines of *Pretty Little Liars* work to expose and unsettle masculine power is through their shared access to the gaze as they collectively deconstruct clues in Bluebeard's forbidden chamber. In Chaps. 2 and 3, I began exploring representations of the girls' gaze, and its capacity to provide an alternative, oppositional perspective. In this chapter, I continue to explore this gaze, but take it further by theorising instances of a collective critical girls' gaze capable of deconstructing and intervening in abuses of masculine power. Television's prioritisation of non—fixity as opposed to closure and multiplicity as opposed to a singular, linear narrative trajectory provides a space for a different set of relations to emerge in relation to the gaze. For instance, Lorraine Gamman's work on the female detective series *Cagney & Lacey* (CBS 1981–1988) argues that women's television series engaged with 'a range of looks—often fragmented and contradictory' (1988, 12). This televisual interplay of female gazes and subject positions proves useful in the context of theorising beyond the limits of the Mulveyan fixed, limited female gaze. Further, because we are offered a multiplicity of looks rather than a monolithic gaze, a range of contestations and resistant ways of looking can arise.

Pretty Little Liars provides representations of moments where the girl group enters Bluebeard's forbidden chamber and investigates masculine violence and the exploitation of feminine bodies in dominant culture. In episode twelve of season four, the sleuths enter one of Bluebeard's darkened lairs. They find that the walls are adorned with garish, shadowy portraits of Alison. Whiteboards are filled with surveillance images and notes about other girls and women. While there are no dead bodies in this forbidden chamber, the portraits and surveillance images represent the girls and women Bluebeard has either already brutalised or intends to brutalise. Furthermore, the 'head shots' of each girl displayed on the whiteboards disturbingly refer back to Bluebeard's disembodied, beheaded women on display. The contemporary forbidden chamber is reinvented in a new media form: while Perrault describes the space filled with 'clotted blood', 'the dead bodies of several women suspended from the walls' with their throats cut ([1697] 2001, 733), the contemporary chamber contains images of girls' fragmented bodies and 'decapitated' heads. There are several levels of trespass that the sleuths commit in order to expose Bluebeard's murderous plot: they break into the forbidden chamber; they unlock secret journals filled with incriminating evidence; and they hack into Bluebeard's state-of-the-art computer system, again emphasising the revisionist new media symbols of this forbidden chamber. These multiple violations of prohibition allow the heroines to exercise their shrewd investigative prowess. Their collective effort to hack into Bluebeard's computer—to deconstruct and decode its contents—leads to their access to files that reveal his identity and the crimes he has committed.

In episode five of season three, sleuths Aria Montgomery and Emily Fields talk on the phone while they examine clues separately. Aria looks through a roll of film, hoping to discover incriminating evidence in the negatives. Meanwhile, Emily goes online to research a drug that was used to spike her drink at a party. As the two sleuths discuss their separate investigations, Aria finds three blue pills in the film canister that she is scrutinising. She describes the pills to Emily, and the sleuths confirm through the online research that these were the same pills used to spike Emily's drink. This allows the heroines to begin investigating where the pills came from and who spiked Emily's drink. The cooperative sharing of information gained through the critical girls' gaze empowers the sleuths to uncover the perpetrator of the crime against Emily. This sharing of the gaze therefore creates an important solidarity between the sleuths, which helps them to identify, critically reflect on and challenge practices such as drink spiking that work to disempower and victimise girls.

This insistence on the sleuths' collective critical reflexivity about their position as girls within patriarchal culture is one of the most feminist aspects of the show, for it is through this critical reflexivity that abuses of adult male power can be identified and then challenged through collective action. Girlhood studies scholar Valerie Hey argues that girls lack:

> a *collective* consciousness/language. After all girls ha[ve] little sustained access to a public 'symbolic political language' capable of reflecting on what it is that is common or shared about their subordinated positioning within the terms of hegemonic masculinity. (1997, 129 original emphasis)

The sleuths' development of their critical gazes can be seen as the 'collective language' that Hey calls for; after all, it is through the shared access to this specific gaze that the sleuths are able to carve out a critical space where they can reflect on their position as subordinate objects within dominant culture, and also expose the practices that hold this subordination in place. I do not suggest that the sleuths of *Pretty Little*

Liars somehow manage to completely evade this male gaze. Rather, I argue that the representation of a variety of girls coming together, with their various perspectives, pieces of information and clues, to collectively interrogate this masculine power, creates the opportunity to expose and therefore unsettle its sexist politics to some extent.

The use of extreme close-ups on deconstructed clues visualises the intensity and power of the sleuths' collective critical gaze. The heroines organise and work together through a shared digital research. The sleuths make records of many of these clues on their phones, cameras, laptops and tablets, and use these technologies to share this information amongst themselves within their all-girl communitas. The theme of girls 'invading domains of adult male power and privilege' (Kearney 2006, 13) is an especially important aspect of the series. They invade and scrutinise areas ordinarily reserved for adult male eyes only, which is particularly evident when the sleuths hack into files that include classified information, including hospital patient files, surveillance camera footage and police files. The structure of this look is an insistently interrogating one—scrutinising in close-up views. Indeed, a policeman suspicious of the sleuths' unofficial investigation accusatorily exclaims 'I guess you girls are used to being in places you're not meant to be' (1.09).

This scrutiny of territories of masculine authority significantly allows the sleuths to uncover the gendered politics of power, revealing and challenging this corruption. For example, in episode three of season four Hanna sneaks into police headquarters. She discovers a whiteboard filled with police evidence and theories about Alison's disappearance. Using her camera phone, she zooms in on the relevant information and snaps a picture, as illustrated in Fig. 4.3. Hanna's critical gaze, zeroing in on the pertinent clues, allows her to scrutinise, select and collect information, illustrated by the concentrated close-up shot she captures on her phone. This use of technology allows the heroines to invade both actual and virtual spaces that are usually off limits to girls.

In capturing this particular set of clues, the sleuths are able to reveal the corrupt actions of detective Wilden, who was revealed to have not only engaged in a sexual relationship with fifteen-year-old Alison before she went missing, but also obsessively stalked her friends, the sleuths. This act of deconstruction, visualised by the close-up and extreme close-up shots on specific sections of the whiteboard, breaks apart the police force's construction of the evidence and exposes Wilden's complicity in the crime. The images are transmitted and shared between the

Fig. 4.3 Hanna scrutinises the clue, zooming in on its relevant information and capturing it on her camera phone (4.03)

communitas through text messaging and email, allowing the sleuths to enact their collective scrutiny. Deconstruction allows the sleuths to create fissures in the power structures that have disempowered and endangered both Alison and themselves. Furthermore, this act of solidarity within liminal communitas seeps into conventional culture in the postliminal phase: once the heroines expose his crimes against girls, he is held accountable by the official justice system. This example shows how liminal communitas has an impact on the heroines' social world, instigating change by ensuring that this corrupt policeman will not continue to terrorise and victimise women.

The use of digital technologies to invade and deconstruct the crime scenes is an important aspect of these scenes of the sleuths investigating Bluebeard's forbidden chamber. As cultural studies scholars have pointed out, boys and men continue to be considered the ideal users of digital technologies (see Kearney 2006, 2010). As Justine Cassell and Meg Cramer argue, contemporary culture's characterisation of the relationship between girls and digital technologies is one of 'panic over young girls at risk...ascrib[ing] roles of naiveté, innocence, or delinquency' (2008, 54). Their research shows that girls often 'turn out to be active and informed consumers and producers of mediated conversations and texts. The important identity construction, self-efficacy, and social net-work production work that they do online is not only largely ignored, but too often condemned' (54–55). They conclude that 'the reason for this exaggeration of danger arises from adult fears about girls' agency... and societal discomfort around girls as power users of technology' (55). In *Pretty Little Liars*, the use of text messaging, emails, computer hack-ing, photography and video provide the heroines with a means to com-municate knowledge within their communitas of girl sleuths. Their exchange of knowledge defies the stereotypes about girls' use of digital media identified by Cassell and Cramer.

Using these technologies also allows the heroines to deconstruct the evidence in Bluebeard's forbidden chamber, particularly through the use of zooming and cropping functions on cameras and mobile phones, freeze-framing videos and isolating sounds in voice recordings. These techniques of digital media are used for subversive purposes. Their use of these technologies in ways that are considered off limits to girls, as pro-ducers and decoders of digital media, challenges the dominant patriar-chal discourse of girlhood that positions girls' use of technology as solely for the traditionally feminine pursuits of gossip, shopping and consum-ing media. This depiction of girls using technology in oppositional ways therefore expands the representational terrain of girlhood on the teen screen, as the heroines agentically intervene into practices and spaces dominated by men and boys. In *Pretty Little Liars*, then, communitas provokes the heroines to unsettle status quo constructions of femininity and adolescence, and girls' access to knowledge and power.

These acts of deconstruction break down the visual economy of the male gaze, in which 'the unseeing gaze of his intended objects...is intrin-sic to the hegemonic control male dominance insists on' (Pomerance 2002, 48). In her later book, *Death 24x a Second* (2006), Mulvey devel-oped her work on the cinematic gaze to argue that contemporary and digital media allows for a new kind of image that encourages interac-tive deciphering engagement. The capacity for media users to freeze frame or zoom in close on specific images and view scenes or sequences repeatedly allows 'key moments and meanings [to] become visible [and] that could not have been perceived' otherwise (147). She writes that this 'decoding is not only essential to the very process of understand-ing but also involves a...moment of detachment, a moment, that is, of self-conscious deciphering' (149). In *Pretty Little Liars*, the heroines' use of zoomed-in, freeze-framed digital media images provides them with a way to deconstruct and decipher the clues under investigation. This accumulation of research through freeze-framed digital images that can be revisited, shared amongst the members of the communitas and closely scrutinised enables this important act of deconstruction that unsettles the dominant power and gaze of the Bluebeard figures under investigation. By actively taking up and maintaining their access to the gaze, the sleuths rebel against the dominance of the male gaze, disrupting the structure that requires its object to be unable to look back. As Jones and Walton comment, many female detective narratives 'place the power dynamics of the gaze itself under surveillance...to subject the gaze to investigation and reformulation' (1999, 159). The sleuths work to uncover Bluebeard's true identity, and challenging their subordination to the authority of his gaze. Through the critical work of communitas and their reformulation of the gaze, the heroines therefore assert a powerful interjection into dominant discourses of girlhood that position the girl as object, and insist on occupying an alternative subjective position.

In the next section of this chapter, I explore how the sleuths challenge dominant discourses of feminine adolescence, particularly those that characterise girls as objects of both suspicion and derision in adult patriarchal culture. The sleuths develop a counter-discourse that disrupts this way of speaking about girls, and I am particularly interested in exploring how this manifests in their subversive use of pretty girl culture objects as a way of conveying this alternative visual language of feminine adolescence.

'WE SEE WHAT THE POLICE DON'T SEE': DECORATIVE AESTHETICS AND THE CRITICAL GIRLS' GAZE

The title *Pretty Little Liars* is made up of words ordinarily used in patriarchal discourses to degrade or even humiliate girls: 'pretty' is often used to designate girls as objects of a desiring masculine gaze; 'little' is a term that diminishes the girl to an infantilised and powerless role; and 'liars' characterises girls as deviant, suspicious and inauthentic, as opposed to the idealised masculine subject who is imagined as a bearer of truth and substance, and a voice of reason and logic. This patriarchal definition of girlhood means that girls are understood as in need of 'monitoring for all too possible deviation or failure' (Driscoll 2002, 127), placing feminine adolescence under the control of adult patriarchal authority. In the narrative of this television series, the heroines confront and challenge this in moments of collective agency and communitas. Their collective gaze searches for alternative girl identities that go beyond dominant definitions of 'girl'.

Pretty Little Liars' moments of feminist politics are often articulated through the medium of pretty aesthetics. Rosalind Galt describes the pretty as an aesthetic relegated 'to a consistent space of exclusion' (2011, 8) in masculinist hierarchies of value. However, the margin or the 'space of exclusion', as Galt calls it, can present an opportunity for opposition to the status quo. The pretty object becomes a critical feminine adolescent semiotic system that eludes the regulatory gaze of the police detectives who refuse to acknowledge the value of these items as clues in the investigation. By eluding this authority and launching a counter-discourse to the official investigation, the sleuths rupture the narrative created by the police about Alison's disappearance and furthermore, as these pretty objects erupt on screen in disruptive spectacular displays, this counter-discourse becomes one that refuses to be silenced. This allows the sleuths to challenge the authority of the male-dominated police force, revealing the corruption and abuses embedded in their power structures. As the heroines decode and examine the clues embedded in pretty objects such as knick-knacks and ornaments, they become conscious of gendered violence and are then prompted to take action against it.

Perrault's representation of Bluebeard's young bride fixes her in a disempowered position in the narrative. Victoria Anderson writes that she is 'unconscious; she does not possess the consciousness to effect her own escape. This lack of consciousness is underscored by the ending, where the success of her new marriage is explicitly identified by its ability to effect her forgetfulness' (2009, 8). Anderson goes on to elucidate that the ending of Perrault's 'Bluebeard' with the girl's new marriage 'reaffirm[s] the wife's subordination. Combined with the unconsciousness of the female protagonist and the cyclical nature of the violence depicted…this creates a suggestion not of resolution but of *perpetuation*; a perpetuation effected through unconsciousness' (8 original emphasis). *Pretty Little Liars'* representation of the girl communitas, and its subversive development of an oppositional and critical language, injects the 'Bluebeard' tale with the empowered feminine consciousness that is, from a contemporary feminist perspective, clearly missing in Perrault's patriarchal narrative. As the heroines become conscious of

Bluebeard's crimes during their liminal communitas, they ensure that he is held accountable in the postliminal phase. While the series does represent multiple Bluebeard figures, it does not represent a perpetual cycle of the torture of women. The purpose of the sleuth's investigation is to break this cycle of violence: with each crime that is solved and with each Bluebeard that is exposed and held accountable, this purpose is achieved.

Like the Bluebeard of Perrault's tale, these contemporary Bluebeards attempt to secure the girl in the role of the guilty party. The police force constructs a narrative that describes Alison as a suspiciously deviant, sexually precocious girl who therefore made herself vulnerable to victimisation. The police also describe the sleuths as suspicious liars and troublesome deviants, continually bringing the girls into the police station for interrogation, attempting to implicate the heroines in the crime and bury the evidence against the police force. To combat this regulatory discourse of girlhood as subject to adult masculine surveillance, control and discipline, the sleuths' pretty counter-discourse allows them to discuss the crimes covertly and work towards eventually exposing the male authority figures responsible for them.

The sleuths' use of decorative clues creates readings that go against the grain of, and are oppositional to, the readings offered by the police. As one of the sleuths, Emily Fields points out, 'we see what the police don't see' (3.22). This rewriting of the 'Bluebeard' narrative provides an opportunity for the exploration of a critical girl's gaze at these dynamics of masculine power, and how it can transform social relations in the postliminal phase of the story by holding these male characters accountable for their actions. The pretty decorative image, which perhaps initially appears to simply reproduce a postfeminist visual landscape of girly consumer products, becomes the perhaps unexpected site where harmful discourses of patriarchal culture are resisted.

The decorative image is routinely associated with frivolity, inauthenticity and cosmetic superficiality, occupying a notoriously low position on the aesthetic hierarchy (Schor 1987; Sparke 1995; Steiner 2001). Considering the terms in which the decorative ornamental has been denigrated throughout art and cinematic history,[6] it is clear that it is inextricably bound up in a denigration of the feminine. Art historian Naomi Schor points out that the detailed object is associated on the one hand with decadent effeminacy and on the other with the domestic interior, ensuring that it is doubly gendered as feminine (1987, 4). The decorative is considered frivolous in its excessive propensity towards embellishment; visual arts scholar Llewellyn Negrin writes that it is associated with the seductive, 'inessential' and 'irrational' (2008, 117), and that the devaluation of this aesthetic means 'at the same time, a dismissal of the feminine as inferior' (117). Galt argues that this extends to the cinematic decorative image, associated with the surface, decorative, ornate and detail, and has thus been denigrated as 'false, shallow, feminine, or apolitical' (2011, 2). This masculinist discourse of contempt for the decorative is evident in the response of the male detectives and police members working on the investigation of Alison's disappearance in *Pretty Little Liars*. These detectives toss the most important clues—those embedded in the decorative object—to the side. They frequently refer to these objects as 'trash', 'useless' and 'junk'—and significantly these objects are usually given to the sleuths in crumpled grey garbage bags as an emphatic reminder of their uselessness. Ironically, it is because the male detectives cannot understand or appreciate the value of the decorative that they cannot solve the case: the most important clues are embedded within these decorative objects. *Pretty Little Liars* reveals a self-consciousness about how the decorative is derided and considered to be meaningless frivolity or 'trash'.

The sleuths revalue these discarded, excluded objects as important clues in their unauthorised investigation, recuperating this derided aspect of girl culture. Instead of accepting 'patriarchal associations of femininity with the realm of appearance over essence and style over substance' (Negrin 2008, 136–137), the sleuths mobilise the pretty objects in new and unexpected directions. These objects are shot in extreme close-up from their perspective, reflecting their close and critical readings of the pretty and the discourse of opposition that it contains, which in turn gives them an opportunity to scrutinise abuses of patriarchal power. A primary clue of the series' first season is a pendant encrusted with pink, peach and violet diamantes, and it becomes an image captured on a camera phone which is covered in a casing decorated with a floral pattern of intertwining vines and leaves, as illustrated in Fig. 4.4.

This image is doubly decorative in its layering of embellished surfaces, appearing to be mere surface frippery. However, this pendant is embedded with a flash drive, and is filled with vital clues about Alison's disappearance. The heroines decode and interpret the information found in the pretty pendant, discovering new suspects to investigate.

Particularly useful to this chapter's theorisation of the decorative is the concept of cinematic excess and spectacle. Film theorists such as

Fig. 4.4   The glittering pendant as decorative clue (1.20)

Christine Gledhill, writing on the cinematic melodrama, have argued that moments of visually spectacular excess can rupture the smoothness of ideologically conservative narratives, bringing oppositional and challenging matters to the surface. These matters are often 'unrepresentable material' that are excluded from the dominant narrative but available in the extravagant 'material [of] the excessive mise-en-scène' (Gledhill 1987, 9). Literary and film theorist Rae Beth Gordon further argues that the purpose of these excesses 'is to carry meaning and intent that have been suppressed or excluded from the central field' (1992, 4). Art historian Wendy Steiner concurs when she writes that the excesses of the decorative, what she calls the 'super-added' and the supplemental, 'threaten at any moment to become the centre, the essence, the heart of the matter' (2001, 121). In this theory, Gledhill, Gordon and Steiner both show that the excess of the decorative image can articulate that which has been marginalised, bringing it forcefully to the surface.

The sleuths produce readings through the decorative clue, going beyond the police detectives' ability to solve the case. The decorative therefore becomes a point of excess in the text, undetected and virtually invisible to the official dominant narrative created by the police detectives. These points of excess, despite being suppressed by this official dominant narrative, forcibly erupt into the *mise en scène*. It disrupts the monolithic male detective's gaze and interjects into the authoritative narrative upon which it relies. In episode seventeen of season one, sleuth Spencer Hastings examines a snow globe for hidden evidence. The snow globe, associated with childish knick-knacks, gaudy souvenirs, glitter and frippery, has evaded the police's gaze. The globe is filled with intricately petalled pale pink rosebuds and soft white-feathered birds, and shimmers with tiny specks of floating glitter. The miniature statue of a ballerina mid-arabesque, as well as the pale green and pink jewellery box worn with use, adds even more decorative detail to the composition. As Spencer squints into the clear glittering globe, the clarity of her view is thrown into relief by the warm white sunlight streaming through the window, thoroughly illuminating the object of visual study, emphasising the clarity of her gaze and her ability to comprehend the clue. She carefully examines its contours and discovers that its base is loose, and when she opens it she finds a mysterious key to a storage unit. When the sleuths arrive at the storage unit and unlock its door in classic 'Bluebeard' style, they find it almost completely empty—but square in the middle of the cold concrete room sits the next decorative layer in the mystery, a hot pink lunchbox that they instantly recognise as Alison's. Adorned with a cartoon Tweety-bird motif and decorative floral pattern, this locked box appears particularly gaudy and girly. The childishness and girlishness of the box's appearance challenges the categorisation of such objects as silly and meaningless, for as the sleuths and the audience know from experience in previous episodes, important information and problem-solving material will be found within it. Opening up the mystery box that Alison left for them to find, yet another flash drive containing important evidence is discovered by the sleuths. The video footage found on it shows Alison being attacked by an adult male teacher from the local high school; the final frames of the video focus on her clenched fist as the struggle ensues. By collecting this clue through the pretty, the heroines are able to identify that the teacher was involved in Alison's disappearance, and they expose his complicity to the community. This disproves the police force's narrative about Alison's disappearance: she was clearly the victim of violence at the hands of multiple adult male authority figures. The spectacular feminine designs of the pendant, snow globe and lunchbox—hot pink, glittery, with imagery associated with juvenile play, the inessential and the cosmetic—are transformed into sites of collective female resistance.

These objects of decorative excess are able to articulate what the police investigation can neither comprehend nor allow: the objects contain within them evidence that implicates the police and other male authority figures such as teachers, doctors and fathers in the crimes perpetrated against Alison. The narrative constructed by the police suppresses the incriminating evidence, which nevertheless erupts to the surface of the text through the decorative objects investigated by the sleuths. In turn, the corruption of the dominant centre is exposed, and the truth about Alison's violation bubbles up to the surface. In so doing, the decorative becomes political, for it not only challenges dominant male authority; it also articulates a language of protest that talks back to it. By encouraging a close, scrutinising gaze, the decorative provides the sleuths with an opportunity to become aware of injustices committed by those male figures in the dominant centre, thus encouraging them to develop oppositional strategies to undermine this power.

COMMUNITAS IN THE SPECTATORIAL REALM: FRAMING DEVICES, *MISE EN SCÈNE* AND EDITING IN *PRETTY LITTLE LIARS*

Through these moments that represent collective agency and oppositional girl gazes, *Pretty Little Liars* presents girl spectators with an invitation to align themselves with the sleuths' shared, deconstructive point of view. I am interested in exploring how the critical work of communitas is extended beyond the diegesis and into the spectatorial realm. Through its framing devices and editing techniques, the series extends an invitation to girl spectators to participate in this communal act of deconstruction. The series' framing and editing—in particular, the three-part shot structure used to depict clues—present this invitation to spectatorial engagement with a collective oppositional girls' gaze. In these moments when spectators are invited to identify with the heroines' visual deconstruction of the evidence against Bluebeard, they are presented with an opportunity to closely examine the power structures that the clues expose. The series' framing and editing techniques therefore foster a potentially feminist viewing position that not only exposes gendered power imbalance but also promotes a critical reading of these politics.

In the first medium or wide shot, the scene is presented in a great amount of visual detail, encouraging a scanning spectatorial look across a range of surfaces and objects. This shot usually pans slowly across the crime scene, allowing the scanning spectatorial look to scrutinise all elements. The superabundance and enormous amount of detail in the *mise en scène* also encourages the eye to scan a range of surfaces and objects. There are multiple objects for spectators to examine as possible clues, including trinkets, stuffed animals, journals and jewellery. This amount of detail encourages a scanning spectatorial look, the eye moving across each potential clue and looking for the meaning it may contain. Anne Friedberg writes that the eye's relationship with the moving image is characterised by movement or 'scanning' across the screen (2006, 78). The movement within the frame, the sequential ordering of frames that work 'to produce movement' and the viewers' eyes moving across these moving images reveals the mobility inherent in 'the framed view' (93).[7] When the framed view is especially cluttered with detail, offering a profusion of several points to visually attend to all at once, the mobility of visual scanning is increased even further as the eye navigates the moving image. Friedberg writes that this mobility is heightened when the screen is fractured into several different images as in 'split-screen or multiple-screen films, inset screens on television, multiple windows on a computer screen—an even more fractured spatiotemporal representational system emerges' (93). *Pretty Little Liars'* representation of multiple screens within the *mise en scène*, which includes mobile phones, tablets, computers and televisions, is evidence of this multiplicity. Further, during the screening of each episode, animated pop-up media appear at the bottom and in the corners of the screen, advertising other television series, fan websites and Twitter comments, creating a further need to visually scan the screen with mobile eyes as the representational system becomes more fractured, multiple and multilayered. *Pretty Little Liars'* representation of this profusion of detail offers a spectatorial position that is mobilised and active, and further mobilises the viewing practice through its use of multiple screens and insets.

The first shot in the depiction of the crime scene promotes this very active mobile look, encouraging spectators to scan their gaze across the screen to find, isolate and identify the next important clue in the case. The second and third shots introduce the clue in a close-up, and then an extreme close-up. Encouraging girl spectators to align their gaze with the diegetic communitas' point of view provides an opportunity to enact a similarly deconstructing look at the clues and the material contained within them. In episode seventeen of season one, the sleuths discover Alison's childhood porcelain dolls. Opening up one of the dolls, they discover mysterious notes from Alison crammed inside. It is the critical, close gaze of the detective that allows the notes to be found, and the framing, camerawork and editing reflect this. The note is unfurled and read by the sleuths, and added to the collection of clues. In the second shot of the sequence, the decorative clue is focused on in a close-up shot. By focusing on the decorative clue through this, the framing encourages close spectatorial engagement with the object. This close engagement with the decorative, and locating meaningful information in it, revalues these previously derided feminine objects, challenging hierarchies of taste and value formed by a masculinist gaze, reconfiguring these terms of value in order to carve out a space for a girl's gaze to emerge. The final shot in this structure pursues the critical gaze even further, in an extreme close-up on the decorative clue. This shot visualises the most rigorously deconstructive and critical moment in the sleuths' collective investigatory look.[8] This identification not only allows for spectatorial engagement with the pretty in innovative ways; it also positions the spectator to participate in the detailed deconstruction of Bluebeard's exploitation of girls and women, provoking responses that may recognise the politics of gendered power that are being revealed on screen.

Spectatorial engagement with the communitas and the heroines' communal critical gaze is clearly reflected in the series' extratextual material. On several *Pretty Little Liars* message boards, blogs and fan sites,[9] fans post images that deconstruct clues presented on the show: freeze-framed, zoomed-in images of clues are posted and the fans provide their own interpretations of what they see as they attempt to solve the crime. In these examples, fans have carefully scanned the image for potential clues, and then deconstructed the image through close-ups and extreme close-ups in order to isolate and interrogate certain elements that may contain the key to solving the crime. Fans also work together to debate the possible meaning of each clue, echoing the communal decoding that occurs in the show's diegesis. Spectators become part of the series' communitas of girl detectives as this collective investigation extends beyond the diegesis and into fan practices. The extension of the three-part visual structure of scanning, close-up and extreme close-up beyond the diegesis and into the extratextual material reveals its importance for spectators and the way they engage with the series, becoming virtual members of the communitas of sleuths. Using this deconstructive technique to break apart the evidence and expose the patriarchal abuses of power embedded within them allows both heroines and spectators to identify with an all-girl communitas that interrogates adult masculine authority's subordination of girls and women in dominant culture. Therefore, I consider these moments as instances of a feminist, oppositional ethos becoming available both at the level of representation and for girl spectators.

Conclusions: The Political Potential of Liminal Communitas

Bluebeard's legacy is evident in teen texts that narrativise a girl's confrontation with a murderous man and the mystery of his locked room. The Bluebeard tale thus often becomes a space to represent feminine adolescent agency in the face of adult male violence. This agency is reflected in the heroine's resourcefulness and her capacity to outwit the Bluebeard figure. She is shown to be exceptional—a final girl or an impossibly clever loner such as Veronica Mars who can defeat the man on her own. While this provides a representation of girlhood agency, it limits that representation to an individual 'special' heroine, suggesting perhaps that these qualities are rare amongst most girls. What makes *Pretty Little Liars* a distinct case is its representation of a group of girls investigating Bluebeard's crimes, expanding the representation of feminine agency in the tale. This also allows for the incorporation of themes of girls' solidarity with one another and communal action against oppression, and this addition to the tale engineers moments of feminist politics for the teen screen. Crossing the threshold of Bluebeard's secret chamber allows the heroines to gain knowledge, and this transgressive act precipitates positive change in their social worlds. In the series, rite-of-passage metamorphoses are primarily figured as the transformations that occur when the girl comes to knowledge, particularly forbidden knowledge that is ordinarily denied her. This is often knowledge about abuses of masculine power, and finding ways to resist it. The girls' transgressive curiosity is therefore revalued as both positive and necessary.

As noted in this chapter, feminist scholars have expressed disappointment that many contemporary revisions of the tale continue to confine themselves to a marriage plot: the heroine often investigates her husband's mysteries and the films close with the husband either absolved or replaced by a new romantic partner. Either way, the agency of the woman's desire to know, and her courageous pursuit of knowledge, is limited to the domestic and the romantic. Teen revisions of 'Bluebeard' are able to sidestep this problem in the sense that the teen girl is too young for marriage, and so the plot often moves away from questions of romantic entanglement and towards other narrative possibilities. Given that many narratives of girlhood rites of passage continue to emphasise heterosexual romance as *the* central and defining factor in the girl's narrative, *Pretty Little Liars*' representation of an all-girl communitas as the most important element of the text becomes a particularly rich area for feminist analysis. By bringing gendered power imbalances to the surface through collective solidarity and shared critical awareness, the heroines are able to identify, name and challenge them together. This representation of collective female insubordination to patriarchal authority not only reveals the instability of the system that works to keep girls subordinated, but it also offers possibilities for cracks to appear in that system of oppression, making room for girls to potentially challenge, disrupt and defy it. Additionally, such cracks in the system provide space for alternative, even feminist, ways of doing girlhood to emerge. The sleuths challenge status quo expectations associated with feminine adolescence: they do not defer to male authority, are able to venture beyond the domestic, can independently experience adventures and are not solely defined by heterosexual romance. Claiming these differences, and therefore challenging dominant assumptions about girlhood, allows the sleuths to occupy a range of alternative subject positions within their rite-of-passage narrative.

I have argued for the political potential of the representation of communitas on the teen screen through an analysis of television series *Pretty Little Liars*. I have explored how the interjection of communitas into the 'Bluebeard' plot creates moments of girls' collective opposition and intervention into adult patriarchal power, with a particular focus on how the heroines work together to expose the violence and exploitation inflicted upon girls and women within dominant culture. Furthermore, I have explored how this dominant system of oppression is unsettled, and at times ruptured, by the heroines' collective work of deconstruction of Bluebeard's crime scenes, exposing the men involved in the crime and ensuring that they are held accountable. Their scrutiny of adult masculine authority figures provokes them to take collective action against their abuses of power, and I have argued that this provides instances of feminist solidarity against girls' subordinate position within patriarchal culture.

Perrault's 'Bluebeard' features a range of completely disempowered women: Bluebeard's wife, her sister and the mutilated corpses of the murderer's previous wives. While the young bride does exercise a measure of agency by unlocking Bluebeard's forbidden chamber and investigating the horrors that lie within it, Perrault undercuts this agency with his focus on the punishment she receives for her 'crime' of curiosity. Furthermore, once her brothers rescue her, she is immediately reincorporated into the dominant order with the second marriage that closes the tale. This reveals Perrault's preoccupation with this patriarchal strategy of containment to limit the feminine figure's agency and power in the narrative. *Pretty Little Liars* revises Perrault's text by interjecting a girl group of investigators who interrogate Bluebeard's crimes and the patriarchal power he represents. Scholarship on cinematic portrayals of the 'Bluebeard' tale found that while these films—especially those of women's cinema of 1940s Hollywood—did attempt to give the female figure on screen access to an empowered gaze, they were unable to sustain it because the cinematic structures they worked within privileged the authority of the male gaze and power. I have argued that *Pretty Little Liars* goes to great lengths to emphasise the female adolescent sleuths' agentic critical gaze through techniques such as the extreme close-up on the clue. Additionally, the series narrativises significant challenges to male authority figures such as policemen, teachers, doctors and fathers, allowing the heroines to scrutinise and challenge the power structures that secure male power and privilege.

This critical and oppositional gaze is represented in the series' formal visual structures, and these formal elements communicate moments of the heroines' opposition to the status quo. The heroines' deconstruction of the crimes committed in Bluebeard's forbidden chamber is visualised through the use of close-ups and extreme close-ups on elements of the crime scenes. The sleuths produce readings of the crime that not only go against the grain of the police's dominant investigation; but their reading from the margins also interrogates the structures of male power, privilege and the gaze, revealing the corruption embedded within them. Their use of technologies such as mobile phones, tablets, laptops and cameras allows them to document and distribute information about the crime amongst themselves. As they deconstruct and break apart each piece of evidence, they expose vital clues about the crimes, and the identity of the Bluebeards under investigation. This subversive use of digital media, which prompts them to confront and expose instances of masculine abuses of power and violence, is a corrosive act because it unsettles this power. Through these acts of deconstruction, the heroines of *Pretty*

Little Liars register their protest against the exploitation of girls and women. Furthermore, the work of deconstruction and scrutiny of the dominant centre done within the liminal realm of communitas continues to impact upon the dominant order in the postliminal phase when each Bluebeard is held accountable for his crimes against girls and women.

The communitas also develops a counter-discourse to this adult patriarchal power through their use of pretty girl culture objects as a mode of liminal communication. By exceeding the comprehension of the policemen's male gaze, the shared understanding of the decorative allows the sleuths to undermine the male gaze's authority, therefore creating a space for a resistant feminine visual language to be articulated. I have read the pretty as a space of opposition to dominant discourses of girlhood, particularly in the representation of how the sleuths disrupt the corrupt police force's characterisation of Alison as a delinquent and liar, a deviant girl whose so-called transgressions made her vulnerable to being assaulted. This is the same victim-blaming tactic used by Bluebeard in Perrault's tale—the girl transgressed and therefore deserves punishment. In *Pretty Little Liars*, the victims of masculine violence can speak back to this tactic and rupture it through their work of deconstruction. Through their counter-discourse embedded in the pretty, they speak otherwise about girlhood. The crimes committed by masculine authority figures like policemen and male teachers are exposed, fracturing the dominance of this patriarchal power. The pretty becomes a site of consciousness about gender inequality for the heroines, and as they become conscious of the crimes committed against girls and women within this dominant system of inequality, they are prompted to take action against it. Therefore, I have argued that the pretty aesthetic can become a feminist image on the teen screen, exploring the political potential of this frequently undervalued aspect of girl culture.

I have also located moments in *Pretty Little Liars* that invites teen spectators to align themselves and identify with the all-girl communitas represented on screen. The series' framing devices and editing techniques in scenes where the sleuths investigate clues in the Bluebeard case encourage a close spectatorial engagement with the heroines' collective, critical and deconstructive gaze. The three-part structure that depicts the clue allows spectators to participate in the act of deconstruction. In the first part of the visual structure, the wide or medium shot of the crime scene allows viewers to scan the space, scrutinising the image for evidence just as the sleuths do. The second and third parts of the visual structure break the clue down into a close-up and then an extreme close-up shot, encouraging a very close spectatorial interrogation of the evidence. As spectators are invited to participate in this breaking down of the evidence against Bluebeard, they are able to confront the gendered power imbalances that the clues expose, providing an opportunity to interrogate and perhaps even oppose these aspects of patriarchal culture. These techniques of framing and editing are therefore significant to a feminist reading of the text, for they reveal the series' investment in exposing these gender imbalances, as well as fostering an oppositional challenging gaze at them from a teen girl point of view. The 'Bluebeard' tale's female investigator is transformed into a victorious figure as she participates in a movement of collective feminine agency and action against the subordination and exploitation of women and girls. Furthermore, spectatorial alignment with this communitas of female investigators provides an opportunity for girl spectators to join the investigation of dominant cultural discourses of girlhood.

The 'Bluebeard' tale's female investigator is transformed into a victorious figure as she participates in a movement of collective feminine agency and action against the subordination and exploitation of women and girls. Furthermore, spectatorial alignment with this communitas of female investigators provides an opportunity for girl spectators to join the investigation of dominant cultural discourses of girlhood. In this chapter, I have explored how communitas provides the heroines of *Pretty Little Liars* with a shared critical gaze through which they can interrogate acts of gendered violence and the exploitation of girls and women in their community. In the next chapter, I further develop my reading of communitas by exploring how the girl group in *Gossip Girl* (The CW 2007–2012) deploys collective displays of masquerade and liminal play, which allow the heroines to experiment with feminine adolescent identities that disrupt and aggravate adult masculine authority and regulation. While the heroines of *Pretty Little Liars* create ruptures in the dominant system by deconstructing and analysing its mechanisms of power, the girl group of *Gossip Girl* experiments with fluid feminine adolescent identities to intrude upon arenas traditionally associated with masculine power, carving out new spaces for the heroines to collectively exercise agency and empowerment. In the series' revision of the 'Cinderella' tale, masquerade, sartorial excess and performance are used not to attract the affections of a Prince, but to explore multiple, even contradictory and challenging, feminine adolescent identities. Turner's work on 'rituals of status elevation' during liminal communitas (1969, 170) is particularly central to the chapter's exploration of this breakdown, which explores the heroines' deployment of masquerade, excess and performance in moments of transgression. I consider how this representation of fluid girlhood identities disrupts and destabilises some of the limits conventionally placed on the girl's rite-of-passage narrative, and how this then expands the representational field of feminine adolescence into alternative territories of signification.

NOTES

1. This television series is based upon a series of sixteen young-adult novels by Sarah Shepard, also entitled *Pretty Little Liars*. The first book in this series of novels was published in 2006, and at the time of writing this book, the most recent was published in 2014.
2. Examples of female crime fiction writers who emerged during and after this period include Sue Grafton, Janet Dawson and Sara Paretsky.
3. Examples of 'Bluebeard'-inflected women's films of classical Hollywood cinema include *The Two Mrs Carrolls* (Godfrey 1947) and *Secret Beyond the Door* (Lang 1947).
4. One exception is Payne (2013).
5. While *Pretty Little Liars* does narrativise romantic relationships (both heterosexual and lesbian), it nevertheless places the female friendship, solidarity and collective work towards discovering what happened to Alison at the centre of the text.
6. There is not enough space within the limits of this chapter to address how this interrelated discourse emerged, particularly within the modernist contempt for the decorative. See BrolinBrolin, Brent C. (1985), Steiner (2001), Galt (2011) for extensive discussions of the history of modernist architectural, art and cinematic debates about the decorative image.
7. This challenges the traditions of apparatus theory (and the psychoanalytic theory that depended on it), which was concerned with theorising cinema spectatorship as static, monocular, fixed and ideologically determined. See for example Jean-Louis BaudryBaudry, Jean Louis (1974) and Stephen Heath (1976).
8. This closeness is heightened even further by the spectatorial practices involved in watching television. As Friedberg writes: 'our physically embodied and subjectively disembodied relation to the screen changes as we engage with the distant, large cinema screen with projected images; the closer and light-emanating television screen; and the even closer computer

screen, one that we put our faces very close to, often touch, one that sites on our laps or in our beds' (2006, 7).
9. See for example: http://prettylittlesecrethints.tumblr.com/, http://plltheories.com/, http://thebestplltheories.tumblr.com/.

Bibliography

Andersen, Victoria. 2009. Introduction: A Perrault in Wolf's Clothing. In *Bluebeard's Legacy: Death and Secrets from Bartók to Hitchcock*, ed. Griselda Pollock and Victoria Andersen, 3–29. London and New York: I.B. Tauris.

Ang, Ien. 1996. *Living Room Wars: Rethinking Media Audiences for a Postmodern World*. London and New York: Routledge.

Atwood, Margaret. [1983] 1986. Bluebeard's Egg. In *Don't Bet on the Prince: Contemporary Fairy Tales in North America and England*, ed. Jack Zipes, 160–82. New York: Routledge.

Bacchilega, Cristina. 1997. *Postmodern Fairy Tales: Gender and Narrative Strategies*. Philadelphia: University of Pennsylvania Press.

Baudry, Jean Louis. 1974. Ideological Effects of the Basic Cinematographic Apparatus. *Film Quarterly* 28 (2): 39–47. doi:10.1525/fq.1974.28.2.04a00080.

Best PLL Theories. 2015. Pretty Little Liars Theories and News. Accessed June 20, 2017. www.thebestplltheories.tumblr.com.

Brolin, Brent C. 1985. *Flight of Fancy: The Banishment and Return of Ornament*. New York: St. Martin's Press.

B & T [pseud.] 2012. Pretty Little Secret Hints. Accessed June 2, 2017. www.prettylittlesecrethints.tumblr.com.

Carter, Angela. [1979] 1996. The Bloody Chamber. In *Burning Your Boats: Collected Short Stories*, 11–143. London: Vintage.

Cassell, Justine, and Meg Cramer. 2008. High Tech or High Risk: Moral Panics about Girls Online. In *Digital Youth, Innovation, and the Unexpected*, ed. Tara McPherson, 53–76. Cambridge, MA: MIT Press.

Clover, Carol J. 1992. *Men, Women and Chain Saws: Gender in the Modern Horror Film*. Princeton, NJ: Princeton University Press.

Cornelius, Michael G. 2012. Configuring Space and Sexuality: Nancy Drew Enters the Bluebeard Room. In *Murdering Miss Marple: Essays on Gender and Sexuality in the New Golden Age of Women's Crime Fiction*, ed. Julie H. Kim, 13–32. Jefferson, NC: McFarland and Co.

Dilley, Kimberly J. 1998. *Busybodies, Meddlers, and Snoops: The Female Hero in Contemporary Women's Mysteries*. Westport, CT and London: Greenwood Press.

Doane, Mary Ann. 1987. *The Desire to Desire: The Woman's Film of the 1940s*. Bloomington and Indianapolis: Indiana University Press.

Driscoll, Catherine. 2002. *Girls: Feminine Adolescence in Popular Culture and Cultural Theory*. New York: Columbia University Press.

Friedberg, Anne. 2006. *The Virtual Window: From Alberti to Microsoft*. Cambridge, MA and London, England: MIT Press.

Gamman, Lorraine. 1988. Watching the Detectives: The Enigma of the Female Gaze. In *The Female Gaze: Women as Viewers of Popular Culture*, ed. Lorraine Gamman and Margaret Marshment, 8–26. London: The Women's Press.

Galt, Rosalind. 2011. *Pretty: Film and the Decorative Image*. New York and Chichester: Columbia University Press.

Gledhill, Christine. 1987. The Melodramatic Field: An Investigation. In *Home is Where the Heart Is: Studies in Melodrama and the Woman's Film*, ed. Christine Gledhill, 5–39. London: BFI Publishing.

Gordon, Rae Beth. 1992. *Ornament, Fantasy, and Desire in Nineteenth-Century French Literature*. Princeton, NJ: Princeton University Press.

Gordon, Tuula. 1996. Citizenship, Difference and Marginality in Schools: Spatial and Embodied Aspects of Gender Construction. In *Equality in the Classroom: Towards Effective Pedagogy for Girls and Boys*, ed. Patricia F. Murphy and Caroline V. Gipps, 33–43. London and Bristol: UNESCO.

Heath, Stephen. 1976. Narrative Space. *Screen* 17 (3): 68–112.

Hey, Valerie. 1997. *The Company She Keeps: An Ethnography of Girls' Friendships*. Buckingham and Philadelphia, PA: Open University Press.

Kearney, Mary Celeste. 2002. Girlfriends and Girl Power: Female Adolescence in Contemporary U.S. Cinema. In *Sugar, Spice, and Everything Nice: Cinemas of Girlhood*, ed. Frances Gateward and Murray Pomerance, 125–142. Detroit, MI: Wayne State University Press.

———. 2006. *Girls Make Media*. New York and London: Routledge.

———. 2010. Pink Technology: Mediamaking Gear for Girls. *Camera Obscura* 25 (2): 1–38. doi:10.1215/02705346-2010-001.

Mulvey, Laura. [1975] 1989. Visual Pleasure and Narrative Cinema. In *Visual and Other Pleasures*, 14–26. Bloomington and Indianapolis: Indiana University Press.

———. 1996. *Fetishism and Curiosity*. Bloomington: Indiana University Press.

———. 2006. *Death 24 a Second: Stillness and the Moving Image*. London: Reaktion.

Negrin, Llewellyn. 2008. *Appearance and Identity: Fashioning the Body in Postmodernity*. New York: Palgrave Macmillan.

Nochimson, Martha. 1992. *No End to Her: Soap Opera and the Female Subject*. Berkeley, Los Angeles and Oxford: University of California Press.

Payne, Jenny Gunnarsson. 2013. Moving Images, Transforming Media: The Mediating Communitas of *HallonTV* and *DYKE HARD*. *International Journal of Cultural Studies* 16 (4): 367–382. doi:10.1177/1367877912460614.

Perrault, Charles. [1697] 2001. Bluebeard. In *The Great Fairy Tale Tradition: From Straparola and Basile to the Brothers Grimm*, trans. and ed. Jack Zipes, 732–735. New York and London: W.W. Norton.

Pretty Little Theories. 2017. Accessed June 20.www.plltheories.com.

Pomerance, Murray. 2002. "Don't understand, my own darling": The Girl Grows Up in Shadow of a Doubt. In *Sugar, Spice, and Everything Nice: Cinemas of Girlhood*, ed. Frances Gateward and Murray Pomerance, 39–53. Detroit, MI: Wayne State University Press.

Schoenfeld, Bethe. 2008. Women Writers Writing About Women Detectives in Twenty-First Century America. *The Journal of Popular Culture* 41 (5): 836–853.

Schor, Naomi. 1987. *Reading in Detail: Aesthetics and the Feminine*. New York and London: Methuen.

Sparke, Penny. 1995. *As Long as It's Pink: The Sexual Politics of Taste*. London: Pandora.

Steiner, Wendy. 2001. *Venus in Exile: The Rejection of Beauty in Twentieth-Century Art*. New York: Free Press.

Tasker, Yvonne. 2002. *Working Girls: Gender and Sexuality in Popular Cinema*. London and New York: Routledge.

Tatar, Maria. 2003. *The Hard Facts of the Grimms' Fairy Tales*, 2nd ed. Princeton, NJ and Oxford: Princeton University Press.

———. 2004. *Secrets Beyond the Door: The Story of Bluebeard and His Wives*. Princeton, NJ and Oxford: Princeton University Press.

———. 2009. Bluebeard's Curse: Repetition and Improvisational Energy in the Bluebeard Tale. In *Bluebeard's Legacy: Death and Secrets from Bartók to Hitchcock*, ed. Griselda Pollock and Victoria Anderson, 15–29. London and New York: I.B. Tauris.

Turner, Victor. 1969. *The Ritual Process: Structure and Anti-Structure*. Chicago: Aldine Publishing Company.

———. 1974. *Dramas, Fields, and Metaphors*. Ithaca, NY and London: Cornell University Press.

———. 1977. Variations on a Theme of Liminality. In *Secular Ritual*, ed. Sally F. Moore and Barbara G. Myerhoff, 40–52. Assen: Van Gorcum.

———. 1982. *From Ritual to Theatre: The Human Seriousness of Play*. New York: Performing Arts Journal Publications.

Walton, Priscilla L., and Manina Jones. 1999. *Detective Agency: Women Rewriting the Hard-Boiled Tradition*. Berkeley, Los Angeles and London: University of California Press.

Warner, Marina. 1989. Bluebeard's Brides: The Dream of the Blue Chamber. *Grand Street* 9 (1): 121–130. http://www.jstor.org/stable/25007307.

———. 1995. *From the Beast to the Blonde: On Fairy Tales and their Tellers*. London: Vintage.

FILMOGRAPHY

Barbe Bleue. Dir. Catherine Breillat. 2009.
Cagney and Lacey. CBS. 1981–1988.
The Glass House. Dir. Daniel Sackheim. 2001.
Gossip Girl. The CW. 2007–2012.
Halloween. Dir. John Carpenter. 1978.
In the Cut. Dir. Jane Campion. 2003.
Nancy Drew. Dir. Andrew Fleming. 2007.
A Nightmare on Elm Street. Dir. Wes Craven. 1984.
The Piano. Dir. Jane Campion. 1994.
Pretty Little Liars. ABC Family. 2010–.
Secret Beyond the Door. Dir. Fritz Lang. 1947.
Slumber Party Massacre. Dir. Amy Holden Jones. 1982.
Twilight. Dir. Catherine Hardwicke. 2008.
The Two Mrs Carrolls. Dir. Peter Godfrey. 1947.
The Uninvited. Dir. The Guard Brothers. 2009.
Veronica Mars. UPN. 2004–2007.
When a Stranger Calls. Dir. Simon West. 2006.

CHAPTER 5

Cinderella's Transformation: Public Liminality and Style as Subversion in *Gossip Girl* (The CW 2007–2012)

Introduction: Performativity and Public Liminality

In the context of contemporary teen girl media, 'Cinderella' is probably the most retold and revised fairy tale, demonstrating the remarkable durability and potency of the narrative. In these retellings, what often endures is the spectacle of the girl's glamorous transformation and how it serves to secure the affections of a male suitor, or to indicate that the girl is worthy of desire. This is the case in teen films such as *She's All That* (Iscove 1999), *A Cinderella Story* (Rosman 2004), *The Princess Diaries* (Marshall 2001), *Cinderella* (Branagh 2015) and *The Prince and Me* (Coolidge 2004). While the heroines of these films are smart, outspoken and active, the romance is prioritised, usurping all other matters initially represented as important in the girl's life. Progressive elements in these texts do exist, but they appear to be in great conflict with the more conservative impulses of the fairy tale princess narrative. As Alexandra Heatwole notes in her analysis of 'progressive' Disney princess texts that have responded to the shift in the contemporary political climate by creating heroines who are 'coded as "modern women" …in the end their stories are tales of self-sacrifice in the interest of heterosexual love' (2016, 5). Even in Disney texts that resolutely avoid the romance plot, such as *Brave* (Andrews, Chapman and Purcell 2012) and *Frozen* (Buck and Lee 2013), these narratives become subsumed by marketing strategies that are at pains to foreground the heroine's hyperfeminine display above all else, suggesting that 'the Disney princess line is not shying away

© The Author(s) 2017
A. Bellas, *Fairy Tales on the Teen Screen*,
DOI 10.1007/978-3-319-64973-3_5

from patriarchal norms just yet' (8). So while contemporary princess culture incorporates progressive notions of the girl as powerful and empowered, it nevertheless tends to also fall back on the familiar formula of
'romance as rescue' (1).

Some teen texts expand the boundaries of the 'Cinderella' tale a little further. Andy Tennant's terrific film *Ever After: A Cinderella Story*
(1998) and Gail Carson Levine's young adult novel *Ella Enchanted*
(1997), as well as the film of the same name (O'Haver 2004), present
narratives about princesses who do not need to be rescued. The made-
for-TV movie *Cinderella* (Iscove 1997), in a very rare example, features
a black Cinderella in a multiracial update of Rodgers and Hammerstein's
musical of 1957, challenging the overwhelming whiteness of the tale. In
her analysis of *Ever After*, fairy tale scholar Christy Williams notes the
film's 'reversal of the damsel-in-distress plot' and heroine Danielle's
agency within the narrative (2010, 102). However, Williams argues that
the film is unable 'to move the "Cinderella" story beyond the structural
misogyny knit into the tale's plot' (102) because it represents female
empowerment in a narrow way, 'reinforc[ing] patriarchal authority by
emphasising individual achievements and isolating one woman, the heroine, as an exception to standard feminine behaviour' (101). Some feminist revisions of the tale deconstruct or disrupt the tale's happily ever
after plot, as in poems such as Anne Sexton's 'Cinderella' (1971) and
Judith Viorst's '...And Then The Prince Knelt Down and Tried to Put
the Glass Slipper on Cinderella's Foot' ([1982] 1986). Others focus
much more strongly on female relationships and community, for example short stories such as Angela Carter's 'Ashputtle' ([1993] 1996)
and Emma Donoghue's 'The Tale of the Shoe' (1997), which queers
the tale. The focus on female community is also evident in contemporary teen television series *Gossip Girl*, a notable exception to the dominant focus on romance in many teen screen retellings of the tale. While
I do not argue that the series is somehow uncomplicatedly feminist, I do
argue that it enacts important shifts in both the representation of feminine spectacle and the romance plot, and that this frequently subverts
the familiar tale of female passivity spun by Charles Perrault (1697) and
Disney (1950).

In this chapter, I continue to deploy the feminist optic in my reading of teen screen aesthetics, and their capacity to articulate a potentially
feminist politics. As Sarah Projansky writes, the purpose of this optic is
to 'develop optimistic readings that push the possibilities of both the

dominant and the alternatives as far as possible toward girlhoods that ... take up public space, and take action' (2014, 222). I use this method to look for the ways in which the heroines of teen television series *Gossip Girl* occupy alternative, shifting and flexible performances of teen girlhood through their deployment of spectacular dress and masquerade. *Gossip Girl* is inflected by the 'Cinderella' fairy tale, especially its most culturally pervasive versions by Perrault and Disney. By revising the tale's sexist association between feminine spectacle, desirability and fulfilment through male approval, *Gossip Girl* carves out a space for oppositional correctives to be explored. In Perrault's canonical 'Cinderella' tale, the girl is characterised as a passive, immaculately dressed spectacle for the Prince. *Gossip Girl* disrupts this aspect of the narrative, representing a communitas of Cinderellas who engineer their sartorial transformations to more challenging, and potentially empowering, ends. The teen communitas unsettles the feminine stereotypes embedded in Perrault's earlier 'Cinderella' text, such as docility, passivity and reliance on heterosexual male approval for economic security and social validation. Through their subversive use of DIY sartorial practices[1] and masquerade, the heroines collectively challenge some of the rituals and regulations that govern contemporary girlhood. Agency is embedded in these performative rebellions, providing an opportunity for the heroines to enact resistant practices through disruptive displays of public liminality. Spectacle and masquerade are the expressive materials through which the heroines confront these gendered relations, pushing the discursive boundaries of girlhood into unexpected territories.

Feminist scholars have explicated the troubling associations between class, consumerism, feminine spectacle and a need for male approval that postfeminist narratives of fashion transformation may espouse. Rachel Moseley posits that the makeover film often works to 'engag[e] in the policing of difference and the construction and validation of hegemonic femininities, in the correcting of "aberrant" femininity' (2002, 405). This policing through the fashion makeover highlights the disciplinary force of 'regimes of the body' that work to define and delimit 'acceptable' expressions of femininity (Skeggs 1997, 109. See also Bordo 1985; Bartky 1990). This image of spectacularised femininity has also been considered in girl's media studies. Mary Celeste Kearney writes that the prevalence of this gendered dynamic in media representations aimed at girl audiences, 'still shaped by patriarchal capitalist ideologies...consistently privilege feminine appearance, encouraging girls to surveil their bodies, find imperfections, and purchase products to overcome these problems, all with the goal of attracting heterosexual male attention' (2006, 215). Many makeover texts reproduce the 'swan' stereotype of femininity in which the transformative beautification process serves to aid the attainment of heterosexual romance through male approval and increased social acceptance.[2] However, the makeover transformation narrative can offer, as Moseley also suggests, 'a space for *difference* to exist' (407 original emphasis). In *Gossip Girl*, sartorial transformations function as moments of excess and masquerade, designed not to comply with patriarchal standards of feminine comportment, beautification, docility and desirability, but rather to unsettle and aggravate these rules and regulations. The heroines do have romantic love interests throughout the course of the series; however, the sartorial displays are rarely in service of impressing prospective love interests, and these romantic relationships are often fleeting. The heroines' constant shifting between love interests and elision of long-term heterosexual romantic relationships suggests their lack of investment in the culturally dominant one-true-love narrative. *Gossip Girl*'s sartorial makeovers are almost always in service of the attainment of either personal or collective power within the girl group, offering a 'Cinderella' fantasy reconfigured for a contemporary teen television audience.

Scholarship on teen television focuses on the destabilising and subversive potential embedded in the medium (Fiske 1998; Bavidge 2004; Stein 2009). For example, in her excellent book *Beyond the Box*, Sharon Ross writes that teen television, by virtue of its serial storytelling structure, promotes 'radical oscillation' (2008, 130). Ross argues that this means teen series are a process of negotiation between 'multiple points of view or "voices"' (130), 'experimentation with pre-set identities' and experimentation with the boundaries that define the status quo (131). This provides what Ross calls an 'expansive experience' of narrative, identity and perspectives (132). Similarly, Moya Luckett suggests that the serial structure and aesthetics of teen television allow for a subversive '*disruption* of identity' because television 'endlessly defer[s]' the resolution of the girl's acculturation into adult heterosexual femininity (1997, 101 and 105 original emphasis). Teen television's seriality, along with its preoccupation with themes of experimentation, liminal thresholds and metamorphosis, provide the space for representing these disruptions of stable identities. In relation to the girl's rite-of-passage narrative in teen television, the unsettling of definitional boundaries around girlhood opens up a more experimental and fluid notion of feminine adolescence, allowing unexpected ways of doing girlhood to arise on screen.

In *Gossip Girl*, the performance of adolescent femininity through dress is frequently constructed as a transgression of dominant discourses of girlhood, a contestation of the boundaries of gender. As Judith Butler writes, 'gender is always a doing' (1999, 34). She elaborates:

> that the gendered body is performative suggests that is has no ontological status apart from the various acts which constitute its reality. This also suggests that if that reality is fabricated as an interior essence, that very interiority is an effect and function of a decidedly public and social discourse, the public regulation of fantasy through the surface politics of the body. (185)

Butler's work reveals how gender itself is produced through public discourses, and these discourses regulate the performance of the gendered body. This means that gender is the repetition of the codes that these discourses inscribe. However, Butler also argues that performances such as masquerade and parody can be subversive when they expose gender as a fabrication, an 'imitative structure' (187). This aspect of Butler's work is important to the field of girlhood studies because, as Currie et al. write, girls are also doing girlhood: they are performing this gendered identity category, and they have a measure of agency in this performance (2009, xv). Chapter 1 invoked Catherine Driscoll's work, which argues that girlhood is 'made up and brought into existence in statements and knowledge about girls' (2002, 5), and this discourse demarcates the borders of this identity category's intelligibility. Girls themselves are also involved in the creation of this discursive formation; they are not simply subjected to it.

Style and clothing are part of the performativity of gender—what Butler calls 'styles of the flesh' (177). Butler shows that performativity is a repetition of acts, gestures, styles and so on that reinforce the gendered norms being performed, thus working as '*a regulated process of repetition* that both conceals itself and enforces its rules precisely through the production of substantialising effects' (185 original emphasis). However, she also points out that within this cycle of repetition, agency can be:

> located within the possibility of a variation on that repetition...If the rules governing signification not only restrict, but enable the assertion of

> alternative domains of cultural intelligibility, i.e., new possibilities for gen-
> der that contest the rigid codes of hierarchical binarisms, then it is only
> *within* the practices of repetitive signifying that a subversion of identity
> becomes possible. (185 original emphasis)

So from within the dominant system of signification, ruptures can be enacted through identity performances that, in some way, unsettle or alter that norm. This is key to my reading of how *Gossip Girl*'s hero-ines use the everyday materials of fashion and dress in new, outrageous combinations that subvert the system of signification from within, unsett-ling dominant ideologies of girlhood and interjecting alternative ways of doing girlhood.

Gossip Girl's heroines deploy collective, public performances of fluid girlhoods through their use of masquerade, outrageous homemade out-fits and the donning of symbolic accessories such as crowns and tiaras as assertions of agency and power as they invade and occupy traditionally adult masculine-dominated spaces. Victor Turner writes that rituals of status elevation are a form of liminality where 'public reflexivity takes the form of a *performance*. The languages through which a group commu-nicates itself to itself are not, of course, confined to talking codes: they include gestures, music, dancing, graphic representation, painting, sculp-ture, and the fashioning of symbolic objects. They are dramatic, that is literally "*doing*" codes' (1979, 465 original emphases). Furthermore, Turner argues that during this liminal performance,

> the factors or elements of culture may be recombined in numerous, often
> grotesque ways, grotesque because they are arrayed in terms of possible
> or fantasied rather than experienced combinations...In other words, in
> liminality people 'play' with the elements of the familiar and defamiliarise
> them. Novelty emerges from unprecedented combinations of familiar ele-
> ments. (1982, 27)

The 'grotesque' and playful combinations of the elements of culture can manifest through masquerade and the presentation of dominant cultural symbols in new patterns and arrangements, defamiliarising their original connotations. Liminality and communitas, therefore, provide an oppor-tunity not only to reflect on dominant cultural structures and hierarchies; during performances such as carnivals, festivals, and masquerades, these structures and hierarchies are turned on their head or rejected entirely. In

Gossip Girl, the use of masquerade, unauthorised and disruptive fashion shows, and the trashing of the school uniform provide a contemporary representation of rituals of status elevation and public liminality. During these performances, elements of culture are recombined in startling new arrangements that rupture the authority of adult masculine power.

Traces of Perrault's 'Cinderella, or the Little Glass Slipper' are clear in *Gossip Girl*'s representation of heroines transforming into 'royalty' by donning masquerades, fancy dress and elaborate garments. In Perrault's text, Cinderella's ascension to the position of royalty is literal, as she becomes a Princess at the conclusion of the tale. In *Gossip Girl*, masquerade and spectacular dress allow the girl group to assume a position of power as a self-declared community of 'queens' within their social world. Perrault's heroine undergoes only one dramatic sartorial transformation because she has achieved the ultimate goal of the masquerade—to find her 'Prince Charming'. Once this goal has been met, there are no further masquerades or transformations to playfully perform. This is amplified in Disney's *Cinderella* (Clyde Geronimi, Wilfred Jackson, Hamilton Luske 1950), where the glamorous transformation serves to make the girl more desirable by emphasising feminine diminutiveness, fragility and smallness through impossibly dainty glass slippers and a dramatically cinched waist. It is only by performing these markers of femininity, along with an upwardly mobile class identity, that the girl becomes acceptable in the eyes of society. As Ilana Nash explicates, this Disney princess model inflects contemporary girls' princess cultures, where glamour and wealth intersect in a fantasy of 'specialness' and 'girl power' (2015, 8). Furthermore, the princess is always in need of her counterpart, the prince, situating princess culture within the domain of romance. And in Perrault and Disney's versions of the story, romantic union is the ultimate goal for the princess.

Gossip Girl is certainly invested in princess culture, but it plays with its boundaries. The show disrupts the romance aspect of the narrative by humorously subverting the centrality of the Prince in the 'Cinderella' tale, and the one-true-love narrative he offers. In episode twelve of season two, at an elaborate fancy dress party, heroine Blair Waldorf jokingly refers to her disappointing date as 'Prince Un-Charming', suggesting the heroine's rejection of the perfect male suitor of the traditional 'Cinderella' transformation narrative. Furthermore, this rejection subverts the normative closure of the romantic paradigm, carving out a space for the heroines to explore other iterations of girlhood that go beyond the imperative of heterosexual male approval. This allows for an expansion of the limits of Perrault's version of the 'Cinderella' tale, beyond the fixity of heteronormative romantic closure, enacting subversions that open the tale up to more resistant possibilities.

The serial televisual medium implements a fluid narrative in which identities, relationships and hierarchies of power are constantly shifting. Working within a medium that promotes the instability of multiplicity and change, and resists the fixity of closure through a gradually unfolding episodic structure, *Gossip Girl*'s revision of the 'Cinderella' tale mobilises a narrative of feminine masquerade that is far more fluid, processual and experimental—and therefore potentially more subversive and destabilising—than Perrault's short tale. As a television text, *Gossip Girl*'s episodic structure is inherently invested in a fluid, ongoing narrative that resists closure and instead fosters opportunities for change and difference to occur. *Gossip Girl* elides the normative impulse of romantic resolution that concludes Perrault's fairy tale through its serially unfolding 121-episode narrative. Instead, it emphasises the heroines' ongoing transformations and multiple performances. As Jennifer Hayward notes in her work on serialised texts, serialisation constitutes a '*refusal* of closure' (1997, 141 original emphasis). Thus, rather than creating a narrative based around the question of how it might end, or whether the heroine will attain her romantic 'happily ever after', Hayward argues that serialised texts provide 'female protagonists [with] space to develop newly defined identities' (183). *Gossip Girl* presents an enormous array of varying and shifting ensembles over its six seasons, suggesting that the temporal structure of the serial allows for the inclusion of many different and even conflicting identity performances. Hayward argues that the 'fluid construction of temporality' allows series' 'to explore shifting identities in ways not possible in more traditional narrative spaces … And they do this within a narrative structure privileging difference over homogeneity, understanding over rejection, open-endedness over closure' (191). This serial temporality of flow and open-endedness allows for many variations to unfold over time. *Gossip Girl* emphasises the heroines' shifting experiments with feminine identities, allowing for a protracted narrative that carves out space for multiple challenges to be launched against adult patriarchal rules and regulations. The series' ability to incorporate so many subversions enacted over an extended period of time creates a representation of girls' persistent destabilisation and deconstruction of some of the gender ideologies that limit feminine adolescence.

Having established how performativity, public liminality and ritu-als of status elevation are embedded in *Gossip Girl*'s rewriting of the 'Cinderella' tale, the next section of this chapter considers how the hero-ines' deployment of these elements intervenes into Perrault's construc-tion of class, heterosexual romance and femininity as passive spectacle. The following section further explores how the girl group constructs performances of subversive style through the use of DIY practices. Through the feminist theory of writers such as Kathleen Rowe (1995) and Jane Gaines (1990), I theorise how the jarringly outrageous and visually over-the-top ensembles interject into scenes dominated by adult male-defined strictures, from school and uniform regulations to the adult male domination of business and economic markets. The fourth sec-tion continues to explore the thread of style as subversion, turning to the girl communitas' preoccupation with masquerade and the mobility it offers, engaging with feminist film theory of masquerade, particularly that of Mary Ann Doane (1982, 1987) and Gaylyn Studlar (1990). I expand on this theory to include a conceptualisation of the performance of masquerade in the teen television text, and the freedom it provides the heroines to invent a proliferation of ever-shifting alternative iden-tities, destabilising status quo constructions of girlhood identities. The fifth and final section of the chapter considers how this subversive onscreen style creates an invitation to spectatorial engagement with a female adolescent version of *flânerie*, which allows girl spectators to identify with the collective, insubordinate girl's culture that invade the male-dominated city streets and enters the public discourse through DIY media-making.

The 'Cinderella' Tale in Feminist Theory

In Perrault's version of the tale, and Disney's culturally pervasive 1950 animation, Cinderella's winning combination of meek passivity, extraor-dinarily elegant garments and physical beauty secure the affections of the Prince. This leads to her ultimate 'fulfilment' through heterosex-ual romantic love, marriage and induction into the Prince's sphere of economic privilege. Many feminist analyses have provided important critiques of the gendered and classed implications of the heroine's trans-formation into a spectacle to win the Prince's affections in Perrault's 'Cinderella' fairy tale (Rowe [1979] 1986; Huang 1990; Preston 1994; Robbins 1998). *Gossip Girl*'s heroines enact important moments of resistance to this construction of feminine spectacle, particularly in their unruly, disruptive responses to such contemporary rite-of-passage rituals as the debutante ball. These oppositional acts shift the 'Cinderella' tale into an alternative representation of feminine spectacle that goes beyond the sexist limitations of Perrault's patriarchal narrative.

Feminist fairy tale scholars such as Karen Rowe and Alexandra Robbins have interrogated the troubling association between Cinderella's idealised passive femininity and her role as spectacle for the heterosexual male gaze of the Prince. Robbins succinctly points out that 'Cinderella's fawning kindness may encourage her to dream of this rescue, but it is her external transformation that allows her to achieve it' (1998, 107). She goes on to argue that this narrative trajectory therefore 'suggests that a woman's function in society is to wait prettily in a passive and docile manner until she is chosen—based on her appearance— for motherhood' (109). Cinderella is therefore required to become this feminine spectacle in order to succeed, but this 'success' is exposed by feminist analysis as 'a myth that romanticises woman's subordinate and domesticated role within the patriarchy' (Huang 1990, 25). It is only through the beautification process that secures Cinderella as spectacle for the male gaze of the Prince that she can gain the 'validation' of heterosexual love, prestige and wealth.

Perrault's tale obsessively centres its attention on Cinderella's sartorial transformation scene, revealing the importance of the spectacle of her beautification to the outcome of her validation through romantic love. Her pumpkin coach is described as 'gilded all over with gold' (17); her footmen are similarly 'all bedaubed with gold and silver' (18); and she is dressed in 'cloth of gold and silver, all beset with jewels … [and] a pair of glass slippers, the prettiest in the whole world' (18). Susan Ohmer points out that 'the transformation scene in Perrault occupies 20% of text and is the most carefully delineated sequence in the narrative' (1993, 233), making it a highly significant passage in the text. The repetition of words such as gilded, gold, silver, jewels and glass in this section of the tale emphasise the importance of opulence and the display of economic privilege, as well as creating a vision of idealised femininity that is both glamorous and spectacular (gold, silver, jewels), as well as delicate, graceful and fragile (glass). Once this transformation takes place, the Prince 'so intently was…busied in gazing on her' (19), clearly delineating Cinderella as the object of a desiring male gaze. The use of fashionable dress and conformity to beauty ideals works to disguise Cinderella's aberrant qualities of poverty and dirtiness (Preston 1994, 32), making her beautification and glamorisation the linchpin of her induction into economic privilege and heterosexual romance.

Cinderella's spectacular transformation, and her subsequent elevation into the position of royalty through her marriage to the Prince, carries gendered and classed implications for a feminist reading of the text. As Rowe powerfully comments:

> *because* the heroine adopts conventional female virtues, that is patience, sacrifice, and dependency, and *because* she submits to patriarchal needs, she consequently receives both the prince and a guarantee of social and financial security through marriage. Status and fortune never result from the female's self-exertion but from passive assimilation into her husband's sphere. (246 original emphases)

Cinderella's elevation of status and economic privilege relies on her capacity to appear desirable, and on the Prince's desire for her, resulting in the wedding that closes the tale—indeed, the wedding is the pinnacle of her achievement and victory within the text. Perrault writes in the final paragraph, 'she was conducted to the young Prince, dressed as she was; he thought her more charming than ever, and, a few days after, married her' (21). It is the pairing of her docility (she was 'conducted to the young Prince', suggesting that her actions were dictated and enforced by others) with her beauty (the Prince 'thought her more charming than ever' and therefore decided to marry her) that Cinderella's 'fulfilment' through marriage—and hence her induction into a normative feminine position of wife and mother—is made possible. Perrault's tale suggests a perfect recipe for feminine desirability: passive compliance with the patriarchal rule and conformity to impossible standards of beauty.

Gossip Girl's revision of the 'Cinderella' tale provides representations of heroines who protest against the construction of idealised feminine beauty, and its instrumental work in the subordination of women to the position of object. In episode ten of season one, the heroines attend a debutante ball dressed in opulent evening gowns. This contemporary rite-of-passage event is intended to mark a young woman's entry into high society and to announce her availability to prospective male suitors—the ultimate manifestation of a Cinderella-inspired heterosexual romance ideology. In this scene, a male partner escorts each debutante towards the centre of the room as her name is called, and she is presented to the attendees. This ritual symbolises the announcement of her availability to male suitors, as well as her acceptance within the upper-class community. The rich gold, mahogany and silver colour palette, coupled with the ornate flower arrangements and immaculately beaded silk ball gowns highlight the ritual's demarcation of the elite, privileged upper class as its exclusive members. Furthermore, in the staging of the scene, each debutante climbs a grand staircase as her name is called and her status within the community is secured. The act of ascending the staircase in this ritual symbolises a promise of elevated status and economic privilege, but only by conforming to the ideology of heterosexual romance. Heroine Serena rebels against this old-fashioned tradition. She exclaims to her grandmother, who has insisted that she attend, 'things aren't the way they were when you were young' and 'I am not just some accessory' to be 'auctioned off'. Serena mocks the ritual as she begrudgingly takes part, making crude jokes and storming out of the ballroom as her name is called, disrupting the party and shocking the elite members of high society in attendance with her rebellion. As she storms out of the party, she bursts into an uncontrollable fit of laughter, further scandalising attendees. Her laughter and mockery of the event register a moment of refusal—she disrupts the ritual that links feminine spectacle, passivity and compliance. This scene's revision of the 'Cinderella' tale for a contemporary audience creates a rupture in its romantic ideology, and in the space of this fracture the heroines explore more flexible constructions of girlhood that go beyond the status quo.

In *Gossip Girl*, these correctives are presented in the heroines' performative use of spectacular dress that emphasises insubordination, defiance and a bid for power, offering moments in which these contemporary Cinderellas transform into oppositional and agentic girls. While Perrault's 'Cinderella' represented spectacle as a method for attracting a desiring male gaze, *Gossip Girl*'s feminine adolescent communitas instead insists on a collective feminine adolescent language of dress as an expression of their resistance to adult masculine authority. Spectacle is redirected to support their collective subversion of the gendered regulations and rules that Perrault's tale held in place. In her work on representations of unruly women in film comedies, Kathleen Rowe argues that:

> visual power flows in multiple directions and...the position of spectacle isn't necessarily one of weakness. Because public power is predicated largely on visibility, men have long understood the need to secure their

power not only by looking but by being seen, or rather, by fashioning – as subject, as author, as artist – a spectacle of themselves. How might women use spectacle to disrupt that power and lay claim to their own? (1995, 11)

Rowe suggests that women 'fashioning...a spectacle of themselves' could be potentially disruptive because it unsettles the power imbalance that contains women through a male gaze that styles them as passive objects. Authoring, as subjects, their own creative spectacle and thereby challenging dominant power structures embedded in the image and spectatorship, this alternative use of spectacle has feminist implications for not only going beyond sexist image-making and spectatorial structures; it may also propose an alternative dynamic of image-making. *Gossip Girl*'s representation of girls' insubordination and subversion of adult male governance emerges in dress as a spectacle purposefully designed to provoke, aggravate and undermine this patriarchal rule. Dress becomes the expressive material through which this contestation is articulated, and thus becomes a site for the articulation of moments of a feminist politics. The next three sections of this chapter explore the potential of this performance of public liminality and disruptive spectacle in detail through an analysis of *Gossip Girl*'s use of style as a subversive element in the text.

STYLE AS SUBVERSION I: SCHOOL UNIFORMS AND DIY DRESS

Gossip Girl represents girls' do-it-yourself (DIY) practices as subversive.[3] The representation of girls' handmade tailoring undermines the cliché assumption that girls' relation to dress is 'merely' consumerist and therefore passive, uncritical and non-political. While *Gossip Girl* certainly delights in the consumerist fare of high-end designer fashion items, it also contains moments that disrupt and unsettle the discourse of consumerism with its emphasis on the heroines' creativity and spontaneity, providing a more complex representation of feminine adolescent engagement with style. This is an example of a 'progressive' or category 'e' text (Comolli and Narboni [1969] 2004, 817), because these contrary elements such as DIY and unauthorised anti-school uniform protests challenge the dominant discourses of patriarchal commodity culture, mainstream fashion and ideologies of 'acceptable' or 'flattering' feminine styles also embedded in the text. While *Gossip Girl*'s engagement with style may 'seem at first sight to belong firmly within the [dominant] ideology and to be completely under its sway' (817), it transgresses these limits and therefore 'partially dismantl[es] the system from within' (817). These outfits are outrageously excessive, and frequently designed and worn for the purpose of collectively aggravating, challenging and undermining the authority of adult, male-defined rules and regulations. Through the feminist optic that 'see[s] other ways of making sense of and imagining girlhood' (Projansky 2014, 223), I look for instances where feminine adolescent deployments of dress become political elements in this text.

Gossip Girl focuses on its heroines' carefully handcrafted sartorial creations, particularly their fantastic alterations to the school uniform and the performance of intrusive fashion shows in unauthorised venues. DIY practices are an important aspect of feminist inquiry into contemporary girlhood, because they demonstrate a 'practice of self-representation' and therefore contain the potential for girls to represent themselves in ways that resist or challenge dominant constructions of girlhood (Kearney 2006, 56). Kirsten Pike argues for an analysis of this practice 'to describe how girls [have] engaged in a kind of civic action and dialogue by circulating their *own* ideas, stories, and opinions to a broader network… Considering that girls have little to no access to traditional forms of citizenship, DIY practices have been (and continue to be) a crucial means through which girls exercise cultural agency' (2011, 68 original emphasis). In *Gossip Girl*, the heroines' ensembles are often engineered to subvert the authority of adult male-dominated culture. These garments therefore register an active and agentic public protest against the rigid rules dictated by this adult male-dominated culture that attempt to restrict what girls can do and where girls can go. Shauna Pomerantz argues that 'the cultural practice of style' can be viewed 'as a threshold of contestation for girls. Rather than something that is done "to" girls, style, as the word *practice* suggests, is something that girls *do*' (2008, 37 original emphases). The practice of tailoring DIY ensembles of excess in *Gossip Girl*—registered in the profusion of colours, textures, layers and patterns—are the very 'threshold of contestation' that Pomerantz identifies in girls' styles. The series frequently stages scenes that emphasise this DIY aesthetic: in Fig. 5.1 is an example of this, showing Jenny in the process of sewing a garment. Jenny's sewing machine, knitting needles, bright pink fabric, thread and tape measure dominate the foreground of the frame, and the remainder of the frame is filled with rows of her handmade ensembles.

Fig. 5.1 DIY creativity and subversive ensembles made by hand (2.09)

The scene then cuts to a close-up shot on Jenny's hands as she runs the fabric through the sewing machine, further emphasising *Gossip Girl*'s focus on the handmade and creative production. Representing the production, rather than just the wearing of the garment, emphasises a creative girl culture that actively shapes and constructs cultural objects. This active engagement with style challenges the dominant conception of fashion—and by extension the femininity it is associated with—as 'mere' conspicuous consumption, devoid of cultural significance or creativity. Rejecting this stereotype, the heroines become active, creative and innovative in their construction of dress.

The theme of style as subversion is clearly articulated in its representation of its heroines' dramatic alterations to the school uniform. Defying the regulatory discourse embedded in it, and the conservative performance of gender it encourages, the heroines collectively cut up and excessively embellish their school uniforms in ways that challenge its adult-governed authority. In her analysis of the school uniform as a technology of control and discipline, Jennifer Craik asserts that 'there are no natural or essential human body techniques...most of the body techniques associated with uniforms entail the acquisition of "not" statements—that is, what to avoid or repress' (2005, 7). Craik point out that through these 'not' statements—for example, skirts not any shorter than to the knee, no non-school colours to be worn, no short haircuts for girls—'the school uniform has several connotations including discipline and authority ... gender training or performativity' (52). As such, Craik argues that 'creating gendered subjectivity is an intrinsic effect of uniforms' (77). If the girls' school uniform is intended to promote a gendered subjectivity around demureness, tastefulness, modesty and so on, deviations from it represent a challenge to these requirements enforced by adult patriarchal culture.

Gossip Girl's heroines exuberantly and excessively elaborate on their uniforms in creative ways, with additions such as bright stockings, oversized necklaces, sequin-studded headbands, high heels, patterned coats, designer handbags and dramatic makeup. Radical deviations from the uniform include cutting up and resewing the dress into a completely new design, adding highly embellished or oversized accessories to the ensemble, shortening the dress, or indeed discarding the dress altogether and vaguely gesturing to the uniform with the inclusion of a loosely knotted tie in an otherwise bright and funky ensemble. These added layers entirely obscure the uniform itself, overwhelming it with the spectacle of these bright and oversized additions. The verisimilitude of the normative high school television plot, and the strict conservatism of the uniform, is engulfed by the spectacle of creatively designed ensembles. Furthermore, the girl group is never punished for their stylistic deviance despite the fact that they are attending Manhattan's most elite, prestigious and strict school where strict rules of punctuality, etiquette and correct uniform would surely apply. The teen communitas collectively works together to create a significant challenge to the regulatory aims and disciplinary force embedded in the uniform, deploying public displays of disruptive dress collectively, with a political effect.

The heroines' deployment of spectacle and excess in *Gossip Girl*'s school scenes generates a challenge to the dominant construction of the schoolgirl identity. Rowe asserts that the 'topos of the unruly woman... reverberates whenever women disrupt the norms of femininity and the social hierarchy of male over female through excess and outrageousness' (1995, 30). The use of spectacular, over-the-top outfits on screen registers the heroines' agency, and is a visual expression of their resistance to this social hierarchy. Fashion and film theorist Stella Bruzzi reads spectacular dress 'against the grain', arguing that 'rather than function as costumes were conventionally meant to do and blend into the character and background, they intrude on, dominate the scenes they are couched in' (2011, 164–165) and *Gossip Girl*'s costuming falls into this category of the spectacular and extravagant. According to Gaines, when the costume exceeds and becomes inconsistent with the narrative—for example, the impracticality of a dress, the improbability of a character's ability to afford the dozens of *haute couture* gowns worn throughout the film, the camera's lingering focus on details of the gown which slow down and obstruct the flow of narrative progression—spectacle becomes an alternative and disruptive storytelling element, drawing attention away from plot and towards the aesthetics of dress (2012, 142–143). In *Gossip Girl*, this aesthetic of excess manifests in lingering close-ups on elements of an ensemble, or compositions dominated by hypersaturated and bright colour palettes, drawing attention away from the school narrative of rules and regulations and instead hyperattentively focusing on the elements of dress that undermine and challenge those rules and regulations. Thus, *Gossip Girl*'s shot choices and aesthetic design, along with the narrative of schoolgirl defiance, create a fantasy of subverting normative school identities and strictures.

DIY provides the medium through which the adolescent heroines' discontent with and challenge to status quo patriarchal power structures emerges, bubbling up to the surface and erupting in a flurry of excess colour, pattern and texture on screen. Indeed, this unruly use of fashion excess on screen has been called 'the smashing dress' (Bruzzi 1997, 17) with a '"much too much" sensibility' (Gaines 1990, 204). In *Gossip Girl*, dress disrupts gendered hierarchies of power, interjecting into its status quo narrative of masculine dominance, superiority and authority. The heroines frequently add headbands covered in opulent materials such as silk, sequins, crystals, ribbons and velvet to their school ensembles. Referring to themselves as 'queens' when they wear these crown-like accessories, they claim a sense of power through their stylistic subversions at school. In a culture dominated by adult male regulations, the emergence of an authoritative adolescent communitas populated with multiple 'queen' identities, which refuses the gendered regulatory power of the uniform and interjects girls' own DIY creations to overshadow that uniform, is significant for a feminist reading of dress in *Gossip Girl*. Asserting themselves as rulers of their school world, the heroines effectively deny this adult authority, and a contestatory bid for power emerges in the practice of DIY dress.

Power relations between women shift from Perrault's earlier text and the contemporary television text, which builds a representation of the girl group as a communitas. Perrault's 'Cinderella' sets up a relationship of competition and jealousy between several women in the tale: Cinderella, her stepmother and stepsisters. Perrault describes the power-hungry stepmother as 'the haughtiest and proudest woman in the world' (449) and the stepsisters as 'detestable' (450). In Perrault's text, there is only one legitimate way for the female characters to gain power: through marriage. In other words, only by being incorporated into a 'man's world' can these women gain social standing and economic security. Within this narrowly defined patriarchal conception of power, limited to the sphere of male privilege, the women have little choice but to compete and conspire against one another in order to gain a measure of power. In the tale, the stepmother and stepsisters conspire to keep Cinderella in her place by forcing her into the role of servant, cruelly delighting in her plight when she is unable to attend the ball to be presented to prospective suitors. Clearly, there are very limited expressions of female power in Perrault's 'Cinderella'. In *Gossip Girl*'s representation of the debutante ball, described earlier in this chapter, the heroines are similarly expected to transition into a conventional feminine role through a reliance upon male approval and heterosexual romance. They are expected to abandon their all-girl communitas for a relationship with their 'Prince', their 'one-true-love'. This would signal an important accomplishment in their adolescent rite of passage. However, the heroines refuse to abide by this expectation, remaining in the all-girl communitas. This subverts the earlier text's power dynamic that forces women to turn against one another. While the series certainly narrativises themes of jealousy and competitiveness between girls, the hierarchy of power is not stable. It is a constantly shifting communitas, allowing the heroines to contest power within their own girl group. Rather than requiring a male figure to validate and incorporate them into a sphere of power, *Gossip Girl*'s heroines experiment with their own power hierarchy separate from men and boys.

In Perrault's 'Cinderella', the heroine's ascension to the position of royalty is enabled through her assimilation into the Prince's world by becoming his wife; *Gossip Girl*'s version of 'royalty' disrupts this gendered discourse of power. The 'queen' heroines of *Gossip Girl* subvert adult patriarchal culture's gendered hierarchies of power, rather than assimilate into it, as Perrault's Cinderella does. Television and film theorist Louisa Stein dubs the fantasy world of *Gossip Girl* a 'matriarchy' in which 'social power play' and 'gendered power politics' are mobilised in 'culturally loaded play' (2009, 117). The shift in power relations between Perrault's earlier text and the contemporary televisual text is significant—the revision challenges the adult patriarchal power exalted in the earlier text by creating a representation of subversive teen girl 'queen' authority that unsettles existing hierarchies of power. Gaines argues that spectacular representations of costume and style on screen can offer examples of 'stylistic deviance' (1990, 206). She writes that the deviant dress can 'engulf' the film narrative, creating 'a rivalry between the dress and the film culminating in the victory of the dress that is the film' (2011, 147). In *Gossip Girl*, the teens' DIY alterations rival the conservatism of the school uniform, rebelling against the adult world's construction of schoolgirl identities as passive, compliant and virtuous. Interjecting into and challenging the narrative of adult patriarchal power, these self-styled ensembles become sites of contestation, expressing the girls' discontent with this imbalance of power. By designing 'queen' identities through the performative deployment of symbolic objects such as tiaras, unauthorised and unexpected schoolgirl identities emerge. The liminal anti-uniform creations are unruly, experimental, expressive and spontaneous—the antithesis of the regulated feminine identity that school uniforms engineer. The creation of new networks of girls' power and opposition through dress in the school setting reveals the capacity for it to not only create an interjection or protest, but also its capacity to generate expressions that go beyond permitted schoolgirl identities.

Dress is also creatively used to rebel against the strictures of elitist high society and class divides. During a society gathering to celebrate wealthy businessman Bart Bass, Jenny and her friends break into the building and take over the elegant cocktail party with a punk-rock-style fashion show, exhibiting Jenny's own unique designs. This unauthorised fashion show unsettles Bart's authority; the interjection of Jenny's DIY creations takes over the scene, undermining Bart's adult masculine authority with the assertion of the teen heroines' disruptive power. The cocktail party's colour palette of warm beige, the candlelight and its soundtrack of soft classical music and polite chatter underscores the conservatism of the scene, but as shown in Fig. 5.2 this is soon usurped by a flurry of colour, noise and motion as Jenny's fashion designs engulf the scene. Fashion takes over, emphasising creativity and performativity.

The fluorescent pinks, greens and yellows of Jenny's unique costumes overwhelm the beige of the room as the models climb onto banquet tables and perform their runway show. Tie-dyed stockings, leather jackets

Fig. 5.2   Jenny's fluorescent fashion show takes over a conservative adult cocktail party (2.09)

and oversized costume jewellery, along with the blaring punk-rock girl-band soundtrack create a bold interjection into the conservative narrative of the cocktail party and the wealthy patriarch that the party honours. The aesthetic of the punk-rock girl-band music and punk-inspired outfits also recalls the aesthetic of the Riot Grrrl movement, which aimed to disrupt both mainstream consumerism and patriarchal capitalist systems. Evoking this aesthetic registers the spirit of girls' defiance and challenge to patriarchal power structures, revealing *Gossip Girls'* self-conscious awareness about the use of fashion performance, style and music as articulations of rebellion.

Spectacle halts the narrative, as Laura Mulvey argues ([1975] 1989, 19–20), but the disruptive quality of spectacle is deployed in a way different to that she describes. In this fashion show sequence, dress engulfs the conservative narrative flow of wealth and patriarchal prestige, asserting itself in the *mise en scène* in a hyperbolic eruption of colour, sound and movement. Jenny takes this moment to advertise her creations by littering the room with business cards, securing her place in the *Gossip Girl* universe as not only a consumer, but also an active, creative producer asserting her authority in the public discourse and business marketplace. The heroines' collective performance of public liminality enables them to invade and occupy these cultural zones ordinarily denied to girls. Jenny sustains this occupation in the postliminal phase by becoming a successful businessperson who is very publicly involved in creative and economic marketplaces, allowing the series to expand the discourse of girlhood beyond the domestic into even more active and agentic territories.

Through this expression of public liminality, Jenny and her friends undermine the dominant cultural hierarchy that celebrates masculine power, symbolised by their invasion of Bart's party. By asserting themselves as producers and businesspeople, the girl communitas creates the 'field' of many options that Turner argues for, making a variety of girlhood identities possible within the narrative. In this scene, dress runs contrary to narrative verisimilitude, and offers an alternative thread to follow in which the heroine's creativity, agency and defiance of rules and regulations are prioritised. The use of DIY has an aggravating effect by allowing the heroines to break this adult male-defined rule, insisting on carving out a space of power for Jenny and her friends.

STYLE AS SUBVERSION II: MASQUERADE AND MOBILITY

Another method of subversion deployed by the heroines of *Gossip Girl* is masquerade. By designing and donning various performative masquerades, represented in elaborate masquerade party scenes as well as their day-to-day lives, the series' heroines move between shifting self-representations, undermining the 'single certainties' enforced in contemporary constructions of girlhood (Pomerantz 2009, 147). If identity cannot be thought of as a 'single certainty', then multiple and fluid performances of feminine adolescence can be experimented with—and the instability of this variation opens up a space for representing different ways of doing girlhood on screen. *Gossip Girl* revises the role of masquerade in the 'Cinderella' narrative, with the heroines collectively using masquerades to gain entry into arenas traditionally associated with masculine power. Girls occupying these zones constitutes an unruly, defiant move because it undermines the status quo, which works to keep girls subordinate by limiting their access to places and positions of power and authority.

In *Gossip Girl*, masquerade serves a disruptive function as a liminal ritual of status elevation, where these normative hierarchies can be challenged and reconfigured. In Perrault's 'Cinderella' the girl's masquerade conceals her lower-class status, allowing her to gain entry into the royal ball and charm the Prince. In this earlier text, masquerade serves a conservative resolution—Cinderella's fulfilment through marriage—and it is by marrying the Prince that she is validated by heterosexual romance and climbs the socio-economic ladder. The girl's temporarily fluid masquerade and mobility serves to ultimately fix her in woman's 'proper' place. In *Gossip Girl*, masquerade shifts into far more resistant territory.

Feminist film scholarship on masquerade has been particularly important for theorising a performative, even resistant, engagement with feminine spectacle. Central to this scholarship is Doane's article 'Film and the Masquerade: Theorising the Female Spectator' (1982) as well as her later book-length study *The Desire to Desire* (1987). Doane's work challenged Mulvey's analysis of spectacle by arguing that representations of feminine masquerades on screen offer distance between the woman and the image of femininity she performs, thus destabilising the visual economy through which women have been compelled to either masochistically or narcissistically align with this spectacularised feminine image. She writes that masquerade:

> constitutes an acknowledgement that it is femininity itself which is constructed as a mask – as a decorative layer which conceals a non-identity...The masquerade, in flaunting femininity, holds it at a distance. Womanliness is a mask which can be worn or removed. The masquerade's resistance to patriarchal positioning would therefore lie in its denial of the production of femininity as closeness, as presence-to-itself, as, precisely, imagistic. (1982, 81–82)

Doane describes these moments as ones 'where the woman appears to produce a re-enactment of femininity, where her gestures are disengaged from their immediate context, made strange' and 'the excessiveness of her role is clearly visible' (1987, 181). It is this exaggeration and excess that 'underlines the absurdity of the woman's status as spectacle' (181). The parodic, excessive performance of the feminine mask, pushed to the point of hyperbole or absurdity in order to reveal its constructedness, destabilises discourses which frame femininity as natural or essential and therefore fixed or stable. Doane argues that 'it is only through a disengagement of women from the roles and gestures of a naturalised femininity that traditional ways of conceptualising sexual difference can be overthrown' (182). Feminine masquerades can be created in ways that have unexpected and disruptive effect because it 'confounds [the] masculine structure of the look. It effects a defamiliarisation of female iconography...as a type of representation which carries a threat, disarticulating male systems of viewing' (82). Through this defamiliarisation of feminine iconography through parody and excess, masquerade provides a crucial distance between the 'woman and her "own" fully feminised gestures' (182).

Following Doane, Rowe suggests that the distance allowed through masquerade '"makes visible" what is supposed to remain concealed: the artifice of femininity, the gap between the impossible role and the woman playing it', and radically 'does not depend on an internal masculine standard, [and thus] circumvents the issue of fetishism that has dominated discussions of gendered spectatorship and implies a different model of subjectivity' (1995, 6). Theorising masquerade allows for a consideration of the ways in which this performance of femininity can be subversively manipulated or altered. Rowe argues that 'as a form of self-representation, masquerade retains the distance necessary for critique, but a distance that is Brechtian and politicised, created by the subject between herself and various forms of representation available to her' (7). The political potential of masquerade as a particular form of self-representation is therefore important to consider, for it offers the agency of control, countering the male power that Mulvey deemed central to the production and stylisation of the image of femininity. Masquerade is a production of the woman's own design, not a production or projection of the determining male gaze, challenging the gendered relations of both the production of the image as well as spectatorial dynamics of viewing that image. As Rowe argues, 'masquerade concerns itself not only with a woman's ability to look, after all, but also with her ability to affect the terms on which she is seen' (11). Performativity opens gender up 'to splittings, self-parody, self-criticism, and those hyperbolic exhibitions of "the natural" that, in their very exaggeration, reveal its fundamentally phantasmatic status' (Butler 1999, 187). Creating a stylised masquerade of femininity can be seen as a performance that disrupts the sexist dynamics of both image construction and the gaze, for it does not rely on the projection of the determining male gaze that Mulvey identified as central to gender imbalance in the cinema. This performance of masquerade therefore contains the potential for disrupting gendered imbalance, making it significant to a feminist reading of the text.

The stylisation of an adolescent feminine masquerade contains within it a threat, a capacity to unsettle the authority of the adult male gaze. Recalling Pomerantz's theorisation of girls' style as a 'threshold of contestation' through which iterations of girls' agency and resistance may emerge (2008, 37), I deploy a feminist optic to look for the contestations embedded in the heroine's use of fancy dress. I highlight masquerade's agentic qualities of performative self-production, critical distance and changeability, which challenge essentialist notions of femininity as fixed or natural. Because they are fluid, they can also be deployed in unexpected, creative and challenging ways that may undermine the ideologies that underpin this gender essentialism. If, as Butler suggests, performativity is 'an account of agency' because 'there is no gender without [the] reproduction of norms that risks undoing or redoing the norm in unexpected ways, thus opening up the possibility of a remaking of gendered reality along new lines' (2009, i), then masquerade can be potentially subversive—for each performance may alter or challenge the norms that define it.

The creation of the self as ironic and knowing through masquerade and performativity is, as Studlar writes, 'part of a process in which the woman obtains power through her knowledge of how others see her' (1990, 243). This knowingness and deliberate construction and manipulation of self-image to pursue specific gains can be seen as a way in which women have been able to access power within dominant culture. However, Studlar argues that masquerade usually serves the 'culturally inculcated wish to attract male attention through an enhancement of [a woman's] own attractiveness. This process helps fulfil the patriarchy's desire to channel women's desires into a "happily-ever-after" heterosexual union privileging male power' (229). Though there is potential for other disruptive identities to emerge in the masquerade process, it is rarely taken up because it works to serve a heterosexual romance plot, and she maintains that the power gained from this knowingness may be limited to the attainment of heterosexual romance (243). However, *Gossip Girl*'s revision of the 'Cinderella' transformation plot avoids the heterosexual script of the 'swan' makeover that Studlar perceives in the masquerade narrative. Instead, it insists on masquerade as a subversive means to gain new access to power through the mobility afforded by disguise.

The girl communitas' preoccupation with masquerade is evident in every episode, as characters constantly shift between identities with ease through costume changes—for example, in one episode, Blair wears an uncharacteristically high-collared plaid dress with pearls to impress Yale representatives for early college admissions interviews; in another, she

Fig. 5.3 Exaggerated feminine identities are revealed as playful masquerades (1.06)

attends church wearing a black veil, only to later admit 'to be truthful, I'm not even a Catholic'. The ease with which Blair shifts between this wide variety of costume changes and identity makeovers reveals the fluidity that masquerade offers her. Furthermore, these effortless shifts between constructed identities that best work to serve Blair's agenda: for example, in the Yale interview described above, Blair wears her finest Ivy League outfit to make a good impression to get into her dream college. In this revision of the makeover trope, the heroines reject the imperative of attracting male approval through feminine masquerade. Instead, their use of masquerade is deployed to fulfil alternative aims— college admissions, business ventures and the distribution of cooperative, creative, artistic projects in the public discourse and economic marketplace.

In its most explicitly 'Cinderella'—inspired episode entitled 'The Handmaiden's Tale', *Gossip Girl* draws attention to the process and construction of masquerade by literally showing the activity of self-adornment and wearing a mask. Making the mask literal through the representation of a masquerade ball allows *Gossip Girl* to explicitly display and comment on issue of self-identity construction. As illustrated in

Fig. 5.3, in a series of close-up shots each character is shown facing the camera and smiling as they put on their elaborate masks.

The spectacular attire of the *Gossip Girl* heroines as they don their masquerade—the pink Marie Antoinette-style 'pouf' wigs; the bejewelled masks; the coloured feathers; the opulent strands of knotted pearls— provides an exaggerated image of masquerade. This stylised, regal masquerade echoes the theme of the teen 'queen' identity explored earlier in the chapter, reinforcing *Gossip Girl*'s association between style, masquerade and access to power and status. Furthermore, in this scene the heroines face the camera, looking directly at the spectator as they don their elaborate masks. This knowing and direct look suggests not only an awareness of the dynamics of display; it also suggests control and power on the part of the looked-at heroine. This 'looking back' suggests a self-conscious construction of spectacle created by the heroines themselves, significantly challenging the traditional sexist dynamics of image-making that have contained women through a male gaze that styles them as passive objects. Continuously stressing the artificiality of this construction creates a distance between the image and the girl. This gap is resistant space; it defamiliarises the iconography of hegemonic femininity by rendering it strange through excess, troubling claims to its 'naturalness' or essence.

The knowing and self-styled masquerade provides a particularly important revision to the 'Cinderella' tale, for it grants the heroines a measure of agency and control over their performance of adolescent femininity. With the help of her friend Vanessa (coded as the episode's fairy godmother), Jenny (coded as Cinderella) constructs a costume and mask for herself to wear to a ball. Jenny's 'Cinderella' transformation is self-engineered and self-produced: she designs and sews the gown herself, constructing her masquerade to her own liking. Jenny's masquerade is elaborate: in addition to a brightly spangled mask and elaborate feathered headdress, she holds an ornate lace fan across her face so that she cannot be recognised. She is allowed into the ball, mistaken for 'queen bee' Serena. Importantly, however, Jenny's Cinderella-esque 'rags to riches' transformation is not in service of securing the affections of a Prince Charming. Instead, Jenny's masquerade ensures her entry into the elite world of the Upper East Side, where she gains power as a popular and innovative fashion designer. Her masquerade secures her induction into this culture, and gives her the ability to pursue her chosen career path with great ease and success. This representation of collective public liminality shifts the 'Cinderella' tale's makeover plot from a story about one special girl who gains the love of a man to one about a group of girls gaining power in the public realm.

STYLE AS SUBVERSION III: MOBILISING A SPECTATORIAL *FLÂNEUSE*

Gossip Girl's heroines use masquerade as a tool that allows them to not only slip into alternative girl identities, but also move subversively into zones ordinarily denied to them. This is significant at the level of the diegesis, and also significant for the construction of spectatorial positions in (at least) two ways: first, it fosters a spectatorship that is constantly made critically aware of the constructed and malleable nature of girlhood identities. Secondly, *Gossip Girl*'s heroines' use of masquerade to move between identities and places allows them to collective occupy the city streets—an arena predominantly reserved for male youth cultures—as creative, active producers and contemporary *flâneuses*. This representation of a girls' street culture through masquerade and DIY creativity is extended to the spectator, who is encouraged to enact a spectatorial and virtual *flânerie* through cinematographic techniques,[4] such as the point of view tracking shot and snippet shots of shop windows, creating a visual language of girls' street cultures for girl spectators to identify with. Because the heroines' identities are always shifting through stylistic subversions, spectators must shift their attention and identification between these many iterations of girlhood. This suggests a creativity and fluidity that challenges the stability and fixity of the category of girlhood and the identity of 'girl', confronting its limits. It also undermines the assumption that girls' spectatorial and viewing practices are passive, fixed and unthinking. Ross writes that teen television's focus on the fluidity and multiplicity of adolescent identities means that 'viewers can take up *various* positions of identification' (2008, 22–23 original emphasis). This fluidity and creativity expands the terrain of possibilities for girlhood and girls, as the spectator is invited to imagine alternative iterations of adolescent femininity.

Gossip Girl's focus on the fluidity of masquerade allows its heroines to access and exercise power in parts of the city that are ordinarily denied to girls. They undertake creative activity on the streets as photographers, writers and mini-movie makers. While access to street life and public discourse has primarily been considered in relation to male youth cultures (see Clarke et al. 1976; Frith 1978; Brake 1980), it is important to consider how the girl communitas of *Gossip Girl* creates a powerful public discourse where girls can contest the limits placed on feminine adolescence. The representation of a girls' street culture also challenges the cliché assumption that girls' culture does not happen on the streets and is solely the domain of the private, domestic realm of the bedroom. *Gossip Girl*'s representation of the street as a space of girl-directed acts of disobedience and agency, and the invitation to spectatorial *flânerie* that accompanies it, asserts a version of girl culture that invades the public domain. This creates a fantasy world that girl spectators can identify with, where girls increase their visibility as active producers within the public discourse.

The *flâneuse*, the female counterpart to the modern *flâneur* described by Walter Benjamin, was 'born' as a consumer as the first modern period's department stores opened and allowed women to stroll in public (Friedberg 1993, 34). Ann Friedberg writes that the *flâneuse* 'was not possible until a woman could wander the city on her own, a freedom linked to the privilege of shopping alone' (1991, 421). Benjamin described the *flâneur* as a wanderer and existential daydreamer for whom 'every street is precipitous. It leads downward—if not into the mythical Mothers, then into a past that can be all the more spellbinding because it is not his own, not private…In the asphalt over which he passes, his steps awaken a surprising resonance' ([1982] 2002, 416). *Flânerie* was a practice of observation and recording, of both people and the commodity culture they were immersed in. Perhaps most importantly, the *flâneur* exercised an 'ambulatory gaze' as he walked the city (Friedberg 1991, 420). While some theorists have considered 'shopping to be a poor imitation of *flânerie*' (Keller 2011, 306), others have shown that shopping afforded women the important freedom to walk alone in the city, to gaze distractedly through shop windows, and this new-found access to agency and freedom for women—limited though it may have been to consumer culture—has therefore been an important avenue of inquiry for feminist historians and theorists.

In the contemporary context, feminist theorists have identified variations on the *flâneuse* in literary, cinematic and televisual representations of female city wanderers (see Mouton 2001; Richards 2003; Ortega 2008). For example, Helen Richards has described popular television series' *Sex and the City*'s (HBO 1998–2004) heroine Carrie Bradshaw as a postmodern *flâneuse*. She asks: 'is it possible that the practice of *flânerie* has survived the transition from the period of modernity into postmodernity? How far has *flânerie* evolved during its transition, and is it now possible that there can be a female *flâneur*, a *flâneuse*?' (2003, 150). Richards argues that *flânerie* has undergone a twofold evolution in the postmodern television text. First, the link between mobility and the fashionable that has undergone a shift; the spectacular outfit worn by the *flâneuse* makes her stand out in the crowd, enhancing her visibility as an important figure in the city landscape (154). And secondly, the *flâneuse* has shifted into the role of the reporter/detective, by recording and publishing her journey through the city (153). This twofold use of the city space is described by Keller as a claiming of the 'right to be in the public sphere and her femininity at the same time, feminising the "man's world" of the public realm' (2011, 303). These new attributes of the postmodern *flâneuse*—her increased visibility and influence, as well as her creative contributions to the cultural discourse through her status as reporter—significantly increase her potential for independence, power and creative subversion, making her an important subject of inquiry for a feminist reading of contemporary texts featuring female city wanderers, such as *Gossip Girl*.

The analysis of girls enacting *flânerie* or mobility in public space has been central to the work of scholars such as Kathleen Rowe Karlyn, Shauna Pomerantz and Erica Carter (1984), particularly in relation to their work on mall culture. Carter writes:

> through their integration into an expanding teenage market, adolescent girls were drawn in increasing numbers into this new public space. The new generation of young consumers were particularly attracted to self-service and department stores, where they were free to look, compare and admire at their leisure, with no immediate compulsion to buy. (197)

Rowe Karlyn similarly proposes that the mobility of mall culture provides 'a postmodern version of public female space where girls gather for recreation and where shopping becomes a cover for the more important work of tending to friendships' (2011, 85). As they travel through the streets, *Gossip Girl*'s heroines document, record and publish their experiences of the city, reflecting the contemporary trend of the *flâneuse* as reporter/detective described earlier. This challenges previous assumptions that girls' access to the mall and the shopping strip is primarily consumerist (McRobbie and Garber [1976] 2000). In *Gossip Girl*, the teens document, through written word, photography and video, their journeys through the city space. These creatively recorded stories are then uploaded via laptops, computers and mobile phones, and published on the Gossip Girl blog; and this information is shared with members of the teen communitas who read the blog, again emphasising the importance of community-building through new media.

This focus on new media interactivity reflects how contemporary teen television emphasises these media forms both within the diegesis and at the extratextual level, extending an invitation to interact with the series online (Ross 2008, 135). Furthermore, this capacity for the communitas of *flâneuses* to record, publish and disseminate their stories about the city space and its inhabitants is particularly interesting and potentially empowering, because it allows these self-constructed stories to be voiced, acknowledged and heard in the public realm. This interjection through media-making not only challenges assumptions that lead to girls' traditional lack of access to media-making equipment, technology and distribution channels. It also challenges what Kearney describes as:

> girls' traditional feminine socialisation [which] has included learning how not to be men, that is, to take up less space, to be 'seen and not heard.' From a young age, female youth are encouraged to manifest their diminution physically – by being thin, restricting their movement, and by keeping their limbs close to their body – as well as sonically – by being silent and not asserting themselves. (2006, 8–9)

This socialisation geared toward girls taking up less space and restricting movement means that girls are not encouraged to collectively create street cultures, while many boys' street cultures thrive. Additionally, the dictate to be silent, to be seen and not heard, suppresses the production and distribution of girls' media making. *Gossip Girl*'s insistence on a collective girl culture based on the streets through creative *flânerie*, as well as the organised production and distribution of digital media created by girls on the streets, interjects into this discourse, and expands the terrain of girlhood as productive and creative, rupturing previous assumptions that limited this possibility.

The construction of this onscreen girls' street culture and *flânerie* creates an invitation to spectatorial *flânerie* through the deployment of techniques such as tracking point of view shots of the street and the heroines' creative media-making process, interspersed with distracted snippet shots of shop windows. Virtual *flânerie* fosters a specific 'visual practice' which 'emphasis[es] mobility and fluid subjectivity' (Friedberg 1993, 16). The gaze of *flânerie* is characterised by distraction, mobility and fluidity. The diegetic *flâneuse* of the *Gossip Girl* universe enacts this mobilised, oscillating gaze: walking the streets of the city, she can direct her vision towards multiple views. She looks out onto the street itself; she window shops; she photographs, videos and writes about city life, and so turns her vision towards her camera or her phone; she also reads, comments on and interacts with the 'Gossip Girl' blog, which reports on the daily lives of the teenage members of the communitas, as she walks. This distracted, mobile and multiple perspective highlights the fluidity and creativity of this *flâneuse*'s subjectivity, a mode of media spectatorship characterised by what Jonathan Crary refers to as 'attention and distraction' flowing on 'a continuum in which the two ceaselessly flow into one another' (2001, 50), resulting in a 'pixilated gaze' (Everett 2003, 8), or distracted attentiveness able to oscillate between points of interest.

The tracking shot that usually initiates these street scenes is presented from the heroine's perspective, anchoring spectatorial identification in her subjectivity and point of view—we see what she sees—and creating an invitation to virtually engage with the heroine's *flânerie*. This allows for an identification with a version of girlhood that actively participates in public life and interjects into the cultural discourse through the publication of DIY media through uploading images, videos and blogs, undermining the 'adultist and patriarchal construction of cultural activity wherein adult men are media producers and young females are media consumers' (Kearney 2006, 23). This mode of creative *flânerie* was quite literally extended to viewers during the show's run: through the Gossip Girl Second Life (GGSL) game, viewers could virtually walk the streets of the *Gossip Girl* universe, filming and uploading mini episodes through the site (Stein 2009, 122), mirroring the media-making *flânerie* exhibited by the series' heroines. Interspersed with these tracking shots of the street and the media created there are short snippet views of shop windows, edited together in a fast-paced montage. In a shopping scene from episode twenty of season two, there is a rapid succession of close-up shots of ornate items, as illustrated in Figs. 5.4 and 5.5: the intricate embellishment of sequins and bugle beads on a garment; a display case filled with colourful accessories and jewellery; and rows of pastel-coloured cocktail dresses.

Fig. 5.4   Extreme close-up on beadwork in a shop window (2.20)

Fig. 5.5   Tracking shots from the *flâneuse*'s point of view are interspersed with extreme close-up views of the shop window (2.20)

This interspersing of a range of images to regard suggests an invitation to spectatorial oscillations of attention, which mirrors the distracted attentiveness of *Gossip Girl*'s diegetic *flâneuse*, who shifts her attention between a variety of feminine masquerades, the street, the shop window and the media she produces and views on her phone or camera. The spectator is thus invited to imaginatively participate in this fluidity, this range of identifications and positions from which to gaze, reflecting the mobility and oscillating perspective of the onscreen *flâneuse*. Driscoll suggests that teen spectatorial practices could be described as being organised around distracted attentiveness, characterised by multiple points of identification, and that this 'concept of distraction actually suggests a mobility of interest' (2002, 224). Such mobility of interest, couched in a girls' street culture that emphasises media-making as an interjection into the public discourse, invites spectatorial participation in an expanded opportunity for the development of a girls' gaze. This new *flâneuse*, who strolls the street and window shops, now also increases her authoritative presence and visibility through a girls' street culture that emphasises the technical prowess of collective girl-produced and published photography, video and text. The shop window provides the opportunity for this subversive movement through the male-dominated street culture to emerge, carving out a space for girls to enter the public discourse in alternative and disruptive ways.

Conclusions: 'Cinderella' for a Contemporary Television Audience

In this chapter, I have redeployed Projansky's feminist optic to focus on *Gossip Girl*'s teen screen aesthetics of dress and adornment, looking for representations of fluid, alternative feminine adolescent identities in these formal visual elements. My analysis of fashion and girls' deployment of style in this teen television series has searched for the moments where the heroines' collective production and performance of feminine masquerade and outrageous ensembles create a rupture in dominant discourses of girlhood. In moments of communitas and public performances of liminality, the heroines reject their subordinate position within dominant culture and create flexible ways of doing girlhood that do not comply with the status quo. I argue that these highly changeable identities and positions expand the representational terrain of the teen screen, providing an example of image-making that can include an alternative, shifting and transformative language of feminine adolescence.

Gossip Girl is a rare case in teen screen revisions of the 'Cinderella' tale, for it shifts the heroine's central focus away from gaining male approval and focuses on the subversive potential of masquerade and collective displays of feminine adolescent liminality instead. As noted in the introduction to this chapter, a number of contemporary 'Cinderella' texts incorporate 'progressive' elements, such as characterising the girl as smart, capable, feisty and in no need of rescue. These texts, to varying degrees of success, attempt to take the representation of girlhood beyond the passive, beautiful heroine embodied in the canonical Perrault and Disney tellings of the tale. However, the vast majority of them remain squarely focused on the spectacle of the girl's transformation into somebody worthy of heterosexual male desire. Furthermore, while some texts eschew this trope—for example, Kenneth Branagh's 2015 *Cinderella* has the prince fall in love with the girl *before* her rags-to-riches makeover—they nevertheless end up styling the girl into a hyperfeminine, demure spectacle and continue to centre the romance as the key to her fulfilment. While *Gossip Girl* relies on many tropes common to the teen makeover text, such as gaining pleasure and power through conspicuous consumption, it also provides an alternative to this, particularly through its focus on DIY and girl-made media. In addition to this, it also represents sartorial transformation and spectacular masquerade as strategies of subversion, rather than as symbols of conformity. These subversions are often undertaken collectively, through the all-girl communitas, and they create change in their social worlds through these unruly performances of public liminality. As a result, *Gossip Girl* contains many moments that incorporate resistant expressions of girlhood into the tale.

Gossip Girl's revision of Perrault's 'Cinderella' fairy tale contributes to the wider contemporary feminist aim to grant Cinderella more agency, power and independence in the narrative. In Perrault's tale, spectacular dress was deployed as a part of a beautification ritual designed to win the approval and admiration of the Prince, securing Cinderella's 'triumph' through heterosexual romantic resolution in marriage and economic security. Feminist fairy tale scholars such as Rowe, Robbins and Preston revealed the patriarchal agenda embedded in the fairy tale structure that required Cinderella's conformity to beauty standards and the feminine 'virtue' of passivity and acquiescence to male authority. Exploring the shift between the earlier literary text and the very contemporary screen text, I have particularly emphasised how the girl communitas rejects the centrality of heterosexual romance to the 'Cinderella' story. Using a feminist optic to search for these alternative feminine adolescent identities within this sartorial aesthetic highlights the moments in which girl heroines rupture the restrictions of the romantic 'happily ever after' and place a representation of a creative all-girl communitas in its stead. *Gossip Girl* insists on the potential for the girl group to deploy dress as a resistant language that challenges the adult male-defined rules and regulations that work to contain and restrict girls' access to agency, power and authority.

The series' mobilisation of dress is important for a feminist reading of the text, for it is through a reading of these styles, what Pomerantz calls the 'threshold of contestation' (2008, 37), that the heroines' most powerful acts of defiance against adult male authority take place. The representation of the heroines as dynamic DIY producers—creators of ensembles, inventive masquerades, businesses and online publications—counters 'the notion of production as a masculine and male activity' and the 'lengthy historical association of femininity and females with the practices of consumption and consumerism' (Kearney 1998, 291). By representing girls as active cultural producers, *Gossip Girl* also creates an image of feminine adolescent heroines who publicly reflect on and respond to dominant culture through their ensembles and publications. These DIY constructions are unauthorised, challenging male power through excess and spectacle, and in so doing, they construct oppositional girl identities that expand the terrain of girlhood into resistant articulations. Furthermore, the fluidity of the television medium allows the series to explore a great variety of contestations and performances over time, creating a persistent aggravation to the adult male systems that work to keep girls subordinate.

To theorise how *Gossip Girl*'s heroines deploy dress as a strategy of opposition and excess, I have engaged closely with the work of feminist writers such as Butler, Doane and Rowe. These writers have provided a theoretical foundation for considering how performativity and masquerade are particularly powerful avenues for feminist analysis of both the cinematic image and spectatorship, because it offers a paradigm in which the iconography of femininity is made strange, thus providing the distance necessary for a critically reflexive consideration of the range of feminine masquerades available for performance. I have argued that in *Gossip Girl* masquerade is deployed as a shifting self-representation that allows the heroines to invade and occupy zones traditionally associated with masculine power, which is an inherently oppositional move since the exclusion of girls from these domains is complicit in the maintenance of girls' subordination in dominant culture. This is particularly evident in Jenny's use of masquerade to gain entry into the creative and economic marketplace as an independent fashion designer. Entering the public discourse as a producer and business owner, Jenny successfully deploys masquerade towards unexpected ends. Rather than donning the mask as a charming accoutrement for a male gaze as her predecessor Cinderella did, Jenny uses it to occupy the alternative girl identity of businessperson, and this carves out a new representational space for girls to be depicted as active cultural producers and participants in the public, economic, realm. The disruptive power of the masquerade is particularly potent in the television medium, for its temporal structure of 121 episodes unfolding over six seasons allows for multiple, conflicting and challenging masquerades to be donned and discarded. This challenges gender essentialist notions of girlhood, providing a point of rupture in which a variety of performative possibilities are offered for many alternative girlhood identities to emerge. Performativity, which recognises the constructedness of femininity, becomes resistant space. Fashioning their own multiple performances of adolescent femininities, *Gossip Girl*'s heroines express significant challenges to the authority of the adult male gaze throughout the series.

The mobilisation of these DIY ensembles and masquerades allow the heroines' access to the streets of the city, where they create a girls' street culture. Whereas Cinderella's liminal public performance of masquerade was short lived, and circumvented with her swift induction into the domestic realm as the Prince's new bride, the heroines of *Gossip Girl* maintain their access to the public realm by creating a street culture founded by an all-girl communitas. Window-shopping provides the pretext for this street culture, allowing for a postmodern version of *flânerie* to occur. As the heroines window shop and stroll down the street, they create photographs, videos and text about their experiences. Uploading this media to the internet, the heroines publish and share their experiences, entering the public discourse and street culture usually coded as male or masculine-dominated. The shot structure that represents this *flâneuse*'s experience encodes a spectatorial identification with the heroine's oscillating attention, variety of objects to be gazed at and stories to be told or created through the camera lens or the mobile phone. Identifying with a girlhood that participates productively in the public sphere, and that is also able to shift fluidly between identities, perspectives and performances, expands the terrain of girlhood beyond the clichés of unproductive consumerism, powerlessness and an inability to critically reflect on the construction of girl identities. Indeed, spectatorial engagement with this contemporary mode of postmodern *flânerie*, creative DIY and subversive masquerade provides an opportunity to identify with representations of oppositional and challenging girlhoods. This expansion of girlhood through subversive style allows *Gossip Girl* to deconstruct and redefine the 'Cinderella' tale for a contemporary television audience.

In each chapter, I have been exploring representations of feminine adolescent liminality on the teen screen, and how these liminal intervals provide moments of rupture where the heroines enact opposition and resistance to the patriarchal status quo. I have analysed the extent to which the oppositions enacted during these moments continue to affect the heroines' worlds in the postliminal phase, and the extent to which these ruptures create lasting, meaningful change in the narrative. While heroines such as Valerie and Bella in *Red Riding Hood* and *Twilight* enact refusals and escape from dominant culture (at least temporarily), the sleuths of *Pretty Little Liars* interrogate and confront, rather than flee from, masculine aggression and violence, and hold its perpetrators accountable for their criminal acts against girls and women. The girl group of *Gossip Girl* takes it a step further, experimenting with fluid feminine adolescent identities and hierarchies of power that unsettle the power structures that uphold adult masculine authority, creating a sustained access to an alternative girl culture. In Chap. 6, I continue to explore this theme of fluid feminine adolescent identities through a close analysis of *Aquamarine* (Allen 2006), pushing the argument further by finding moments in the text where the heroines imagine and pursue positive, empowered feminist futures.

Endnotes

1. This chapter uses the words 'sartorial,' 'dress' and 'style' to define the costumes and the heroine's use of garments and accessories within *Gossip Girl*'s *mise en scène*. The word 'fashion' is used specifically in relation to the fashion industry and fashion shows. As Valerie Steele writes, 'fashion is a particular kind of clothing that is "in style"' (1997, 3).

2. For further explorations of the 'swan' makeover paradigm on television, particularly makeovers on reality TV, see Heller (2007); Weber (2009); Palmer (2008).

3. Girls' DIY practices have been extensively researched in relation to the Riot Grrrl movement of the early 1990s, which was typified by an anti-capitalist, antimainstream media ethos (see Kearney 2006; Piepmier 2009). Examples of Riot Grrrl DIY creations include feminist-inflected punk rock music, zines and videos.

4. Scholars have noted that contemporary televisual viewing practices themselves constitute a kind of *flânerie*. For instance, Ann Friedberg writes that cinema and television offer the viewer 'a mobilised gaze that conducts a *flânerie* through an imaginary other place and time' (1991, 420). Relatedly, Susan Buck-Morss elaborates that 'in our time, television provides [*flânerie*] in an optical, non-ambulatory form. In the United States particularly the format of television news-programmes approaches the distracted, impressionistic, physiognomic viewing of the *flâneur*, as the sights purveyed take one around the world' (2006, 38).

BIBLIOGRAPHY

Bartky, Sandra Lee. 1990. *Femininity and Domination: Studies in the Phenomenology of Oppression*. New York and London: Routledge.

Bavidge, Jenny. 2004. Chosen Ones: Reading the Contemporary Teen Heroine. In *Teen TV: Genre, Consumption, Identity*, ed. Glyn Davis, and Kay Dickinson, 41–53. London: BFI Publishing.

Benjamin, Walter. [1982] 2002. *The Arcades Project*, trans. Howard Eiland and Kevin McLaughlin. Cambridge, MA: Harvard University Press.

Bordo, Susan. 1985. Anorexia Nervosa: Psychopathology as the Crystallisation of Culture. *The Philosophical Forum* 17 (2): 73–104.

Brake, Mike. 1980. *The Sociology of Youth Culture and Youth Subcultures: Sex and Drugs and Rock 'n Roll*. London: Routledge & Kegan Paul.

Bruzzi, Stella. 1997. *Undressing Cinema: Clothing and Identity in the Movies*. London and New York: Routledge.

———. 2011. "It Will Be a Magnificent Obsession": Femininity, Desire, and the New Look in 1950s Hollywood Melodrama.' In *Fashion in Film*, ed. Adrienne Munich, 160–180. Bloomington: Indiana University Press.

Buck-Morss, Susan. 2006. The *Flaneur*, the Sandwichman and the Whore: The Politics of Loitering. In *Walter Benjamin and the Arcades Project*, ed. Beatrice Hanssen, 33–69. London and New York: Continuum.

Butler, Judith. 1999. *Gender Trouble: Feminism and the Subversion of Identity*. New York: Routledge.

———. 2009. Performativity, Precarity and Sexual Politics. *AIBR* 4 (3): 1–13.

Carter, Angela. [1993] 1996. Ashputtle. In *Burning Your Boats: Collected Short Stories*, 390–396. London: Vintage.

Carter, Erica. 1984. Alice in Consumer Wonderland. In *Gender and Generation*, ed. Angela McRobbie and Mica Nava, 185–214. London: Macmillan.

Clarke, John, Stuart Hall, Tony Jefferson, and Brian Roberts (eds.). 1976. *Resistance Through Rituals*. London: Hutchison.

Comolli, Jean-Louis and Jean Narboni. [1969] 2004. Cinema/Ideology/ Criticism. In *Film Theory and Criticism: Introductory Readings*, ed. Leo Braudy and Marshall Cohen, 812–819. New York: Oxford University Press.

Craik, Jennifer. 2005. *Uniforms Exposed: From Conformity to Transgression*. Oxford and New York: Berg.

Crary, Jonathan. 2001. *Suspensions of Perception: Attention, Spectacle, and Modern Culture*. Cambridge, MA: MIT Press.

Currie, Dawn H., Deirdre M. Kelly, and Shauna Pomerantz. 2009. *'Girl Power': Girls Reinventing Girlhood*. New York: Peter Lang.

Doane, Mary Ann. 1982. Film and the Masquerade: Theorising the Female Spectator. *Screen* 23 (3–4): 74–87.

———. 1987. *The Desire to Desire: The Woman's Film of the 1940s*. Bloomington and Indianapolis: Indiana University Press.

Donoghue, Emma. 1997. The Tale of the Shoe. *Kissing the Witch: Old Tales in New Skins*, 1–10. New York: Harper Collins.

Driscoll, Catherine. 2002. *Girls: Feminine Adolescence in Popular Culture and Cultural Theory*. New York: Columbia University Press.

Everett, Anna. 2003. Digitextuality and Click Theory: Theses on Convergence Media in the Digital Age. In *New Media: Theories and Practices of Digitextuality*, ed. Anna Everett and John T. Caldwell, 3–28. New York and London: Routledge.

Fiske, John. 1998. MTV: Post-Structural, Post-Modern. In *The Postmodern Presence: Readings on Postmodernism in American Culture and Society*, ed. Arthur Asa Berger, 166–174. Walnut Creek, CA, London, New Delhi: Altamira Press.

Friedberg, Anne. 1991. Les Flaneurs du Ma(l): Cinema and the Postmodern Condition. *Publications of the Modern Language Association of America* 106 (3): 419–431.

———. 1993. *Window Shopping: Cinema and the Postmodern*. Berkeley: University of California Press.

Frith, Simon. 1978. *The Sociology of Rock*. London: Constable.

Gaines, Jane M. 1990. Costume and Narrative: How Dress Tells the Woman's Story. In *Fabrications: Costume and the Female Body*, ed. Jane Gaines and Charlotte Herzog, 180–211. New York and London: Routledge.

———. 2011. Wanting to Wear Seeing: Gilbert Adrian at MGM. In *Fashion in Film*, ed. Adrienne Munich, 135–159. Bloomington: Indiana University Press.

Hayward, Jennifer. 1997. *Consuming Pleasures: Active Audiences and Serial Fictions from Dickens to Soap Opera*. Lexington: University Press of Kentucky.

Heatwole, Alexandra. 2016. Disney Girlhood: Princess Generations and *Once Upon a Time*. *Studies in Humanities* 43 (1): 1–19.

Heller, Dana (ed.). 2007. *Makeover Television: Realities Remodelled*. London and New York: I.B. Tauris.

Huang, Mei. 1990. *Transforming the Cinderella Dream: From Frances Burney to Charlotte Brontë*. New Brunswick, NJ and London: Rutgers University Press.

Kearney, Mary Celeste. 1998. Producing Girls: Rethinking the Study of Female Youth Culture. In *Delinquents and Debutantes: Twentieth-Century American Girls' Cultures*, ed. Sherrie A. Inness, 285–310. New York and London: New York University Press.

———. 2006. *Girls Make Media*. New York and London: Routledge.

Keller, Susan. 2011. Compact Resistance: Public Powdering and *Flânerie* in the Modern City. *Women's Studies* 40: 299–335. doi:10.1080/00497878.2011.5 55670.

Levine, Gail Carson. 1997. *Ella Enchanted*. New York: HarperCollins.

Luckett, Moya. 1997. Girl Watchers: Patty Duke and Teen TV. In *The Revolution Wasn't Televised: Sixties Television and Social Conflict*, ed. Lynn Spigel and Michael Curtin, 95–116. New York and London: Routledge.

McRobbie, Angela and Jenny Garber. [1976] 2000. Girls and Subcultures. In *Feminism and Youth Culture*, 2nd ed., ed. Angela McRobbie, 12–25. London: Macmillan Press.

Moseley, Rachel. 2002. Glamorous Witchcraft: Gender and Magic in Teen Film and Television. *Screen* 43 (4): 403–422.

Mulvey, Laura. [1975] 1989. Visual Pleasure and Narrative Cinema. In *Visual and Other Pleasures*, 14–26. Bloomington and Indianapolis: Indiana University Press.

Nash, Ilana. 2015. The Princess and the Teen Witch: Fantasies of the Essential Self. In *Princess Cultures: Mediating Girls' Imaginations and Identities*, ed. Miriam Forman-Brunell and Rebecca C. Haines, 3–23. New York: Peter Lang.

Ohmer, Susan. 1993. "That Rags to Riches Stuff": Disney's *Cinderella* and the Cultural Space of Animation. *Film History* 5: 231–249. http://www.jstor.org/stable/27670722.

Palmer, Gareth (ed.). 2008. *Exposing Lifestyle Television: The Big Reveal*. Aldershot and Burlington: Ashgate.

Perrault, Charles. [1697] 1982. Cinderella, or the Little Glass Slipper. In *Cinderella: A Folklore Casebook*, ed. Alan Dundes and trans. Andrew Lang, 14–21. New York and London: Garland.

Piepmeier, Alison. 2009. *Girl Zines: Making Media, Doing Feminism*. New York and London: New York University Press.

Pike, Kirsten. 2011. "The New Activists": Girls and Discourses of Citizenship, Liberation, and Femininity in *Seventeen*, 1968–1977. In *Mediated Girlhoods: New Explorations of Girls' Media Culture*, ed. Mary Celeste Kearney, 55–73. New York: Peter Lang.

Pomerantz, Shauna. 2008. *Girls, Style, and School Identities: Dressing the Part*. New York and Basingstoke: Palgrave Macmillan.

———. 2009. Between a Rock and a Hard Place: Un/Defining the "Girl". *Jeunesse: Young People, Texts, Cultures* 1 (2): 147–158.

Preston, Cathy Lynn. 1994. "Cinderella" as a Dirty Joke: Gender, Multivocality, and the Polysemic Text. *Western Folklore* 53 (1): 27–49. http://www.jstor.org/stable/1499651.

Projansky, Sarah. 2014. *Spectacular Girls: Media Fascination and Celebrity Culture*. New York and London: New York University Press.

Richards, Helen. 2003. *Sex and the City:* A Visible *Flâneuse* for the Postmodern Era? *Continuum: Journal of Media & Cultural Studies* 17 (2): 147–157. doi:10.1080/1030431031000112749.

Robbins, Alexandra. 1998. The Fairy-Tale Façade: *Cinderella's* Anti-grotesque Dream. *Journal of Popular Culture* 32 (3): 101–115.

Ross, Sharon Marie. 2008. *Beyond the Box: Television and the Internet*. Malden, MA, Oxford and Victoria: Blackwell.

Rowe, Kathleen. 1995. *The Unruly Woman: Gender and the Genres of Laughter*. Austin: University of Texas Press.

Rowe Karlyn, Kathleen. 2011. *Unruly Girls, Unrepentant Mothers: Redefining Feminism on Screen*. Austin: University of Texas Press.

Rowe, Karen E. [1979] 1986. Feminism and Fairy Tales. In *Don't Bet on the Prince: Contemporary Feminist Fairy Tales in North America and England*, ed. Jack Zipes, 209–226. Aldershot and New York: Gower.

Skeggs, Beverley. 1997. *Formations of Class and Gender: Becoming Respectable*. London, Thousand Oaks, CA, New Delhi: SAGE.

Sexton, Ann. 1971. Cinderella. In *Transformations*, 53–58. Boston and New York: Mariner.

Steele, Valerie. 1997. *Fifty Years of Fashion: From New Look to Now*. New Haven, CT: Yale University Press.

Stein, Louisa. 2009. Playing Dress-Up: Digital Fashion and Gamic Extensions of Televisual Experience in *Gossip Girl's Second Life*. *Cinema Journal* 48 (3): 116–122.

Studlar, Gaylyn. 1990. Masochism, Masquerade, and the Erotic Metamorphoses of Marlene Dietrich. In *Fabrications: Costume and the Female Body*, ed. Jane Gaines and Charlotte Herzog, 229–249. New York and London: Routledge.

Turner, Victor. 1979. Frame, Flow and Reflection: Ritual and Drama as Public Liminality. *Japanese Journal of Religious Studies* 6 (4): 465–499. http://www.jstor.org/stable/30233219.

———. 1982. *From Ritual to Theatre: The Human Seriousness of Play*. New York: Performing Arts Journal Publications.

Viorst, Judith. [1982] 1986. … And Then The Prince Knelt Down and Tried to Put the Glass Slipper on Cinderella's Foot. In *Don't Bet on the Prince: Contemporary Feminist Fairy Tales in North America and England*, ed. Jack Zipes, 73. Aldershot and New York: Gower.

Weber, Brenda R. 2009. *Makeover TV: Selfhood, Citizenship, and Celebrity*. Durham, NC: Duke University Press.

Williams, Christy. 2010. The Shoe Still Fits: *Ever After* and the Pursuit of a Feminist Cinderella. In *Fairy Tale Films: Visions of Ambiguity*, ed. Pauline Greenhill and Sidney Eve Matrix, 99–115. Logan, UT: Utah State University Press.

Filmography

Aquamarine. Dir. Elizabeth Allen. 2006.

Brave. Dirs. Mark Andrews, Brenda Chapman, Steve Purcell. 2012.

Cinderella. Dirs. Clyde Geronimi, Wilfred Jackson, Hamilton Luske. 1950.

Cinderella. Dir. Robert Iscove. 1997.

Cinderella. Dir. Kenneth Branagh. 2015.

A Cinderella Story. Dir. Mark Rosman. 2004.

Ella Enchanted. Dir. Tommy O'Haver. 2004.

Ever After: A Cinderella Story. Dir. Andy Tennant. 1998.

Frozen. Dir. Chris Buck and Jennifer Lee. 2013.

Gossip Girl. The CW. 2007–2012.

The Prince and Me. Dir. Martha Coolidge. 2004.

The Princess Diaries. Dir. Garry Marshall. 2001.

Sex and the City. HBO. 1998–2004.

She's All That. Dir. Robert Iscove. 1999.

CHAPTER 6

The Mermaid's Tale: Ultraliminality and Feminist Futures in *Aquamarine* (Allen 2006)

INTRODUCTION: ULTRALIMINALITY AND FEMINIST FUTURES

The mermaid remains a popular mainstay in contemporary girls' visual culture, continuing to be particularly influenced by the legacy of Disney's enormously popular film *The Little Mermaid* (Musker and Clements 1989). Television series such as *H2O Just Add Water* (ABC 2006–2010), its spinoffs *Mako: Island of Secrets* (ZDF Enterprises 2013–) and Netflix original *H2O: Mermaid Adventures* (2015–); films such as Elizabeth Allen's *Aquamarine* (2006) based on the young adult novel of the same name by Alice Hoffman (2001), *A Mermaid's Tale* (Rikert 2016) and the upcoming live action film *The Little Mermaid* (Bouchard and Harris 2017); and the TV movie *Mermaids* (Barry 2003) attest to this enduring interest in the narrative of the girl's rite of passage as imagined in this tale. Hans Christian Andersen's story of 'The Little Mermaid' ([1837] 2008), in its characterisation of a girl who undergoes a painful journey to win a man's affection, is often seen as a metaphor for the process of female maturation. In her work on Disney's depiction of the tale, Susan White asserts that in contemporary screen culture 'the mermaid has become a pervasive cinematic symbol of the girl's difficult rite of passage to womanhood' (1993, 186). In many of the texts listed above, the mermaid is confronted with the process of transforming into the role of 'girl' when she arrives on land, negotiating what it means to take up this position.

© The Author(s) 2017
A. Bellas, *Fairy Tales on the Teen Screen*,
DOI 10.1007/978-3-319-64973-3_6

A number of feminist revisions of the tale interrogate the conditions by which the feminine adolescent rite of passage is conceived of as a necessarily painful process of acquiescing to the agendas of patriarchal culture, as in short stories such as Emma Donoghue's 'The Tale of the Voice' (1997) and Melissa Lee Shaw's 'The Sea Hag' (1999), as well as novels such as Samantha Hunt's *The Seas* (2004), and poems such as '...And Although the Little Mermaid Sacrificed Everything to Win the Love of the Prince, the Prince (Alas) Decided to Wed Another' by Judith Viorst (1984) and Joanna Russ 'Russalka, or the Seacoast of Bohemia' ([1978] 1986). The surreal Polish horror-musical film *The Lure* (Smoczynska 2015) represents the figure of the mermaid beyond the confines of the romance plot, instead imagining its mermaids as murderous sirens. While one of the mermaids, Silver, sacrifices her tail, voice and ultimately her life for the man she loves, as in Andersen's familiar version, the film provides an alternative vision of the feminine rite of passage through the character of Gold, who refuses to comply with the strictures of the human world and fiercely protects her independence. As in the feminist revisions of other tales explored throughout this book, these writers and filmmakers often attempt to imagine the fairy tale heroine as a more agentic and active character within the coming-of-age narrative.

The mermaid is also reimagined in girls' media culture. Disney's Ariel is a feistier, more agentic heroine than such classic heroines as Cinderella and Aurora. Indeed, as Marina Warner notes in her analysis of Disney's *The Little Mermaid*, 'the issue of female desire dominates the film, and may account for its tremendous popularity among little girls – the verb "want" falls from the lips of Ariel, the Little Mermaid, more often than any other – until her tongue is cut out' (1995, 403). Nevertheless, the film 'suggests that the ultimate adventure is traditional romance' and ensures that the girl's rite of passage centres on attaining the love of a man (Nash 2015, 12). Thus any progressive qualities that this updated Disney heroine embodies remain in service of the same conservative ends found in earlier fairy tale princess films. Meanwhile, more recent texts such as *H2O Just Add Water* and *Aquamarine* focus much more strongly on the friendship of a group of adolescent mermaids who support one another in their journeys of transformation. What sets *Aquamarine* apart is its representation of heroines who band together to actively critique and reject some of the limited rituals of girlhood inscribed in the earlier text, performing a demure, acquiescent emphasised femininity in order to be deemed desirable. I am interested in what shifts this displacement of the romance enables in the representation of girlhood rites of passage on the teen screen.

In this chapter, I return full circle to the teen screen fantasy of permanent liminality or 'ultraliminality' that I explored in the second chapter. Like *Red Riding Hood*, *Aquamarine* provides a representation of heroines who 'opt out' (Turner 1969, 112) of dominant culture and escape into an otherworldly space to pursue alternative girl identities. In *Red Riding Hood*, this otherworld is represented as a forest, while in *Aquamarine* it is represented as an ocean. There are two major differences that distinguish the representation of ultraliminality in these two texts. The first difference is that in *Aquamarine* communitas is central to the heroines' expression of noncompliance: they collectively act against adult masculine authority and support one another's explorations of alternative ways of doing girlhood. The second difference is that ultraliminality is represented as a zone to explore malleable feminine adolescent identities; the heroines' exploration of flexible, alternative girlhoods is aligned with the highly symbolic imagery of the ocean that the mermaids swim through, and the iridescent flowing streams of sparkles and bubbles that represent the activation of the heroines' magical underwater powers. In this representation of communitas and fluidity, *Aquamarine* provides a field of possibilities where the heroines collectively imagine and pursue feminist futures.

Aquamarine is a clear revision of Andersen's tale: in both texts, the mermaid longs for a life on land. Her father grants her leave to do so, giving her a three-day deadline to find true love with a man. She will only be granted permanent access to land if she fulfils this demand. In Andersen's tale, the mermaid cannot win the Prince's affection, so she turns into sea foam at the end of the three-day deadline. In *Aquamarine*, the mermaid finally refuses her father's demand and finds true love within her all-girl communitas instead. By opposing her father, and the centrality of heterosexual romance to her fulfilment, this contemporary mermaid finds an alternative way of doing girlhood. In my analysis of *Aquamarine*'s representation of ultraliminality and its potential for becoming a space of unruliness, I explore how the film's revision of Andersen's tale interjects resistant feminine adolescent voices and identities into the fairy tale's narrative. My feminist reading of Andersen's tale critiques its representation of a glamorous, yet passive youthful femininity, and its reliance upon heterosexual romance as the key to the heroine's fulfilment. The communitas of girl mermaids collectively resists and challenges this construction of femininity, and then escapes to the ultraliminal terrain of the ocean where they foster networks of solidarity.

While *Red Riding Hood*'s heroine, Valerie, enacted her escape from dominant culture on her own, the mermaid heroines of *Aquamarine* form a supportive communitas in their departure from the status quo. Because communitas is a multitude of voices talking back to dominant culture and can therefore become a collective movement that instigates change, it is all the more powerful. In communitas, Victor Turner writes that ritual subjects enter into an experience of 'anti-structure', encountering 'symbols...[which] not only reflect it but contribute to creating it' (1974, 270). Furthermore, this free play in the field of anti-structure allows the communitas to 'innovate new patterns...or to assent into innovation' (14–15). Communitas is therefore a collective act of innovation where alternatives to the status quo are imagined, explored and acted upon. Turner writes that theorising liminality allows us to perceive:

> liminal...situations as the settings in which new models, symbols, paradigms, etc., arise – as the seedbeds of cultural creativity in fact. These new symbols and constructions then feed back into the 'central' economic and politico-legal domains and arenas, supplying them with goals, aspirations, incentives, structural models. (1982, 28)

In the fantasy of ultraliminality, this creativity is even more powerful because it provides a space for ongoing interventions into dominant culture and for continuous innovations to be enacted. *Aquamarine's* narrativisation of ultraliminality in the girls' rite of passage allows for the representation of girls who pursue multiple, subversive feminine identities and enact multiple, ongoing oppositions to dominant patriarchal power. This makes ultraliminality particularly corrosive and politically potent, and a particularly important arena for imagining and representing social change on the teen screen.

The contemporary teen mermaid narrative provides an opportunity to critique the 'difficult rite-of-passage' that White identifies as central to the tale, because the mermaid must literally transform from mythical hybrid sea creature to glamorous girl, an identity that is completely unfamiliar to her. The mermaids of *Aquamarine* exaggeratedly perform and speak back to the vernacular of contemporary society, interrogating the use of sexist language in a world organised according to adult masculine agendas and desires. They undermine this language structure through their deployment of explosive laughter at and mockery of its conventions, creating fissures in conventional gendered speech to locate collective, alternative voices of their own. They also perform excessive public displays of emphasised femininity that parody the image of glamorous desirability. Finally resisting this paradigm of desirability, the mermaids construct unruly images of prettiness in the film's ultraliminal 'glitter aesthetic', manifesting onscreen as bubbles and iridescent magic sparkles, which represent the active and agentic use of their magical underwater powers. This unsettling of patriarchal constructions of both language and glamour in 'The Little Mermaid' tale opens up the terrain of girlhood to new representational fields of possibility.

The defamiliarisation of the codes of emphasised femininity provides both *Aquamarine*'s comedy and critique, because it exposes and parodies power structures that keep girls subordinate. Furthermore, the defamiliarisation of these codes provokes unruly laughter at them, both within the diegesis and for the spectator, creating critical distance between the girl and the performance. This critical distance fractures the authority of these normative codes, and provides space for the emergence of challenging alternatives. Critical reflexivity about these limits, and the potential for the transgression of those limits, forms a central theme of *Aquamarine*. As in the other teen fairy tales analysed throughout this book, the violation of prohibition is positively valued in this contemporary text. It is through this disruption that the heroines are able to metamorphose and pursue a fairy tale ending where they can go beyond the boundaries of the everyday. It is through their desire to know and critically reflect that they are able to challenge and protest those limits. If girlhood is a performative gender category, then it follows that girls can author iterations of this performance that test its confines.

The mermaid's multiple performances of femininity, varying from exaggerated imitations of cliché versions of emphasised femininity to alternative constructions of girlhood, reveal the constructedness of this gender role. Aquamarine, Hayley and Claire all experiment with multiple versions of doing girlhood. Butler writes that 'the multiplication of gender possibilities expose and disrupt the binary reifications of gender', thus potentially constituting a subversion (1999, 160). Butler has shown how gender is a contingent 'imitative structure' (175), containing the potential for imitations that produce contrary and subversive performances. Through Butler's work on performativity, girlhood studies scholars Emma Renold and Jessica Ringrose have argued that 'in the repetitions, spaces emerge, and it is the productive potential of the ambivalence, contradiction and perpetual displacement produced within these spaces that we are interested in exploring further' (2008, 317). Within narrative, the liminal can become the site for the contradictions that Renold and Ringrose identify as potential sites of contestation, troubling conventional notions of girlhood and disrupting the smooth veneer of its construction.

Within the field of ultraliminality, *Aquamarine*'s heroines intervene into fixed constructions of the girlhood rite of passage. The next section of this chapter considers feminist responses to Andersen's 'The Little Mermaid', before going on to explicate the ways in which *Aquamarine* revises these elements of the tale. The third section explores how *Aquamarine* constructs an alternative to the tale's theme of voicelessness, especially through the heroines' unruly deployment of assertive shouting and singing, as well as laughter at the conventions of sexist language structures. I argue that their subversive use of language and voice allows them to critique patriarchal discourses of girlhood, as well as create an alternative language of feminine adolescence that redefines their access to power. The fourth and final section of the chapter addresses the heroines' opposition to the demands of the emphasised femininity enforced in Andersen's earlier text. As the heroines journey through the flexible zone of the ocean, they are able to occupy and experiment with a fluid range of girlhoods, including the adoption of 'tomboy' identities, the creation of a supportive all-girl communitas and a rejection of adult patriarchal power. Through my redeployment of the feminist optic (Projansky 2014), I then examine the glitter aesthetic that represents the ultraliminal ocean. In my analysis, I argue that the pretty elements of flowing colours, gleaming bubbles and glittering sparkles are political images that visualise the activation of the heroines' magic powers, and also provide a representational terrain of fluidity where the heroines expand the terrain of girlhood into previously uncharted territories.

SILENCE AND GLAMOUR: FEMINIST RESPONSES TO 'THE LITTLE MERMAID'

Feminist critics have shown the ways in which 'The Little Mermaid' tale creates a narrative of female subservience to patriarchal authority, specifically through its silencing of the heroine's voice, the adoption of strict codes of feminine glamour and desirability, and the mobilisation of the conservative marriage plot (Trites 1991; Sells 1995; Warner 1995).

Andersen's tale formulates feminine desirability through a punishing ritual of beautification and silencing. The mermaid gives up the autonomy of her voice in order to gain a desirable human figure, and this is done in service of attracting and securing the affections of a man, subscribing to a heteronormative narrative in which female suffering is the price for the ultimate reward that the tale promises—a 'happily ever after'. As Warner dryly notes, 'romance constitutes the ultimate redemption, and romantic love, personified by the prince, the justification of desire' in 'The Little Mermaid' (1995, 404). The young mermaid strikes a bargain with the sea witch, exchanging her tongue and voice for a spell that will grant her legs so that she may walk on land. If she is able to attract the Prince's love and affection within three days, she will be granted an eternal soul and life on land. If not, she will perish and turn into sea foam. Undergoing the torture of having her tongue removed and the excruciating pain of bifurcating her legs, which many scholars agree represents the pain of menarche and its attendant pressures of femininity (Sells 1995; Williams 2010; Cowdy 2012), the mermaid attempts to woo her Prince but to no avail, and he marries another. The mermaid dissolves into a 'daughter of the air', intent on working hard for three hundred years doing good deeds in the hope that she may attain an eternal soul. Disney's version elides this morbid ending by rewarding the mermaid with marriage to the Prince, further emphasising the centrality of heterosexual romance as the ultimate fulfilment and validation of the girl's rite of passage.

One of the most profoundly disturbing aspects of 'The Little Mermaid' tale is its portrayal of voicelessness, forbearance, demureness and helplessness as an ideal version of femininity. In Andersen's tale, the mermaid trades her voice for legs, exclaiming to the sea witch:

> But if you take my voice away…what will I have left?' 'Your lovely figure,' said the witch, 'your graceful movements, and your expressive eyes. With all that you can easily enchant a human heart. Well, where's your courage? Stick out your little tongue and let me cut it off in payment. ([1837] 2008, 144)

The mermaid, metamorphosing into an idealised feminine form, must surrender her ability to articulate herself in exchange for a glamorous feminine body. The interlacing of suffering and voicelessness as a formula for feminine desirability in this tale creates a scenario in which the demands of patriarchal culture secure the heroine in the role of power-lessness and self-sacrifice (Golden 1998, 19). As Roberta Trites writes of both the Andersen and Disney versions of the tale, the mermaids:

> agree to be voiceless, to give up their physical forms, and to separate them-selves from their cultures...Both of them believe that they can gain love by suppressing their true identities. But because they have no verbal commu-nication skills and are illiterate, they can express their personalities only by relying on their appearances. (1991, para. 31)

The mermaid's attractiveness is secured through an obliteration of per-sonal freedom, signified by her inability to express her true feelings or thoughts, and an investment solely in the outward appearance of glamor-ous femininity. She is rendered mute, docile and unable to speak for her-self. Warner writes that the tale reveals cultural ideals of womanhood that equate 'silence with virtue, of forbearance with femininity' (1995, 394). Andersen's representation of the silent mermaid reproduces an idealised femininity that is aligned with helplessness, suffering and powerlessness.

To explicate the issues at stake in the silence of the mermaid repre-sented on the screen, I turn to the feminist film theory of scholars such as Kaja Silverman (1988) and Mary Ann Doane (1980), who have exam-ined the ways in which women on screen have been frequently rendered voiceless, without a clear place from which to articulate themselves, their stories or their points of view. Silverman writes that in classical Hollywood cinema, woman is denied a position of 'symbolic power and privilege'—the powers and privileges of holding an authoritative position from which to act, speak, and look. Simultaneously, woman must acqui-esce, obey and be 'receptive' to the demands of the male gaze and the authority of the male voice (1988, 31–32). She writes:

> the female subject's gaze is depicted as partial, flawed, unreliable, and self-entrapping...Woman's words are shown to be even less her own that are her 'looks.' They are scripted for her, extracted from her by an exter-nal agency, or uttered by her in a trancelike state. Her voice also reveals a remarkable facility for self-disparagement and self-incrimination...Even when she speaks without apparent coercion, she is always spoken from the place of the sexual other. (31)

Silverman argues that as a result of this diminutive and compromised position, woman in classical Hollywood cinema is unable to attain 'the invisible agency of enunciation' (32). Her description fittingly speaks to the plight of Andersen's mermaid: unable to articulate herself, she is helpless. Receptive to the commands and desires of the patriarchal authority figures, her father and the Prince, the mermaid is subjected to the power of the male voice without commanding her own. In this text, the silenced, glamorous woman is receptive, undemanding, docile and without agency.[1]

Holding her comb and mirror, the mermaid becomes the ultimate symbol of 'vanity and heartlessness,' a reminder of 'the perils of female beauty' (Norris 1998, 327). In the tale, becoming glamorous requires the heroine to undergo extreme pain, suffering and sacrifice in order to attract and secure the affections of a man and to become 'marriage material'. The sea witch explains the process that the mermaid must go through in order to become the feminine ideal:

> Your tail will then split in two and shrink into what human beings call pretty legs. But it will hurt. It will feel like a sharp sword passing through you. Everyone who sees you will say that you are the loveliest human child they have ever encountered...but every step you take will make you feel as if you were treading on a sharp knife, enough to make your feet bleed. ([1837] 2008, 143)

Andersen's focus on the mermaid's pain and suffering suggests a patriarchal association between disempowerment and glamour, a lack of agency in the face of the desiring, straight male gaze. The mermaid's transformation into a feminine, desirable figure comes at a high price of pain and suffering, and this disempowering process glamorises weakness, for as White writes, 'the transformation of the body towards desirability has involved, up to the present, a process of *weakening* the woman in order to render her sexually desirable' (1993, 189 original emphasis). While Andersen's tale rightly acknowledges the difficulty of adolescent feminine glamorisation, it marks it as a necessary and even desirable process, for it is through this glamorisation that the mermaid aims to achieve her most desired goal—being accepted and validated by her beloved Prince.

This containment of woman to the role of object, rather than subject, is embedded in standards of feminine glamour and the cosmetic, because these standards often prescribe and delimit a particularly pernicious version of acceptable femininity. After Mulvey's groundbreaking work on the male gaze in classical Hollywood cinema, feminist scholars such as Susan Bordo (1993, 1985) and Sandra Lee Bartky (1990) revealed how Western processes of feminine beautification and glamorisation work to control, regulate and manipulate the feminine body in other cultural arenas such as advertising and television. Bordo's Foucauldian analysis of the link between Western beauty culture and the prevalence of anorexia and bulimia nervosa among women argues that the body is 'constantly "in the grip"…of cultural practices' (1985, 76) which demand a very specific feminine form—slenderness (74), fitness (75) and subservience to 'fashion tyranny' (90). This is a fantasy of an 'ideal femininity, from which all threatening elements have been purged' and 'women have mutilated themselves *internally* to attain' this ideal (93 original emphasis). Bordo argues that this 'grip' of control is one of contemporary culture's ways of regulating, monitoring and manipulating the female body 'as an absolutely central strategy in the maintenance of power relations between the sexes' (76–77). Feminine glamour is therefore considered an avenue for the subjugation of women, for it reinforces sexist stereotypes that position women as objects, not subjects, as icons, not agents.

More recently, scholars have begun to consider potentially subversive rewritings of 'The Little Mermaid' tale in contemporary young adult (YA) fiction and teen film (White 1993; Williams 2010; Cowdy 2012), and *Aquamarine* has begun to be considered as part of this new wave of mermaid narratives. Fairy tale scholar Christy Williams has shown that rewritings such as *Aquamarine* revise the tale to tell a story of feminine adolescent transformation that incorporates female empowerment, friendship and personal transformation into the narrative (2010, 195). Furthermore, *Aquamarine* does not rely on romantic narrative closure in order to reward a long-suffering heroine—indeed, the heroines reject heterosexual romance in favour of explorations of independence, as well as building supportive communities with other girls. This provides a positive space for a feminist reading of the film, going beyond the kind of analysis offered in Silverman's work on classical cinema. In Andersen's fairy tale, the heroine's process of feminine transformation requires the obliteration of self—the mermaid must sacrifice her tongue to the witch's knife, she must tolerate excruciating pain as she sheds her tail and grows legs, she must give up the power of her voice—in order to gain entry to dry land and gain the love of a man. In extreme contrast, the contemporary teen screen revision of 'The Little Mermaid' tale mobilises the mermaid narrative in order to tell a story in which the mermaid rebels against the heteronormative scripts and rituals that the culture compels her to adopt and internalise. I argue that *Aquamarine*'s revision of Andersen's tale rupture these scripts and rituals, firstly through an interrogation of language and the gendered limits imposed on girls as speaking subjects, and secondly through a contestation of the politics of glamour. These disruptions expose the limits of 'acceptability' placed upon girls in patriarchal culture, and make these limits vulnerable to rupture and expansion in the realm of ultraliminal opposition. This presents a significant opportunity for expanding the horizon of girlhood into alternative articulations on the teen screen.

THE SIREN'S SONG: VOICE AND LANGUAGE IN *AQUAMARINE*

In Andersen's tale, the mermaid loses her voice and therefore becomes disempowered and infantilised, while the male characters of the tale retain and wield the agency of speech, setting up a clearly gendered divide through language and voice. One of *Aquamarine*'s most important revisions of the tale is its interrogation of this gendering of access to voice and language, rendering the heroines triumphant as they find ways to subversively refuse to be defined by this sexist structure of language and begin articulating and expressing themselves in alternative ways. As Williams has shown, 'in contrast to Andersen's...telling, the mermaids of...*Aquamarine* retain their voices on land; they express their desires, symbolically preserving the autonomy lost to the silent mermaids' (2010, 195). This aspect of the film's revision of the tale is therefore vital to its reconfiguration of gender, power and agency. The adolescent heroines critically reflect on the constructedness of this gendered performance of language. I turn to the feminist film theory of writers such as Doane (1980), Amy Lawrence (1991) and Kathleen Rowe (1995) in order to explicate the ways in which female voice can be mobilised in oppositional ways on the teen screen. In *Aquamarine*, voice and language are mobilised as sites of the heroines' negotiation of gender and power. In her work on teen film, Lesley Speed argues that teen girl characters 'are subject to a double domination, firstly by adults and secondly by male teenagers' (1995, 24), and I explore how this adult patriarchal domination plays out in linguistic control and the authority of voice in *Aquamarine*. I interpret *Aquamarine*'s representations of girls screaming, laughing and singing as unruly expressions that articulate the heroines' refusal of emphasised femininity, and how in this resistant space of refusal, innovative articulations of girlhood can be expressed.

Doane writes that sound poses a threat to the unity of film, for it 'carries with it the potential risk of exposing the material heterogeneity of the medium; attempts to contain that risk surface in the language of the ideology of organic unity' (1980, 35). Her article 'The Voice in the Cinema' considers the use of the '*disembodied* voice' in the cinema (1980, 42 original emphasis), particularly utilised in the voice-over of documentary films, as the most radical. Doane writes that while techniques such as 'the voice off, the voice-over during a flashback, or the interior monologue…work to affirm the homogeneity and dominance of diegetic space, the voice-over commentary is necessarily presented as outside of that space. It is its radical otherness with respect to the diegesis which endows this voice with a certain authority' (42). Doane describes this disembodied voice of the voice-over as 'privileged', imbued with the characteristics of 'activity', 'interpretation' and the 'possession of knowledge' (42). This distanced privilege means that 'because the voice is not localisable, because it cannot be yoked to a body, that it is capable of interpreting the image, producing its truth' (42). While Doane's work on the disembodied voice could open up avenues for considering more 'radical' examples of the feminine in the cinema, it nevertheless, like Silverman's work, privileges an aesthetic hierarchy in which the 'disembodied' voice is favoured as radical, distanced, critical as opposed to the 'embodied' voice which is too aligned with 'the claustral confinement within the female body' (Silverman 1988, 186). Some film theorists such as Britta Sjorgen (2006) and Amy Lawrence have rightly pointed out that Doane and Silverman perhaps problematically privilege a 'transcendent distance' as 'synonymous with subjective power', which 'clearly reflect[s] a view of "masculine-coded" subjectivity' (Sjorgen 2006, 13; See also Lawrence 1991, 2), but their work nevertheless reveals the political value of gaining critical distance from the circumstances by which women's subordination is sustained. While the heroines of *Aquamarine* never achieve the levels of the most radical deployment of voice according to Doane and Silverman's paradigms, they are certainly able to knowingly, exaggeratedly perform and critically challenge the structures of gendered language as they experience them. Interventions into gendered language and voice are politically important because they can oppose the ways in which girls and women are spoken about in patriarchal culture.

As I have been arguing, the term 'doing girlhood' recognises that girls actively participate in the construction of girlhood, while also acknowledging the cultural constraints that determine acceptable expressions of adolescent femininity (see Currie et al. 2009, xvii). Silverman and Doane show how classical Hollywood cinema denied the woman on screen a place from which to speak with authority, to interpret or contest the structure and meanings of gendered language. In the contemporary example of *Aquamarine*, however, the active process of doing girlhood allows Aquamarine, Hayley and Claire to challenge, critique and unsettle the very language codes they mock and laugh at in disruptive displays of public liminality. Doing girlhood is a knowing, active process and therefore holds within it the capacity for critical reflexivity—to push the boundaries of gendered language and to push the boundaries of what and how girls can speak. The heroines' techniques of deconstructing and interrogating voice and language are an important aspect of the film's revisionary powers, confronting the silence of Andersen's mermaid. This narrativises the contemporary mermaids' abilities to deconstruct the cultural forces that ordinarily silence girls, claiming disruptive ways of articulating themselves in the face of patriarchal oppression.

One of the most important ways that the heroines disrupt patriarchal language is through their deconstruction of how it enforces 'acceptable' expressions of femininity. The revelation that gendered speech is performative and requires work to understand and practise, exposes its constructedness. Aquamarine does not fully understand the way human language works, particularly when it comes to the 'language of love' and the cultural rituals of heterosexual dating. She constantly speaks out of turn, says the 'wrong' thing or misinterprets ambiguous words unfamiliar to the mermaid world. In their first encounter, Aquamarine assertively approaches lifeguard Raymond, the 'Prince' in this contemporary 'Little Mermaid' tale, and says 'Hi Raymond! Do you love me?' Raymond, confused by the question as this is their first meeting, responds as he slowly scans her body with his eyes, 'Well, no. But I think you're hot...*really* hot!' Aquamarine returns to her friends Hayley and Claire and repeats Raymond's 'compliment' with grave disappointment: 'He said I was hot. How would he know? Do I feel hot to you?' she asks, as she raises Claire's hand to her forehead. Aquamarine misunderstands the contemporary gendered courtship language at play, with 'hot' designated to mean physical attractiveness. Even when this definition is explained to Aquamarine, she remains confused and troubled by it, refusing to take on its meaning. This scene of misunderstanding profoundly achieves an exposure of the unnaturalness of this use of language—it is revealed as a performance, a construction and a limiting one that confines Aquamarine to the role of object of masculine desire in this instance. As Lawrence argues, this is important, because when the unnaturalness of language and sound is revealed, 'its role in the patriarchal construction of woman [is also] exposed' (1991, 111). In questioning and rejecting this gendered language, Aquamarine refuses to accept this ritual objectification and categorisation of her body. In this moment of disobedience and opposition to this language, Aquamarine is claiming her agency. While the mermaid of Andersen's tale gave up the agency of voice in order to receive the approval and desire of the Prince, the contemporary mermaid refuses this powerlessness. By rejecting this normative way of categorising the feminine body through language, Aquamarine opens up the potential for alternative vocabularies and languages of girlhood to emerge in the film.

The exposure and mockery of this gendered language registers a refusal to participate in the reproduction of sexist forms of speech—an act of insubordination and noncompliance. Lawrence writes that the use of comic and parodic styles of language in the cinema allows heroines to 'reflect [words] back on themselves in order to expose' their constructedness and therefore enact 'a refusal of "their" discourse and its dominance' (1991, 53). In the example of misunderstanding the word 'hot', both Aquamarine's onscreen friends and the spectator become aware of its comic quality, provoking laughter at its constructedness and drawing attention to the gendered identities it inscribes—in this instance, the word 'hot' promotes the internalisation of patriarchal standards of female attractiveness so that male approval and validation can be won. The act of mockery depicted through the heroines' laughter, and the laughter encouraged on the part of the spectator, subverts the authority of the word. Laughter and mockery is therefore an act of disobedience and dissent, a refusal of the sexist meanings encoded into this language. Speed's work similarly analyses the importance of laughter in teen girl films. She writes that it signifies the girl's unruliness, and calls for the consideration of 'the feminist significance of female disobedience' through representations of 'vocal excess' on the teen screen (2002, 226). As Rowe writes in her work on women's comedy films and television series, women's laughter at 'the language of their oppressors' challenges 'the social and symbolic systems that would keep women in their place' (1995, 2–3). In *Aquamarine*, this act of unruly laughter creates distance between the girls and the words that invoke particularly restrictive forms of femininity, and critical reflexivity flourishes in this gap.

In *Aquamarine*, speaking from the place of 'girl' is represented as a strategic process, a performative negotiation of gendered power. In another scene that defamiliarises the gendered codes of language, Hayley and Claire try to help Aquamarine understand and reproduce the codes of romance and romantic desirability by gleaning information and advice from teen magazines together. The words contained within these pages present the heroines with a particularly narrow representation of doing girlhood—they focus exclusively on girlhood as an identity centred on the codes of feminine desirability and heterosexual romance. Feminist studies of teen girl magazines have explored how these postfeminist texts, as Angela McRobbie writes, often cast girls as 'passive, conformist, willing subjects of romantic ideology, easily persuaded by the various seductions of advertising and consumption' (2008, 535). Girlhood studies scholar Marnina Gonick elaborates that:

> teen magazines, although they do not all do so in the same way, participate in the construction of particular meanings about what it is to be an adolescent girl…The magazines employ powerful hegemonic discourses of femininity, heterosexuality, romance and morality. At the level of culture the magazines are an explicit attempt to win consent to the dominant order. (1997, 72)

As the heroines read the magazines, they encounter these postfeminist discourses identified by McRobbie and Gonick; however, they also enact a deconstruction of these discourses. The search for male approval as the means for women to 'obtain satisfaction in the world' is at the root of Andersen's tale (White 1993, 191), and *Aquamarine*'s revision of the tale works to critique this sexist paradigm through a deconstruction of language.

The magazines that the heroines read in *Aquamarine* clearly reproduce the heterosexual romance paradigm that demands the performance of emphasised femininity. Claire drags a large pile of the magazines onto her bed and the girls begin reading them. During this scene, the editing speeds up to a frantic pace and the framing tightens, primarily focusing on snippets of the pages, and extreme close-ups on the heroines' eyes as they move across the page, as shown in Figs. 6.1 and 6.2.

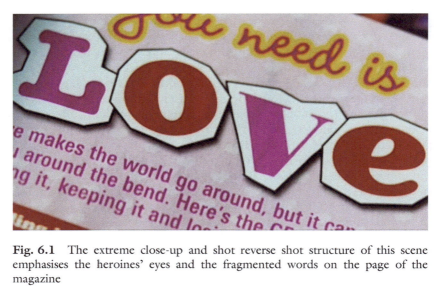

Fig. 6.1 The extreme close-up and shot reverse shot structure of this scene emphasises the heroines' eyes and the fragmented words on the page of the magazine

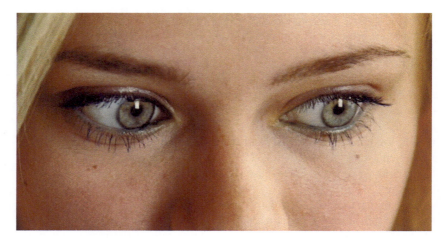

Fig. 6.2 The extreme close-up and shot reverse shot structure of this scene emphasises the heroines' eyes and the fragmented words on the page of the magazine

The flamboyant display of bright pinks, reds and oranges in the colour palette, the illustrations of bright stars and neon love hearts littering the page and the glossy sheen of the paper draw attention to the words on the page. The ultra-fast editing of this sequence generates discomfort and a moment of disruption, which Dickinson writes is typical of the rapid-fire editing of the MTV aesthetic (2003, 143, 146). This discomforting, dizzying effect of the rapid editing gives the impression of visual overload for both the heroines and the spectator. Through this use of rapid-paced montage, the magazine's pages are represented as a visual affront, accosting the reader with an overwhelming amount of information that inscribes a very narrow construction of hegemonic emphasised femininity. The heroines experience an information and image overload, frantically reading dozens of articles with titles such as 'Love Stories: Serious Chemistry', 'Get a Man's Attention', 'Sex Education' and 'All You Need is Love'. The visual style of the scene matches this frantic information overload, interpolating the viewer into the heroines' point of view and reading process. The spectator is aligned with their gaze and perspective, and is positioned to experience the difficulty of this moment. This excess performs a critical function: the intense close ups, garish colour scheme and rapid editing style all create a confrontational image that visually deconstructs the ideology contained within the magazine's pages.

While the heroines read the magazine articles with frenzied intensity, which suggests an immersive and seductive absorption of its language, they articulate frustrations with and critiques of the language provided within its pages that opposes the language they are confronted with. The magazines certainly encourage the heroines to adopt a particular language of girlhood and desirability—a particular gendered way of expressing the self through emphasised femininity. However, *Aquamarine*'s heroines deconstruct this language, and this is visually represented with each extreme close-up focusing on a shot of a particular word (Love; Sex; Chemistry; Guys; Hearts) intercut with extreme close-ups on the heroines' eyes, which move across the pages of the magazines. This focus on the heroines' active eyes as they scan, read and analyse the content suggests a much more complex dynamic. The great amount of visual detail and fast-paced cutting style promotes a spectatorial position of an active, scanning, critical look to match the intensity of the scene. This spectatorial positioning is generated through the sequence's MTV-style filmic techniques of superabundance and fast-paced editing. As John Fiske points out, the fragmenting of images in the MTV aesthetic is 'oppositional to the fixed world of the established', containing within it the capacity to resist (1998, 170). *Aquamarine* uses this fragmentation to break apart the gendered discourse of romance: the extreme close-up shots on single words draw attention to their structure as they are broken down by the camera and the heroines' collective deconstructive gaze. Fiske writes that this fragmented aesthetic 'necessarily resists dominant ideology, in which the invisibility of the process is the essential condition for the naturalisation of the product' (171). This visual deconstruction of the words on the page therefore represents a critical practice for the heroines, creating a spectatorial position that works in the same critically reflexive manner. The film presents the heroines as knowing subjects, as the *mise en scène*, framing and editing represents their critical perspective as they scrutinise the magazine's pages.

Despite the magazines' incitement to speak exclusively of heterosexual feminine desire, romance, and one-true-love narratives, the heroines of *Aquamarine* challenge this language, and even interrogate and speak back to it as they visually deconstruct the phrases presented within their pages. Indeed, Aquamarine exclaims in frustration, 'How do you remember all this? You have to be flirty but demure, devoted but not desperate, available but elusive? It's so annoying!' Aquamarine points out the ridiculous contradictions of the gendered performance she is being called to assume, and her contestation also reveals the possibility of refusing to perform these codes, posing a significant rupture. The heroines' collective contestation of these gendered language codes, and the limiting rituals of femininity they inscribe, suggest their contingency and vulnerability to contestation in the realm of liminal communitas. Through their critically reflexive interrogation of the words littered across the magazine's pages, the heroines not only reject this sexist language, but also enact the agency of choosing other more oppositional modes of expression that exceed the language that would contain them.

Once the heroines realise the constructedness of gendered language performance, they also enjoy finding new ways to articulate themselves— for example, through shouting, singing and laughing. *Aquamarine* revises Andersen's troubling narrative in which the heroine progresses from clear articulation to the sacrifice of silence. In extreme contrast, in *Aquamarine* 'finding your voice' becomes an important theme of feminine empowerment. As Leslie Dunn and Nancy A. Jones have argued in their work on the representation of women's voices in Western culture,

> feminists have used the word 'voice' to refer to a wide range of aspirations: cultural agency, political enfranchisement, sexual autonomy, and expressive freedom, all of which have been historically denied to women. In this context, 'voice' has become a metaphor for textual authority, and alludes to the efforts of women to reclaim their own experience through writing ('having a voice') or to the specific qualities of their literary and cultural expression ('in a different voice'). (1994, 1; See also Lawrence 1991, 3–11)

The theme of 'finding your voice' is central to Aquamarine, Hayley and Claire's access to empowerment. At the beginning of the film, before the onset of liminal communitas, Hayley and Claire find it difficult to clearly articulate themselves. For example, they quietly suppress their squeals of delight as they gaze at handsome lifeguard Raymond. When high school bullies make fun of them, they are unable to 'talk back' or stand up for themselves, remaining silent throughout and enduring cruel taunts. But when Aquamarine magically attains access to land, and liminal communitas is activated, Hayley and Claire embark upon an alternative rite-of-passage journey towards assertiveness and 'finding a voice'. Aquamarine encourages them to 'just be yourself', and as the heroines gain confidence and self-assuredness, their capacity to talk back and even yell loudly increases.

Aquamarine also finds her voice at the end of the film when she loudly and firmly interjects 'NO' when Raymond asks her to remain on land with him in order to be his girlfriend. Additionally, she also shouts 'NO' to her tyrannical father. He demands that she must find true love within a three-day period, otherwise he will not relinquish his control over her or allow her to independently explore her considerable magic powers in the ocean. By loudly declaring her refusal to both these men, she finds a language that allows her to redefine her access to power in the social realm. Claire also shows this progression towards empowerment in the use of voice through her version of the siren's song. She is afraid of swimming in the ocean since experiencing the trauma of her parents dying in a boating accident when she was a child. By the end of the film, Claire has gained the confidence to plunge into the water and 'find her fins' in the flexible, fluid waves of the ultraliminal ocean, if not literally

then metaphorically. Fading out of this image of Claire floating and lux-
uriating, mermaid-like, in the turquoise waves of the ocean, the screen
fades to black as the end credits play. During these end credits, Claire's
voice appears as she sings a pop song called 'Island in the Sun'. This
final moment of the film links Claire to the liminal transformation into
a 'mermaid' both in the image track and the soundtrack as she sings her
Siren's song. 'Finding your voice' comes to represent feminine empowerment and agency in *Aquamarine*, particularly in relation to assertive,
disruptive or unruly vocal expressions such as singing, shouting, yelling
and laughing. All of these examples occur in the ultraliminal zone of the
ocean, aligning this space with the heroines' unruly interjections into
patriarchal power. The fantasy of ultraliminality therefore provides the
heroines with an opportunity to enact multiple, ongoing interventions
into the dominant order.

THE GLITTER AESTHETIC: SPARKLES AND COLOUR IN *AQUAMARINE*'S *MISE EN SCÈNE*

Aquamarine's rewriting of 'The Little Mermaid' also destabilises the sexist visual economy of glamour that Andersen idealised and reified. The
film's heroines construct exaggerated public performances of glamorous
femininity as Aquamarine and her friends begin to learn how to behave,
dress and appear desirable on land. Furthermore, the film presents several different ways of engaging with glamorous girlhood through
heroines such as Cecilia who performs an exaggerated femininity, in
contrast with Hayley who adopts a more alternative 'tomboy' identity.
Aquamarine also constructs an alternative image of prettiness as she
resists glamour's paradigm of desirability, instead creating a glitter aesthetic which arises in images of bubbles and dazzling sparkles which represent the active, independent and agentic use of her underwater powers.
The imagery of flow and fluidity is symbolised by the iridescent waves of
the ocean that the mermaids swim through, and the pretty shimmering
bubbles that appear when the mermaids activate their magical underwater powers. The heroines map their exploration of alternative, fluid girlhood identities onto their ocean adventure, aligning the pretty image
with the girls' empowerment. Pretty images therefore visualise the heroines' critique of emphasised femininity and the normative, acceptable
performances of girlhood that it encodes, while also offering alternative
constructions of prettiness in film.

Feminist film theorists have been correct to point out the connection between glamour—which includes sparkles, glitter and sequins—and the potentially disempowering role of the showgirl, the woman on display to be looked at (Mulvey [1975] 1989, 19). Mulvey's work reveals how the woman on screen is burdened with 'glamorous characteristics' (20) that cement her in the role of erotic object on display for the male gaze, both within the diegesis and for the spectator (19). Jane Gaines takes up this thesis of the showgirl on display in her writing on the use of spectacular fashion in classical Hollywood cinema, powerfully commenting that 'bugle beads, sequins, and rhinestones have a long history of signifying the side-show and burlesque side of sexualised entertainment, relying on a stabilised caricature of money and finery' (2011, 149–150). This cosmetic image of the woman as spectacle, made up and stylised as a glittering and glamorous object on display for the male gaze, relies on the sexist ideals of the woman as showgirl and icon, an opulent and Othered image, a caricature onto which masculine desires and fears can be projected, negotiated, managed and allayed.

Aquamarine's heroines challenge this construction of glamour, as well as the representation of the mermaid that relies on sexist stereotypes of feminine vapidity and narcissism. Aquamarine finds it deeply difficult to mimic the codes of 'appropriate' feminine appearance. Indeed, she dryly rehashes the definition: 'Mermaid: best known for sitting on rocks, staring into mirrors and obsessively combing our hair. Blah blah blah.' At the beginning of the film, Aquamarine believes that she must nevertheless learn these codes of feminine desirability in order to win the love and affection of handsome lifeguard Raymond, attempting to work the trap of femininity. She goes through the process of 'gender acquisition', but she finds the rules difficult to memorise and learn, exposing the persistent work required to perform heteronormative girlhood and emphasised femininity (Williams 2010, 201). In one scene, Aquamarine attempts to attract Raymond's attention, performing a code of desirability learned from the pages of a magazine: 'the laugh and pass: casually walk past him, laughing'. The heroines 'casually' walk past Raymond, twirling their hair and laughing hysterically.

As illustrated in Fig. 6.3, this gesture is so exaggerated and artificially synchronised that it reveals itself as a gendered performance. The scene is set at a carnival teeming with clowns and other circus performers, drawing further attention to the girls' gestures as a performative display of public liminality. The revelation that gender is performed, and therefore

Fig. 6.3 Hyperconscious displays of femininity generate both humour and insightful critique of gendered performance

unstable, contains within it the potential for the destabilisation of that very performance. Butler argues that 'performativity has to do with repetition, very often with the repetition of oppressive and painful gender norms to force them to resignify. This is not freedom, but a question of how to work the trap that one is inevitably in' (quoted in Kotz 1992, 84). Butler denies the existence of a way out of this cultural ensnarement, but she does point out that one can 'work the trap'. At the beginning of the film, *Aquamarine*'s heroines work the trap by playing up and showing up the conditions by which this performance is negotiated, produced and maintained. Codes of feminine desirability are rendered ridiculous, appearing unnatural and humorously hyperbolic. This opens them up to critique and even transgression, which occurs when the heroines enter the ultraliminal zone in the second half of the film.

Cecilia, who presents an excessive embodiment of this performance of glamorous girlhood, similarly shows up and exposes the work of emphasised femininity. With her baby-pink sartorial ensembles, T-shirts studded with the rhinestone slogan 'PRINCESS' and her Barbie-esque pink convertible car (which humorously also bears the extravagant stamp 'PRINCESS' on its licence plate), Cecilia performs girlhood in a highly self-conscious and exaggerated way. Her method of doing girlhood is spectacular and excessive, amplifying the codes of glamorous femininity. This excessive way of doing girlhood, of working the trap, emphasises that glamour is carefully constructed and performed. Through the excessive figure of Cecilia, the film is able to bring this gendered cultural construction of glamorous femininity to the surface of the text, providing a way to critically reflect on the processes involved in constructing this dominant version of girlhood. Bringing these demands to the surface of the text undermines the supposed natural neutrality of this gendered ideological structure, exposing how it works and the processes required in order to successfully comply with it. The work of performing normative femininity and glamorous girlhood lies in the 'invisibilisation' of its processes, rules and disciplines. As girlhood scholars Kelly and Pomerantz observe, the rules of adolescent femininity must be followed in such a way that invisibilises the process and struggle, so that girls seems to acquire normative femininity 'without seeming to follow any rules at all' (2009, 5). Excess ensures that these hidden processes are revealed and this exposure threatens them, for they rely on a seemingly natural neutrality to operate.

Excess exposes the process and strategic work involved in acquiring and performing normative femininity—in Cecilia's case, internalising the demands of objectification, disciplining the body, conforming to stereotypes of youthful femininity—bringing it to the surface of *Aquamarine*. The rules of performing glamorous girlhood, just under the surface of Cecilia's constructed spectacle, rise to the surface and are made available for critically reflexive exploration. By bringing the workings of glamour to the surface, and thereby exposing how it is governed, enforced and performed, the film provides an opportunity to question, critique, reconfigure and alter this gendered performance. For example, the heroines do not wish to conform to the ideals of glamorous feminine display. Hayley in particular is coded as a 'tomboy', donning cargo shorts and baggy gender-neutral coloured T-shirts. Bullies cruelly taunt Hayley's divergent way of doing girlhood, asking if she has 'something against *girl's* clothes'. Hayley shrugs off this remark and continues to do girlhood differently. This scene reveals a critical reflexivity that the heroines practise, in their capacity to identify and sustain other ways of doing girlhood that do not conform to glamorous feminine ideals.

The heroines of *Aquamarine* also create alternative engagements with prettiness in ways that challenge the edicts of emphasised femininity and desirability for a male gaze. In the wake of theory by Mulvey, Bordo,

Bartky and others, feminist theorists have sought to consider surfaces, decoration and images of excess in new ways in order to account for its capacity to provide a feminist image. Throughout this book, I have redeployed Projansky's feminist optic to look for the ways that girl heroines use elements of prettiness, glamour and adornment to construct alternative feminine identities that oppose conventional culture and adult masculine authority. The films and television series under analysis use these formal screen elements to include girl's points of view, gazes, alternative identities and instances of feminine adolescent insubordination in the face of patriarchal oppression. Scholars such as Rosalind Galt (2011) have argued that disparaged screen aesthetics such as the 'pretty' may 'be uniquely able to develop a politics that engages gender, sexuality, and geographical alterity at a formal level rather than simply as a problem for representation' (6). I have been exploring Galt's theorisation of pretty cinematic aesthetics throughout this book, and in this chapter, I unpack her theorisation of glitter as an element of this aesthetic (67). She writes that glitter is associated with the disparaged categories of 'commodification' and 'fashionable patterns' as opposed to 'aesthetic purity'—firmly locating it in the realm of the feminine (67). Galt concludes that 'we see...the rhetoric of glitter and duplicity that underwrites aesthetically the discursive formation of a bad feminine culture' (253). The sparkling surface is a 'light catcher' and 'scene stealer', which brings the eye to the surface, the materiality of the image (Gaines 2011, 149). The glittery, pretty image is over the top, an embellishment, associated with femininity, play, childhood, tackiness and frivolity. As art historian Penny Sparke writes, glitter is an aesthetic of excess, linked with the trivial, the unnecessary and brash display (1995, 15). But the pretty image can indeed be articulate material charged with critical, even political potential. I argue that *Aquamarine*'s glitter aesthetic defies the sexist connotations of glamour and availability for a male gaze, and instead constructs a pretty image that visualises the heroine's autonomous and independent exploration of her magical powers.

Teen screen media's deployment of the glitter aesthetic arises in its use of sequin-studded sartorial ensembles, shimmering make-up, a glossy *mise en scène* dominated by bright candy colour palettes, and the use of glamorous sparkles that shimmer across the screen in magical moments. This aesthetic category of teen film has been disparaged as both inanely superficial and dangerously seductive to the teen viewer (see DeVaney 2002; Fox-Kales 2011). Emily Fox-Kales' media-effects study laments this 'sparkling sunny world' that teen heroines inhabit, 'enhanced by the film's standard production design featuring vibrant colours, sparkling lighting and stylish sets accompanied by bouncy soundtracks playing "bubble-gum" music and pop rock tunes' (2011, 121). She concludes that whatever challenge or critique of contemporary girlhood that may be embedded at a deeper level in the teen text is overrun by the seductive and meaningless surface of the film, which is so overwhelming that 'unfortunately [these deeper messages are] lost on many adolescent moviegoers' (122). This analysis suggests that the prettiness of teen film's images is somehow both totally empty of any significant meaning and yet simultaneously overflowing with the potential to seduce and compel a vulnerable teen audience. Fox-Kales does not acknowledge that teen film's glittering images of excess can act as a commentary on the ideologies that construct adolescence, nor does she account for the fact that teens are critical viewers with the capacity to engage in critical reflexivity.

While the use of glitter and sparkles has not yet been fully considered in relation to teen screen aesthetics, Mary Celeste Kearney's (2015) and Rachel Moseley's (2002) work offer excellent starting points. In her work on sparkles in postfeminist girl's media, Kearney writes that the sparkle 'is so ubiquitous in mainstream girls' culture...it vies with pink as the primary signifier of youthful femininity' (2015, 263). Sparkles, Kearney observes, are usually represented 'via girls' bodies, which are commonly adorned with glittery makeup, clothing and accessories' (263). While Kearney acknowledges the problems inherent in linking female agency with 'the body and marketplace given the history of women's and girls' construction as merely objects available for male pleasure and thus our epic exploitation as consumers of fashion-beauty products' (270), she also notes 'the pronounced superficiality, theatricality and ironic knowingness of postfeminist glamour' and the complex ways in which 'girls are negotiating the contradictory messages of postfeminist culture...[and undertaking] critical reclamations of femininity' (270). As I argued earlier in this chapter, *Aquamarine*'s heroines demonstrate the 'ironic knowingness' of codes of glamour that Kearney observes within contemporary postfeminist media. Crucially, Kearney also notes the potential that the distance of irony and theatricality holds for negotiations and possible 'critical reclamations' of feminine aesthetics. Similarly, Moseley investigates the formal element of the sparkle in teen witch television series and films. She writes that:

the glamorous sparkle – whether of eyes, teeth, cosmetics or dress – is a conventional sign of femininity, but for teen witches it also signals power made manifest as audiovisual effect, or spectacle. Herein lies the paradox of glamour in the texts, and perhaps in the postfeminist project. While the sparkle is powerfully spectacular and grabs the viewer's attention, it is also highly ephemeral, drawing the eye to the surface of the text. The textual sparkle as a marker of glamour in all its senses emphasises surface: through glamour, feminine power in these texts is located in and articulated through appearance. (408–409)

Moseley's work offers a way in which to consider how the sparkle of glitter aesthetics in teen screen media has been tethered to narrative moments of the heroine's empowerment and magical capabilities. Her work reveals that in these teen witch texts the spectacle of the sparkle, though it 'emphasises surface', can also visually articulate the heroine's power and empowerment.

In *Aquamarine*, the emphasis on the ocean, the iridescent surface of the water, glistening waves, colourful bubbles and floating sparkles provides a glitter aesthetic that represents a flexible, shifting, fluid, flowing image. As the heroines navigate this ultraliminal, shifting otherworld that is not bound to the rules and strictures of the everyday, they are able to imagine and enact alternative versions of girlhood. Turner argues that 'unruliness itself is a mark of the ultraliminal, of the perilous realm of possibility of "anything *may* go" which threatens any social order and seems the more threatening, the more *that* order *seems* rigorous and secure' (1979, 478 original emphases). In the unsettled zone of ultraliminality, any alternative arrangements or patterns may be innovated and acted upon, therefore providing a field of possibilities where routine categories and identities are done away with. This fluidity, unruliness and sense of the heroines' sustained access to expansive alternative possibilities is visualised in the glitter aesthetic of the ultraliminal ocean space.

The glitter aesthetic constitutes an exuberant pretty image. Crowding the frame with sparkles, glitter, luminous bubbles and shimmering light, this aesthetic brings attention to the surface of the image. These images of shimmering glittering prettiness are not mobilised in service of a display of emphasised femininity presented for a male gaze; instead, prettiness is revised as a site for the expression of the girl's agency as she navigates the waters and exercises her magical powers when she escapes to the ocean with the communitas of mermaids. This renegotiation of

Fig. 6.4 The glitter aesthetic is revealed in the opening shots of *Aquamarine*, with the mermaid's magical powers visualised through images of sparkles, bubbles, iridescent colours and glitter

prettiness and its relation to girlhood reveals that the pretty image can contain and sustain a political intervention into the configuration of girlhood on screen, becoming a site of transgression. In the opening shots of *Aquamarine*, the camera glides through the ocean, which is a hypersaturated, hyper real turquoise blue. Recording the visual perspective of the mermaid Aquamarine, the camera drifts across the ocean floor. As illustrated in Fig. 6.4, the frame is crowded with a profusion of colours: the turquoise water, tiny fuchsia pink and violet coloured fish, golden coral and emerald green moss. Gleaming bubbles float into frame, radiantly sparkling and glittering.

The magic sparkle appears in the *mise en scène* and crowds the frame when the heroine is using her mermaid powers, investing the pretty glittering image as a visual display of the theme of feminine agency and power. This image of the girl's liminal transformation into a mermaid provides a representation of the girl as a malleable, shifting identity category: her body momentarily becomes watery, composed of twinkling sparkles and floating bubbles. By visualising this flexibility and power through the glitter aesthetic, *Aquamarine* creates a new constellation of associations to emerge from the pretty that shimmers across the screen as a visual manifestation of girls' agency, innovation and access to alternative femininities.

Aquamarine, Hayley and Claire initially play with but ultimately reject the performance of emphasised femininity and glamorous girlhood. Their hyperconscious, over-the-top performance of emphasised femininity's codes works to expose its constructedness, and their ultimate rejection of it reveals the possibility of finding alternatives to it. The refusal to participate in glamorous girlhood is particularly evident in the heroines' rejection of beautification and feminine adornment as a means to win the attention and approval of male characters. While Andersen's mermaid agreed to suffer extreme pain to beautify herself to gain the love of the Prince, *Aquamarine*'s mermaids self-reflexively deconstruct and resist this construction of femininity. The glitter aesthetic provides an alternative version of prettiness. It gives representational space to the girl's contestation of glamorous girlhood as she constructs a new version of prettiness that does not rely upon attracting the male gaze. This gives the heroines a space through which to navigate and critically reflect upon these ambivalences. The pretty can indeed be a locus for bringing the contradictions and demands of girlhood to the surface, creating an aesthetic that can incorporate a critique of these conflicting demands. Therefore, the glitter aesthetic offers a critically reflexive space to explore and challenge these constructions of girlhood. Aquamarine, in her protest against and refusal to conform to the gender norms required of her, does not fulfil her father's task of finding true love with a man in the three-day period. Instead, she finds unconditional love in her friendship with Hayley and Claire, articulating an alternative way of doing girlhood that does not rely on romance scripts but rather fosters solidarity between girls. She is able to do girlhood differently, avoiding the language and glamour of romance she critiqued in the magazines. Aquamarine has gained freedom from her controlling father's grip, and chooses to return permanently to the ultraliminal field of the ocean. Instead of entering into the constraints of conservative romantic resolution, she decides to swim to Fiji and have adventures, literally distancing herself from the stability and domesticity of this resolution.

Furthermore, the pretty glitter aesthetic also provides a representation of the heroines' empowerment and navigation of ultraliminality, and the fluid girlhood identities available in this space. In this zone, the heroines explore alternative girlhoods such as tomboy identities, refusals of heterosexual romantic ideology, focus on building and sustaining a positive, supportive, all-girl communitas and pursuing adventures beyond the confines of hegemonic femininity. By constructing a permanent access to the magical, ultraliminal zone of the ocean, the heroines are able to imagine and pursue feminist futures that include sustained female solidarity, experimentation with alternative feminine identities, and undertaking independent adventures of self-discovery and self-empowerment. The pretty glitter aesthetic is a political image in this film, an image that not only comments on and protests against rigid cultural constructions of contemporary girlhood, but also provides a representation of girls building empowering futures for themselves and their girl group community. Returning to her mermaid state, Aquamarine rejects the prescribed limitations imposed by her father and instead inventing another way for herself to find happiness in her liminal mermaid state. As Laura Sells writes, in the contemporary mermaid tale, 'to be definned is to be defined' and 'the mermaid fantasy is a means of prolonging the period when girls are allowed free movement and more far-ranging identification' (1995, 192). Rewriting the fiction of girlhood (Walkerdine 1993), which demands that the girl present herself as a romantic, heterosexual object for male affection, *Aquamarine* proposes another way of doing girlhood that is contrary to hegemonic femininity. Aquamarine's way of doing girlhood is mobile and fluid, as she navigates the waters of her adventure on her own at times and with the all-girl communitas at other times.

Sociologist Arpad Szakolczai has recently considered the importance of Turner's concept of permanent liminality or ultraliminality. He posits that 'the crucial question' about permanent liminality 'concerns the large-scale social impact of the phenomenon' (2013, 16). He writes that 'the confusing character of liminal conditions, the absence of stability and structure' can allow ritual subjects to create an 'ideal...without limits...which means permanent liminality' (2012, 175). For Szakolczai, ultraliminality's capacity to 'play with boundaries' (2012, 187) holds a promise of social change, where the pliable limits of dominant culture can be perforated, shifted, and moved in new directions, in ways that may impact upon the status quo. To transform 'a liminal situation...into a permanent condition' (2007, 22), Szakolczai argues that a liminal figure must instigate and perpetuate the situation through play, trickery, the confusion of 'meaningful order,' excitement and 'generating hectic movements in the social body' (22). *Aquamarine*'s heroines, who slip between the identities of mermaid and girl, and between the locations of land and sea, perpetuate the liminal situation in this magical state of flux. The confusion this generates in the dominant order breaks down any singular, hegemonic definition of 'girl' in their social world, as their friends, family and townspeople are confronted with the presence of this 'new' flexible form of girlhood. This shift creates a state of permanent liminality, and an attendant effect of social change, because the conventional definitions of femininity can no longer apply in the town. The mermaid heroines create the 'hectic' movement identified by Szakolczai, dissolving old boundaries around girlhood and generating an expansive, flexible, liminal experience of feminine adolescence in its place.

CONCLUSIONS: GIRLHOOD'S 'CIRCUMFERENCE OF THE VISIBLE'

In this chapter, I have returned to the theme of permanent or ultraliminality that I explored towards the beginning of the book. In both *Red Riding Hood* and *Aquamarine*, ultraliminality is represented as a zone of escape and freedom for the heroines who want to overcome the limits imposed upon them within dominant culture. However, there are two major differences between these texts: the first is that while *Red Riding Hood*'s Valerie pursues a solitary journey into the forest, in *Aquamarine* the escape into permanent liminality is a shared experience of the all-girl communitas. *Aquamarine* represents ultraliminality as a space for girls to cooperatively, continuously create ruptures in the status quo, suggesting a collective, sustained and therefore politically powerful intervention into the strictures of hegemonic girlhood. Secondly, the ocean is represented as a space of flow, fluidity and flexibility through imagery of glistening rolling waves, colourful bubbles and twinkling sparkles that depict the activation of the mermaid's magic powers. As they occupy this space of flow and flexibility, the heroines are able to imagine and construct a variety of alternative girlhoods to experiment with, creating a language of fluid feminine adolescent identity. This allows the heroines to go beyond binary definitions and closed categorisations, and into more expansive territories. These differences have led me to argue that *Aquamarine*'s representation of adolescent ultraliminality presents even more of a significant, sustained rupture in the fairy tale's feminine rite-of-passage narrative.

While some contemporary girls' mermaid texts continue to narrativise the girl's transformation through the lens of heterosexual romance, there is a growing trend of teen texts that elide Andersen's and Disney's canonical representations. *Aquamarine* is a particularly clear and progressive example of this, with its heroines actively and self-reflexively protesting against the male characters who attempt to diminish them to damsels in need of romance and rescue. A text such as *Aquamarine* provides a refreshing alternative to the princess narratives contained in dominant tellings of this girls' rite-of-passage journey. The film's all-girl communitas of mermaids confronts the boundaries of what it is possible to be, say and do from the position of 'girl' in contemporary culture. This is because communitas in ultraliminality promotes both critical reflexivity and sustained opposition to the status quo, as well as the enactment of innovations that shift the boundaries of the dominant system into new, uncharted and expansive territories.

For a time, Andersen's and Disney's mermaids do access a liminal space by roaming freely through the fluid space of the ocean and temporarily eluding patriarchal expectations about their girlhood rites of passage. But this access is brief, and circumvented by conservative narrative conclusions that fix the girl in a passive position. Any unruly and experimental energy of liminality that exists in these tellings is finally contained as the girl takes up her 'appropriate' feminine position. Meanwhile, *Aquamarine* revises the tale to tell a story about girls who reject dominant culture and pursue a permanent escape instead, opening up the possibilities of the liminal, rather than foreclosing on them. *Aquamarine* provides a revision of Andersen's fairy tale 'The Little Mermaid' through its construction of ultraliminality and the heroines' access to flexible girlhood identities. While Andersen's mermaid profoundly sacrifices her voice and endures excruciating pain in order to gain a perfect glamorous body and to woo the Prince, *Aquamarine*'s heroines refuse to accept this heteronormative construction of femininity. The all-girl communitas of mermaids confronts the boundaries of what it is possible to be, say and do from the position of 'girl' in contemporary culture. This is because communitas in ultraliminality promotes both critical reflexivity and sustained opposition to the status quo, as well as the enactment of innovations that shift the boundaries of the dominant system into new, uncharted, expansive territories.

In this contemporary rewriting, the mythical figure of the mermaid becomes a fantasy site for imagining girlhood beyond the strictures of the everyday. In that expansive ultraliminal zone, the heroines imagine and pursue futures beyond attaining the desire and validation of a prince. If, as Sells argues, in mermaid narratives, 'to be definned is to be defined' (1995, 192), then *Aquamarine*'s elision of such a narrative conclusion allows its heroines to remain in an unsettled zone where definitions of 'girl' are unstable and shifting. In this revised version of 'The Little Mermaid' tale, the mermaid figure charts a process of feminine adolescent transformation, a fantasy of broadening the potentialities of doing girlhood. Ultraliminality is presented not only as a field of possibilities, but a space of sustained intervention into dominant culture. As the heroines navigate the ocean's waves together, they construct alternative girlhoods that impact upon their social world: through their pursuit of nondominant expressions of femininity, they expand the circumference of the visible of what it is possible to be and do as girls on the teen screen. Furthermore, by pursuing feminist futures, they promise to continue to enact unruly oppositions, sustaining their access to agency in their rite-of-passage adventure.

I have argued that the heroines' capacity to critically reflect on the gendered dynamics of voice and language allows them to oppose the place from which they are being prompted to speak by dominant culture. Through their public performances of disruptive shouting, singing and explosive laughter at sexist language codes, the heroines express an unruly language of feminine adolescence that articulates the girl as capable of negotiating dominant structures of gendered oppression. The heroines confront the words and other verbal expressions deployed by men to fix girls in a diminished role—for example, the label of 'hot', which demands a patriarchal standard of feminine attractiveness. As I have argued, the heroines deploy critical strategies such as laughter in the face of this labelling, which exposes the ridiculousness of the language and renders it strange. The distance that this defamiliarisation opens up is a critical space, a fissure in the dominant system of this language. Within the space of rupture, the heroines develop alternative strategies of verbal assertiveness, for example by shouting the word 'NO' to adult male authority figures. By doing this, the heroines find ways to negotiate language and voice in ways that challenge and go beyond the sexist language structures they encounter. While Andersen's mermaid acquiesced to a powerless position of voiceless and silent supplication, the heroines of *Aquamarine* gain critical distance from the system that enforces this silence, creating opportunities for girls' unruly articulations on the teen screen.

Another point of unruliness in this revised mermaid tale arises in images of glitter, bubbles, and sparkles—what I have called the glitter aesthetic. *Aquamarine*'s heroines critically reflect on the performance of glamorous femininity, experimenting with exaggerated and hyperbolic performances of glamour that exposes the constructedness of this category, and therefore making it vulnerable to deconstruction. Through this act of critical deconstruction, the heroines reject this performance of emphasised femininity and adopt alternative forms of adolescent femininity, including Hayley's sustained deployment of a 'tomboy' aesthetic. Aquamarine similarly rejects glamorous femininity as she finally refuses to participate in sexist codes that govern feminine attractiveness and the privileging of heteronormative masculine desires. Rejecting these codes, and the romantic advances of the 'Prince' Raymond, Aquamarine instead escapes to the ultraliminal ocean space with her communitas of Hayley and Claire.

While they swim through the glittering waves and activate their magical mermaid powers, colourful bubbles and glittering sparkles surround them and crowd the frame. These images of glitter and sparkles are dissociated from emphasised femininity, the primary purpose of which is to secure the attention and affection of men. Instead, the exuberant bubbles and sparkles overwhelm the frame as a visualisation and signifier of the heroines' access to collective power, autonomy and agency. Furthermore, these floating, bubbling images align the mermaid heroines with a sense of free-flowing flexibility as they pursue alternative girlhood identities in this space. In this space of ultraliminality, Aquamarine and her friends imagine and pursue feminist futures for themselves: they reject heterosexual romance as the defining factor of their rite of passage; they resist adult patriarchal authority; they construct an all-girl communitas of support and solidarity; and they undertake brave and independent adventures. The glitter aesthetic presents a resistant image that sustains a critical function, rejecting status quo constructions of glamorous girlhood and constructing a visual language of the girl's agency and power.

These audio-visual constructions of adolescent ultraliminality intervene the clear 'single certainties' that work to govern girlhood and its rigid boundaries (Pomerantz 2008), providing an opportunity to perforate and expand these boundaries on the teen screen. Single certainties only allow for patriarchal constructions of hegemonic girlhood; as Pomerantz writes, they deny the potential for fluid representations of girls and 'seek to paint girlhood with one brush and in one colour' (161). Throughout the film, the heroines strategically perform exaggerated public displays of femininity that render the performance strange, and then rebel against the single certainties of girlhood that they are expected to adopt. In particular, I have argued that they resist the primacy of glamorous femininity and the importance of gaining male approval through romance and the one-true-love narrative. *Aquamarine* therefore demonstrates a capacity to challenge these single certainties through the deployment of ultraliminality and acts of noncompliance. Through these ruptures, the heroines find ways to expand the field of girlhood as they chart flexible feminine adolescent identities and voices. In this way, *Aquamarine* is able to increase the 'circumference of the visible' of girlhood (Haraway quoted in Pomerantz 2009, 155), to go beyond the dominant hegemonic models and engineer a feminist mermaid tale for the contemporary teen screen.

NOTE

1. The silent woman in the cinema has also been conceived of in some instances as a figure of protest against gendered norms and expectations, as in Jane Campion's *The Piano* (1994).

BIBLIOGRAPHY

Andersen, Hans Christian. [1837] 2008. The Little Mermaid. In *The Annotated Hans Christian Andersen*, trans. Maria Tatar and Julie K. Allen and ed. Maria Tatar, 119–155. New York and London: W.W. Norton and Co.

Bartky, Sandra Lee. 1990. *Femininity and Domination: Studies in the Phenomenology of Oppression*. New York and London: Routledge.

Bordo, Susan. 1985. Anorexia Nervosa: Psychopathology as the Crystallisation of Culture. *The Philosophical Forum* 17 (2): 73–104.

———. 1993. *Unbearable Weight: Feminism, Western Culture, and the Body*. Berkeley: University of California Press.

Butler, Judith. 1999. *Gender Trouble: Feminism and the Subversion of Identity*. New York: Routledge.

Cowdy, Cheryl. 2012. Resistant Rituals: Self-mutilation and the Female Adolescent Body in Fairy Tales and Young Adult Fiction. *Bookbird: A Journal of International Children's Literature* 50 (1): 42–52. doi:10.1353/bkb.2012.0003.

Currie, Dawn H., Deirdre M. Kelly, and Shauna Pomerantz. 2009. *'Girl Power': Girls Reinventing Girlhood*. New York: Peter Lang.

DeVaney, Ann. 2002. Pretty in Pink? John Hughes Reinscribes Daddy's Girl in Homes and Schools. In *Sugar, Spice and Everything Nice: Cinemas of*

Girlhood, ed. Murray Pomerance and Frances Gateward, 201–215. Detroit, MI: Wayne State University Press.

Dickinson, Kay. 2003. Pop, Speed, Teenagers and the "MTV Aesthetic". In *Movie Music, The Film Reader*, ed. Kay Dickinson, 143–151. London and New York: Routledge.

Doane, Mary Ann. 1980. The Voice in the Cinema: The Articulation of Body and Space. *Yale French Studies* 60: 33–50.

Donoghue, Emma. 1997. The Tale of the Voice. In *Kissing the Witch: Old Tales in New Skins*, 185–206. New York: Harper Collins.

Dunn, Leslie and Nancy A. Jones. 1994. Introduction. In *Embodied Voices: Representing Female Vocality in Western Culture*, ed. Leslie Dunn and Nancy A. Jones, 1–13. Cambridge: Cambridge University Press.

Fiske, John. 1998. MTV: Post-structural, Post-modern. In *The Postmodern Presence: Readings on Postmodernism in American Culture and Society*, ed. Arthur Asa Berger, 166–174. Walnut Creek, CA, London, New Delhi: Altamira Press.

Fox-Kales, Emily. 2011. *Body Shots: Hollywood and the Culture of Eating Disorders*. Albany: State University of New York Press.

Galt, Rosalind. 2011. *Pretty: Film and the Decorative Image*. New York and Chichester: Columbia University Press.

Gaines, Jane. 2011. Wanting to Wear Seeing: Gilbert Adrian at MGM. In *Fashion in Film*, ed. Adrienne Munich, 135–159. Bloomington: Indiana University Press.

Golden, Stephanie. 1998. *Slaying the Mermaid: Women and the Culture of Sacrifice*. New York: Harmony Books.

Gonick, Marnina. 1997. Reading Selves, Re-fashioning Identity: Teen Magazines and their Readers. *Curriculum Studies* 5 (1): 69–86.

Hoffman, Alice. 2001. *Aquamarine*. New York: Scholastic.

Hunt, Samantha. 2004. *The Seas*. New York: Picador.

Kearney, Mary Celeste. 2015. Sparkle: Luminosity and Post-Girl Power in Media. *Continuum* 29 (3): 263–273.

Kelly, Deirdre M. and Shauna Pomerantz. 2009. Mean, Wild, and Alienated: Girls and the State of Feminism in Popular Culture. *Girlhood Studies* 2 (1): 1–19. doi:10.3167/ghs.2009020102.

Kotz, Liz. 1992. The Body You Want: Liz Kotz Interviews Judith Butler. *Artforum* 31: 82–89.

Lawrence, Amy. 1991. *Echo and Narcissus: Women's Voices in Classical Hollywood Cinema*. Berkeley, Los Angeles and Oxford: University of California Press.

McRobbie, Angela. 2008. Young Women and Consumer Culture: An Intervention. *Cultural Studies* 22 (5): 531–550. doi:10.1080/09502380802245803.

Moseley, Rachel. 2002. Glamorous Witchcraft: Gender and Magic in Teen Film and Television. *Screen* 43 (4): 403–422.

Mulvey, Laura. [1975] 1989. Visual Pleasure and Narrative Cinema. In *Visual and Other Pleasures*, 14–26. Bloomington and Indianapolis: Indiana University Press.

Nash, Ilana. 2015. The Princess and the Teen Witch: Fantasies of the Essential Self. In *Princess Cultures: Mediating Girls' Imaginations and Identities*, ed. Miriam Forman-Brunell and Rebecca C. Haines, 3–23. New York: Peter Lang.

Norris, Pamela. 1998. *The Story of Eve*. London and Basingstoke: Picador.

Pomerantz, Shauna. 2008. *Girls, Style, and School Identities: Dressing the Part*. New York and Basingstoke: Palgrave Macmillan.

———. 2009. Between a Rock and a Hard Place: Un/Defining the "Girl". *Jeunesse: Young People, Texts, Cultures* 1 (2): 147–158.

Projansky, Sarah. 2014. *Spectacular Girls: Media Fascination and Celebrity Culture*. New York and London: New York University Press.

Renold, Emma and Jessica Ringrose. 2008. Regulation and Rupture: Mapping Tween and Teenage Girls' Resistance to the Heterosexual Matrix. *Feminist Theory* 9: 313–338. doi:10.1177/1464700108095854.

Rowe, Kathleen. 1995. *The Unruly Woman: Gender and the Genres of Laughter*. Austin: University of Texas Press.

Russ, Joanna. [1978] 1986. Russalka *or* The Seacoast of Bohemia. In *Don't Bet on the Prince: Contemporary Feminist Fairy Tales in North America and England*, ed. Jack Zipes, 88–94. Aldershot and New York: Gower.

Sells, Laura. 1995. "Where Do the Mermaids Stand?" Voice and Body in *The Little Mermaid*. In *From Mouse to Mermaid: The Politics of Film, Gender and Culture*, ed. Elizabeth Bell, Lynda Haas, and Laura Sells, 175–192. Bloomington and Indianapolis: Indiana University Press.

Shaw, Melissa Lee. 1999. The Sea Hag. In *Silver Birch, Blood Moon*, ed. Ellen Datlow and Terri Windling. New York: Open Road.

Silverman, Kaja. 1988. *The Acoustic Mirror: The Female Voice in Psychoanalysis and Cinema*. Bloomington and Indianapolis: Indiana University Press.

Sjorgren, Britta. 2006. *Into the Vortex: Female Voice and Paradox in Film*. Urbana and Chicago: University of Illinois Press.

Sparke, Penny. 1995. *As Long as it's Pink: The Sexual Politics of Taste*. London: Pandora.

Speed, Lesley. 1995. Good Fun and Bad Hair Days: Girls in Teen Film. *Metro Magazine* 101: 24–30.

———. 2002. Reading, Writing, and Unruliness: Female Education in the *St. Trinian's* Films. *International Journal of Cultural Studies* 5: 221–238. doi:10.1177/1367877902005002572.

Szakolczai, Arpad. 2007. Image-Magic in *A Midsummer Night's Dream*: Power and Modernity from Weber to Shakespeare. *History of the Human Sciences* 20 (4): 1–26. doi:10.1177/0952695107082488.

———. 2012. *Comedy and the Public Sphere: The Rebirth of Theatre as Comedy and the Genealogy of the Modern Public Arena*. Hoboken, NJ: Taylor and Francis.

———. 2013. *The Genesis of Modernity*. Hoboken, NJ: Taylor and Francis.

Trites, Roberta. 1991. Disney's Sub/Version of Andersen's *The Little Mermaid*. *Journal of Popular Film and Television* 18 (4): 145–152.

Turner, Victor. 1969. *The Ritual Process: Structure and Anti-structure*. Chicago: Aldine Publishing Company.

———. 1974. *Dramas, Fields, and Metaphors*. Ithaca, NY and London: Cornell University Press.

———. 1982. *From Ritual to Theatre: The Human Seriousness of Play*. New York: Performing Arts Journal Publications.

Viorst, Judith. 1984. ...And Although the Little Mermaid Sacrificed Everything to Win the Love of the Prince, the Prince (Alas) Decided to Wed Another. In *If I Were In Charge of the World and Other Worries*, 30–31. New York: Aladdin Paperbacks.

Walkerdine, Valerie. 1993. Girlhood through the Looking Glass. In *Girls, Girlhood and Girls' Studies in Transition*, ed. Marion de Ras and Mieke Lunenberg, 9–24. Amsterdam: Het Spinhuis.

Warner, Marina. 1995. *From the Beast to the Blonde: On Fairy Tales and their Tellers*. London: Vintage.

White, Susan. 1993. Split Skins: Female Agency and Bodily Mutilation in *The Little Mermaid*. In *Film Theory Goes to the Movies*, ed. Jim Collins, Hilary Radner, and Ava Collins Preacher, 182–195. New York and London: Routledge.

Williams, Christy. 2010. Mermaid Tales on Screen: Splash, The Little Mermaid, and Aquamarine. In *Beyond Adaptation: Essays on Radical Transformations of Original Works*, ed. Phyllis Frus and Christy Williams, 194–205. Jefferson, NC and London: McFarland and Co.

Filmography

Aquamarine. Dir. Elizabeth Allen. 2006.

H2O Just Add Water. ABC. 2006–2010.

H2O: Mermaid Adventures. Netflix. 2015– .

The Little Mermaid. Dirs. Ron Clements and John Musker. 1989.

The Little Mermaid. Dirs. Chris Bouchard and Blake Harris. 2017.

The Lure. Dir. Agnieszka Smoczynska. 2015.

Mako: Island of Secrets. ZDF Enterprises. 2013– .

Mermaids. Dir. Ian Barry. 2003.

A Mermaid's Tale. Dir. Dustin Rikert. 2016.

The Piano. Dir. Jane Campion. 1994.

Red Riding Hood. Dir. Catherine Hardwicke. 2011.

CHAPTER 7

Conclusion: Rituals of Girlhood Transformed on the Teen Screen

The fairy tale, as Marina Warner writes, contradictorily bends 'towards acquiescence on the one hand and rebellion on the other' (1995, 409). While the fairy tale has been mobilised for profoundly conservative purposes, it also contains an interest in 'forbidden territories' where 'received ideas' can be attacked and 'potential conduits of another way of seeing the world, of telling an alternative story,' are explored (415). This contradiction is at the heart of this book, which has explored the ways in which the fairy tale provides constrained images of the girlhood rite of passage, and yet at the same time how its narrativisation of unruly transgressions of prohibition can come to include positive representations of girls who resist such constraints. I have charted the phase of adolescent liminality in the feminine fairy tale rite-of-passage narrative, where conventional rules and restrictions temporarily dissolve. Violating prohibitions precipitates change, or metamorphosis, which is a key theme of the fairy tale. In the teen fairy tales under analysis, metamorphosis is principally figured as the transformation that occurs when the girl comes to knowledge, particularly forbidden knowledge that is ordinarily denied her. This is often knowledge about mechanisms and abuses of masculine power, and discovering ways to resist it. Where the canonical fairy tale characterises the girl's curiosity and desire to know as a punishable vice, these revisions work to characterise knowledge as power and an instigator of social change in the heroine's world.

Resistance is a key theme in the revisions, and it takes place in the liminal portion of the girl's rite-of-passage journey. Liminality's energy of

© The Author(s) 2017
A. Bellas, *Fairy Tales on the Teen Screen*,
DOI 10.1007/978-3-319-64973-3_7

upheaval, flux, play, rebellion, protest and experimentation produces representations that unsettle received ideas about girlhood. And as a result of this destabilisation, a range of alternative rituals of girlhood emerge on the teen screen. These alternative rituals include fostering solidarity and community building between girls; critically reflecting on and countering the demands of emphasised femininity; carving out new spaces to occupy in traditionally male-dominated arenas such as city streets and the economic marketplace; and creating and distributing girl-authored media online. The fantasy production of alternative ways of doing girlhood is a key aspect of these teen screen representations of liminality. Theorising liminality for a feminist agenda offers a way of reading the political potential of the teen screen's representations of girls' rites of passage. The liminal journey is a flight from conventional culture and an opening up to the unknown, where the ritual subject can experiment with multiple different ways of being and behaving. Crossing the threshold from the everyday into the magical forest, the ocean, the chamber of secrets and the world of dreams provides expansive realms in which other ways of doing girlhood are made possible for the heroines.

While princess culture is certainly a pervasive part of contemporary girls' fairy tale narratives, there are also important alternatives that run throughout these stories of transformation. One-true-love fantasies, makeover narratives that focus on the girl becoming desirable and cautionary tales that idealise feminine adolescent docility and compliance are still frequently reproduced in contemporary teen fairy tale screen media, and seem to be particularly influenced by the enduring legacy of Disney's authoritative versions of the tales. At the same time, the transgressive potential at the heart of the fairy tale can also provide a space to imagine more resistant rituals of girlhood. These dual impulses frequently seem to be in play in contemporary revisions of the tales. As Cristina Bacchilega writes, there are fairy tale texts 'actively selling the idea that in our hypermodern citified lives, girls and women wish to be consumed by fairy tales that buy us a pink and glittery happiness', but that there are films on the other end of the spectrum, that 'kindle a sense of opportunity' to go beyond these limits (2013, 83–84). Importantly, she notes that 'hegemonic and counterhegemonic uses of the fairy tale are not in binary opposition to each other' in film, but rather produce 'multiple images of the fairy-tale genre and its phantasmatic relation to our social world, images that do not replace one another in a narrative of progress but are in active competition with one another' (107).

Twenty-first-century teen texts often contain both hegemonic and counter-hegemonic deployments of the fairy tale, demonstrating not only the flexibility of this narrative form, but also the contemporary ambivalence about feminine adolescence and the girlhood rite of passage towards womanhood.

Contemporary teen fairy tales often reflect the ambivalence noted by Bacchilega. Within the postfeminist media culture that these texts circulate in, girls' coming-of-age narratives often celebrate 'girl power', but often only when the girl remains within the confines of conventional femininity. So while the girls of *A Cinderella Story*, Bill Condon's recent film *Beauty and the Beast* and *The Princess Diaries* may be represented as clever, brave, outspoken and able to save themselves when in danger, attaining heterosexual romance and male approval are frequently depicted as the pinnacle of success and fulfilment in their rites of passage. They are girl-powerful, but within limits. Furthermore, while these fairy tale journeys contain moments of liminal upheaval, they are also at pains to completely circumvent it by the end of the story, producing a reassuring and conventional narrative of linear progress towards womanhood. In this book, I have chosen to examine texts that significantly extend the liminal period, either through the promise of ultraliminality that continues beyond the close of the narrative, as in *Red Riding Hood* and *Aquamarine*, or through a serial narrative format that delays narrative closure, as in *Twilight*, *Pretty Little Liars* and *Gossip Girl*. This liminal space is one of ambiguity and flux, where the girl often takes on roles beyond those conventionally assigned her. The girls in the texts under analysis in this book are witches, hunters, travellers, investigators, authors and creators, and often articulate a protest or resistance to the ways in which their progress towards womanhood is monitored and judged by adult patriarchal culture.

I have found moments of feminist politics being articulated on the teen screen, but I also acknowledge the limits of these articulations of feminism. For example, while *Twilight*'s Bella does rebel against some of the normalising strictures of feminine adolescent development, she is nevertheless inducted into the roles of wife and mother at the end of her rite of passage, and while *Gossip Girl*'s heroines construct a variety of protests against adult male power, the text also represents conspicuous consumption and makeover rituals as key to their power and pleasure. Rather than seeing these ambivalences and contradictions as an undermining of potentially progressive elements in the text, it is fruitful to attend to the ways that discourses of girlhood are both delimited and disrupted on the teen screen. This allows us to consider the complex ways in which postfeminist and feminist discourses circulate within girls' media culture, and how both these discourses inform how girls are represented onscreen. As Mary Celeste Kearney writes, 'while many previous research projects on girls' media culture have used feminist theory to understand the construction of gender in media texts, producers, and consumers, few scholars have focused specifically on the role of feminist politics in girls' media culture' (2011, 5). By examining how girls' interventions into patriarchal culture can be represented on the teen screen, I have read teen screen media to highlight their potential feminist political function, particularly by focusing on texts that feature heroines who critically reflect on and challenge their subordinate position as girls in contemporary patriarchal culture.

The texts under analysis challenge and revise the limiting, prescriptive feminine rite-of-passage narratives of canonical literary fairy tales written by Charles Perrault, the Brothers Grimm and Hans Christian Andersen. I claim that these earlier texts become sites for moments of feminist intervention into conservative and hegemonic rituals of feminine acculturation on the contemporary teen screen. In *Red Riding Hood*, *Twilight*, *Pretty Little Liars*, *Gossip Girl* and *Aquamarine* the heroines confront the patriarchal order by challenging the conventional rites of passage and rituals of 'acceptable' adolescent femininity as defined by this order. These screen texts represent teen girls who refuse to perform many of these social codes and rituals, which include the privileging of heterosexual romance as central to the girl's fulfilment; styling and presenting the feminine body for a male gaze in ways deemed attractive by dominant patriarchal standards; acquiescing to adult masculine authority; and keeping out of spaces traditionally defined as male dominated. These moments of noncompliance and resistance are evidence that the teen screen can indeed include representations of feminine adolescent opposition to the status quo.

The teen films and television series under analysis all work to create new narratives out of older texts for a contemporary teen girl audience. Theorising this confrontation between the contemporary screen text and the earlier literary fairy tale texts of Perrault, the Brothers Grimm and Andersen has required wide research that ranges across feminist fairy tale scholarship, feminist cultural, film and television theory, and girlhood studies. The scope and range of this research is grounded in an interrogation of the position of women and girls in patriarchal fairy tale narratives across literature, film and television, as well as theorising how these structures can be challenged and renegotiated. Inspired by Jean-Louis Comolli and Jean Narboni's work on the 'progressive text' ([1969] 2004) and the feminist 'against the grain' analyses that developed in its wake (see de Lauretis 1984; Klinger 1984, 1994; Gledhill 1987), I have developed a similar mode of analysis that looks for the gaps, fissures and political potential for ruptures in screen texts that may initially appear 'ideologically conservative' (Klinger 1984, 38). Focusing on teen screen aesthetics and paying close attention to representations of girls' voices and use of language has highlighted subversive moments in which the heroines not only talk back to patriarchal power figures, but also articulate alternative configurations of girlhood. Through unruly vocal interjections such as shouting, singing and laughing, as well as dominating the soundtrack through omniscient voice-over narration, the heroines of these texts create resistant counter-discourses. Through the development of a feminist optic that focuses on teen screen aesthetics, I have also argued that the heroines in these texts create visual languages of opposition through their deployment of spectacle, excess, fashion and prettiness. The pretty's ability to unsettle patriarchal imagery and structures of the gaze carves out a space for a new visual language of feminine adolescent subjectivity, opposition and power to be expressed on the teen screen. By using the feminist optic to develop close readings of undervalued formal elements of teen screen texts such as glitter, hypersaturated colours, girl culture objects and fashion as sites of potential political potency, I hope to have provided an innovative, feminist formal analysis that enriches teen screen studies, girlhood studies and feminist screen studies in general because it expands the possibilities for identifying the articulation of a feminist politics on the teen screen.

While most of the major studies of the teen screen to date do not attend to the formal structure of the texts under analysis in great detail, I have countered this dominant research method throughout this book. I have closely analysed teen film and television's formal audiovisual structures for sites of rupture and dislocation in hegemonic representations and narratives of femininity. As resistant space, this rupture is the precise location of the teen text's feminist, political potential because it provides the opportunity for girls to exceed the confines of hegemonic femininity and pursue identities that go beyond these confines. This approach to the formal analysis of the teen screen has enabled me to identify and read important threads of agency, critique and rebellion in girl culture objects, aesthetics and visual motifs, thus contributing to the wider contemporary feminist project that seeks to interrogate the dismissal of these screen elements as well as revalue them and their political potential.

'DOING GIRLHOOD' ON SCREEN

I have mobilised a feminist poststructuralist methodology that analyses onscreen expressions of 'doing girlhood' (Currie et al. 2009), examining how the agency and resistance made possible by doing girlhood can disrupt the status quo. I argue that this theoretical concept diversifies how girls and girlhoods are thought about, including previously unconsidered and challenging possibilities and therefore expanding the field of feminine adolescence into new territories of power and empowerment. As I have elaborated in detail, feminist poststructuralism is invested in both deconstructing the means by which women and girls are oppressed in patriarchal culture, as well as looking for the gaps and fissures in this structure that hold the potential for transformation of gendered power imbalance and inequality. Locating attention in these disruptive gaps and fissures uncovers the moments at which the strictures of patriarchal culture are ruptured and contested on the teen screen.

My feminist poststructuralist methodology has built on Foucault's theorisation of power and transgression. I have used these concepts to theorise how girls are not simply subjugated by official and institutionalised power structures of dominant patriarchal culture, but also agents within the power network. Like other girlhood studies scholars such as Shauna Pomerantz (2008), Mary Celeste Kearney (2010) and Catherine Driscoll (2002), I have used Michel Foucault's theorisation of power because it can be reinterpreted in the context of patriarchal power, and how this governmentality keeps girls and women subordinate. Redeploying Foucault's theory within the context of feminist poststructuralist analysis allows for an account of how this gendered subordination occurs, and how patriarchal power works. I hope to have illuminated this through analyses of the politics of the male and panoptic gazes, abuses of adult masculine power, the regulation of girlhood through beauty regimes, adult panoptic constructions of feminine development and the enforcement of compulsory heterosexuality in the texts. However, like the feminist theorists listed above, I have also used Foucault's theorisation of the narrow margin of transgression that emerges in moving 'between power's threads' (1980, 98). I have argued that in this narrow margin it is possible for the heroines of the texts under analysis to enact gestures of noncompliance to this power as they contest institutionalised and official channels of governance and authority. Feminine adolescence emerges as a phase and stage that is both constrained, limited, surveiled and monitored by adult masculine regulation and authority, but also expanding and shifting through girls' gestures of opposition, resistance, questioning and refusal in the face of that power. I have argued that in this marginal space the heroines are able to enact their opposition and protest most clearly and powerfully, and that these resistances represent feminist interventions into patriarchal constructions of hegemonic femininity.

I have also engaged very closely with Victor Turner's theorisation of liminality as a form of in-betweenness, an interstructural or even antistructural moment where everyday hierarchies and power structures temporarily dissolve, breaking down into an unsettled field of possibilities. I have redeployed Turner's theory to explore the potential for opposition, resistance and transformation in liminality on the teen screen, and the extent to which it can impact upon the heroine's reincorporation into conventional culture in the postliminal phase. An exciting prospect is what Turner calls 'a kind of institutional capsule or pocket which contains the germ of future social developments, of societal change' within liminality (1982, 45). The innovations enacted in the liminal zone hold within them the potential to create social change. This possibility is staged more successfully in some of the texts under analysis than others, and I have argued that it is in the texts that represent female solidarity in all-girl communitas'—collectives of liminal ritual subjects—that the heroines are able to create a particularly meaningful and lasting impact on their postliminal return to dominant culture. I argue that an analysis of communitas in teen girl screen media provides a new paradigm for analysing representations of girls' friendships, solidarity and collective action against the status quo.

THE FAIRY TALE'S NEW UNRULY PATHS

The screen texts under analysis hybridise the fairy tale and teen genres to produce new outcomes for the representation of the feminine adolescent rite of passage. By narrativising moments of rupture these revisions of the fairy tale are able to unleash the subversive voices, narratives and identities that the earlier literary fairy tale texts by Perrault, the Grimms and Andersen excluded or repressed. This act of splitting or rupturing represents a moment of feminist intervention into the gendered politics of these canonical narratives, and the myths they perpetuate about girls and women.

These teen screen revisions counteract the fairy tale narrative which is traditionally structured around masculine authority, often embodied by the valiant Prince and the interdicting narrator's moral resolution to the tale, coupled with the relative powerlessness and vulnerability of the young female character, especially in those versions written by Perrault, the Brothers Grimm and Andersen. From a contemporary feminist perspective, these earlier fairy tale texts rely upon a clear gender inequality that consistently and clearly narrativises the girl's acquiescence to masculine power. Karlyn Crowley and John Pennington rightly argue that the best contemporary feminist rewritings of fairy tales 'rattle the foundational cages of the tale where the power structures reside' (2010, 304). The female-authored revisions under analysis reveal a self-reflexive awareness of the structural inequalities that govern the girl's position in the fairy tale narrative, as well as a desire to create alternatives to these dominant structures. In each teen screen text under analysis, the revised fairy tale rite of passage narrative hinges on a resistant challenge and refusal of the conventional power structures that govern and delimit the heroine's life, followed by an innovative and agentic assertion of alternative ways of doing girlhood.

Each chapter has charted unruly liminal paths through the fairy tale. These paths include escape routes from conventional culture (*Red Riding Hood*; *Twilight*); acts of trespass and violations of prohibition that provoke heroines to take action against instances of patriarchal violence (*Pretty Little Liars*); invasion of domains traditionally associated with masculine power (*Gossip Girl*); and expansive, flexible terrains that make way for feminist futures (*Aquamarine*). These new paths through the fairy tale create opportunities to explore and chart new, previously unconsidered territories in these narratives. Whereas all the earlier literary fairy tale texts under analysis maintained girls in positions of acquiescence, powerlessness and voicelessness—as helpless maidens, comatose beauties or glamorous damsels—the contemporary heroines' navigation of new paths through the fairy tale narrative allow them to contest these limiting positions, pushing against them and working to expand beyond them. Bacchilega argues that contemporary 'disenchantments' of the fairy tale are 'directly related to a now-public dissatisfaction with its magic as trick or (ultimately disempowering) deception, a disillusionment with the reality of the social conditions that canonised tales of magic idealise' (2013, 5). To counter these idealised social conditions, Bacchilega writes that contemporary revisions of fairy tales offer a 'symbolic enactment of possibilities ... to explore alternatives we hope for' (5). Here Bacchilega identifies a contemporary tendency to disenchant the earlier text's magic spell, a refusal of its illusions. But rather than necessarily breaking the spell, its magic can be transformed and redirected towards a different outcome. As she elaborates, 'magic and pacifying enchantment are not the only poetics of the fairy tale', and that we must equally attend to the element of wonder that magic generates (5). Of this she writes, '[f]airy tales can invite us to dwell is astonishment and explore new possibilities, to engage in *wondering* and *wandering*. It is in this symbolic enactment of possibilities ... and taking us *ex-cursus*, off course or off socially sanctioned paths...[that fairy tales are] wonder producing' (5 original emphases). The use of fairy tale wonder to explore possibilities, unexpected narrative paths and new configurations of the girl's rite-of-passage journey invites us to contemplate girlhood beyond the conventional and the dominant.

The unsettled and undecided zone of fairy tale liminality provides a location for the heroines under analysis to intervene into rituals of girlhood in innovative and oppositional ways. The heroines of these contemporary revisions all enact multiple possibilities and alternatives for new iterations of girlhood, to use Bacchilega's formulation. These alternatives include the challenging iterations found in the screen texts under analysis, allowing the fairy tale heroine to step into the revisionary roles of hunter, lone traveller, detective and reporter. Resisting, protesting against and exposing the systemic abuses of violence against girls and women in the power structures of dominant culture, these heroines find ways to creatively intervene into realms in which girls have been traditionally disempowered. These teen screen revisions of fairy tales are especially interesting for the ways in which the girl's narrative rite of passage unfolds, expanding the possibilities beyond the binary fairy tale closure of conventional heterosexual romantic fulfilment as reward or violent death as punishment. I have argued that this expansion pushes the fairy tale's representation of the feminine rite of passage into more challenging terrains, as the heroines find ways to seize both personal and collective girl-centred power in the liminal realm.

Opposition and Agency: Expanding the Terrain in Future Research

All of the primary screen texts I discussed in this book were produced in the US context, and all were relatively mainstream productions. My intention has been to highlight the fact that teen fairy tale narratives, even those in the mainstream, can include representations of alternative girls. An account of girls' fairy tale media must go beyond automatic assumptions that mainstream texts are inherently regressive or conservative, and instead look for points of ambivalence and resistance wherever they arise. To expand on this project, future work on teen screen revisions of fairy tales could explore a range of other national and historical contexts, media formats and media makers. Fairy tale films about girls such as Australia's *Girl Asleep* (Myers 2015), Catherine Breillat's French films *Barbe Bleue* (2009) and *La Belle Endormie* (2010), Guillermo del Toro's Spanish film *Pan's Labyrinth* (2016), Korean horror films *A Tale of Two Sisters* (Jee-woon Kim 2003) and *Sin-de-rel-la* (Man-dae Bong 2006), the Polish horror musical *The Lure* (Smoczynska 2015), the Danish werewolf film *When Animals Dream* (Arnby 2014) and the Japanese animations *Ponyo* (Miyazaki 2008) and *The Tale of the Princess Kaguya* (Takahata 2013) demonstrate that the interest in fairy tale feminine rites of passage extend beyond the US context. Queer girls' fairy tale texts such as Hulu's recent online short *Rosaline* (Errico 2016) and Jamie Babbit's short *Sleeping Beauties* (1999) provide an opportunity to consider contemporary interventions into the heterosexist narrative outcomes of the authoritative versions of fairy tales by Perrault, the Grimms and Andersen, as well as Disney. These texts focus on a range of girls' points of view, voices and gazes, and an analysis of how these elements may work to create alternative, challenging, oppositional and agentic representations of girlhood on the teen screen would continue to enrich and expand the analysis of the teen screen that I have conducted in this book.

The methodology established in this book offers a base for further research and the continued expansion of the field. This methodology explicates the emergence of alternative iterations of girl's voices and identities that unsettle dominant constructions of feminine adolescence. Therefore, many other alternative expressions and experiences of adolescent femininity that do not conform to a straight, white, middle-class perspective can be explored further. For example, many girlhood studies scholars are starting to point out the relative absence of queer girls, 'crip'[1] girls and girls of colour in girlhood and teen film studies (Mazzarella and Pecora 2007, 117; Kearney 2011, 11; Berridge 2013, 480). Such an absence invisibilises and silences these diverse experiences and perspectives of girls who may not conform to a variety of status quo expectations of what a 'girl' should be, look like and behave.[2] To begin to remedy this gap in the discourse, Projansky argues that it is of political importance for feminist scholars to seek out and write about non-hegemonic girls in media such as film, television and celebrity gossip magazines (2014, 11). This is vital because the identification of these alternative girlhoods validates and makes them visible, thus activating their cultural power. As Projansky writes, 'various alternative girls—often girls of colour and/or queer girls—are right there, right in front of us in the vast mediascape' (17). Attending to these alternatives is a positive move for further scholarly research into fairy tale revisions in teen girl screen media.

This would contribute to the feminist project of going beyond status quo assumptions about girls and 'appropriate' or 'acceptable' femininities more generally, combating the ways in which many expressions of feminine adolescence are invisibilised, minimised and even excluded from the discussion of girlhood.

Furthermore, in order to emphasise and advance the study of 'doing girlhood' on the teen screen, the analysis of contemporary girl filmmakers' active work of producing representations of adolescent femininity could fruitfully expand the discourse in powerful ways. Some scholars have analysed the cinema of girl filmmakers such as Sadie Benning and other members of the riot grrrl movement, in the 1990s and early 2000s (see for example Carter 1998; Milliken 2002). This work has been important in the shift towards recognising girls as agentic cultural producers, challenging discourses that position girls as 'mere' consumers of screen media. Other work considering girls as 'prosumers' of popular culture has also emerged more recently, exploring girl-made media such as fan fiction, zines, fan videos and blogs (Black 2008; Piepmeier 2009; Burwell 2010; Parrish 2010; Day 2014).However, far more work can be done in this field, especially through a feminist poststructuralist methodology, in the exploration of how contemporary girl filmmakers present their multiple versions of doing girlhood onscreen. Kearney has strongly advocated the development of this scholarship, writing that girls' filmmaking can powerfully 'engage directly with the ideologies of gender and generation prevalent in popular culture and contradictorily experienced by female youth' (2003, 32). This work would also further the theorisation of girls' DIY, which was elaborated in Chap. 5 exploration of sartorial design on *Gossip Girl*. As Kearney argues:

> if scholars involved in the field of girls' studies desire to keep current with the state of female youth and their cultural practices, we must expand the focus of our analyses to include not only texts produced for girls by the adult-run mainstream culture industries, but also those cultural artefacts created by girls. (1998, 286)

An analysis of girl-made media would further the feminist project's focus on female authorship, because it would continue to expand the discourse on, and draw attention to, the work of female film and media-makers of multiple generations. It would also counter the imbalance of power relations in which girls have been traditionally afforded little control over image-making processes, thus opening up new networks of relations between media production, the gaze and spectatorship in ways that may be beneficial to girls. This book has worked to challenge this imbalance by focusing on representations of girls who produce and establish authority over the screen image. However, a further focus on the analysis of girl-made media would also contribute greatly to correcting this disparity because it would assert the importance of girls as cultural producers, negotiating and remaking rituals of girlhood through creative practice. This would also attune feminist analyses to important new resistances and innovations in the production and reception of the field of possibilities for girlhood on screen.

NOTES

1. Disability studies scholar Carrie Sandahl writes that the term 'crip' 'has expanded to include not only those with physical impairments but those with sensory or mental impairments as well' (2003, 27).
2. This is not to suggest that analyses of these varieties of representations of girls have been completely absent in the scholarship. For example, writers such as Moya Luckett (1997), Alison Burgess (2008), Susan Driver (2007) and Kirsten Pike (2011) have examined representations of queer girls in film and television.

Bibliography

Bacchilega, Cristina. 2013. *Fairy Tales Transformed? Twenty-First-Century Adaptations and the Politics of Wonder*. Detroit, MI: Wayne State University Press.

Berridge, Susan. 2013. Teen Heroine TV: Narrative Complexity and Sexual Violence in Female-Fronted Teen Drama Series. *New Review of Film and Television Studies* 11 (4): 477–496. doi:10.3366/jbctv.2013.0175.

Black, Rebecca W. 2008. *Adolescents and Online Fan Fiction*. New York: Peter Lang.

Burgess, Allison. 2008. There's Something Queer Going on in Orange County: The Representation of Queer Women's Sexuality in *The O.C.* In *Televising Queer Women: A Reader*, ed. Rebecca Beirne, 211–227. New York and Basingstoke: Palgrave Macmillan.

Burwell, Catherine. 2010. Rewriting the Script: Toward a Politics of Young People's Digital Media Participation. *The Review of Education, Pedagogy, and Cultural Studies* 32: 382–402. doi:10.1080/10714413.2010.510354.

Carter, Mia. 1998. The Politics of Pleasure: Cross-Cultural Autobiographic Performance in the Video Works of Sadie Benning. *Signs* 23 (3): 745–769. http://www.jstor.org/stable/3175309.

Comolli, Jean-Louis and Jean Narboni. [1969] 2004. Cinema/Ideology/Criticism. In *Film Theory and Criticism: Introductory Readings*, ed. Leo Braudy and Marshall Cohen, 812–819. New York: Oxford University Press.

Crowley, Karlyn, and John Pennington. 2010. Feminist Frauds on the Fairies? Didacticism and Liberation in Recent Retellings of *Cinderella*. *Marvels & Tales* 24 (2): 297–313.

Currie, Dawn H., Deirdre M. Kelly, and Shauna Pomerantz. 2009. *'Girl Power': Girls Reinventing Girlhood*. New York: Peter Lang.

Day, Sarah K. 2014. Pure Passion: The Twilight Saga, 'Abstinence Porn', and Adolescent Women's Fan Fiction. *Children's Literature Association Quarterly* 39 (1): 28–48. doi:10.1353/chq.2014.0014.

de Lauretis, Teresa. 1984. *Alice Doesn't: Feminism, Semiotics, Cinema*. Bloomington: Indiana University Press.

Driscoll, Catherine. 2002. *Girls: Feminine Adolescence in Popular Culture and Cultural Theory*. New York: Columbia University Press.

Driver, Susan. 2007. Girls Look at Girls Looking for Girls: The Visual Pleasures and Social Empowerment of Queer Teen Romance Flicks. In *Youth Culture and Global Cinema*, ed. Timothy Shary and Alexandra Seibel, 241–255. Austin: University of Texas Press.

Foucault, Michel. 1980. *The History of Sexuality:*, vol. One. London: Penguin.

Gledhill, Christine (ed.). 1987. *Home is Where the Heart Is: Studies in Melodrama and the Woman's Film*. London: BFI Publishing.

Kearney, Mary Celeste. 1998. Producing Girls: Rethinking the Study of Female Youth Culture. In *Delinquents and Debutantes: Twentieth-Century American Girls' Cultures*, ed. Sherrie A. Inness, 285–310. New York and London: New York University Press.

———. 2003. Girls Make Movies. In *Youth Cultures: Texts, Images, and Identities*, ed. Kerry Mallan and Sharyn Pearce, 17–34. Westport, CT: Praeger.

———. 2010. Pink Technology: Mediamaking Gear for Girls. *Camera Obscura* 25 (2): 1–38. doi:10.1215/02705346-2010-001.

———. 2011. Introduction: Girls' Media Studies 2.0. In *Mediated Girlhoods: New Explorations of Girls' Media Culture*, ed. Mary Celeste Kearney, 1–16. New York: Peter Lang.

Klinger, Barbara. 1984. "Cinema/Ideology/Criticism" Revisited: The Progressive Text. *Screen* 25 (1): 30–44.

———. 1994. *Melodrama and Meaning: History, Culture, and the Films of Douglas Sirk*. Bloomington and Indianapolis: Indiana University Press.

Luckett, Moya. 1997. Girl Watchers: Patty Duke and Teen TV. In *The Revolution Wasn't Televised: Sixties Television and Social Conflict*, ed. Lynn Spigel and Michael Curtin, 95–116. New York and London: Routledge.

Mazzarella, Sharon R., and Norma Pecora. 2007. Revisiting Girls Studies'. *Journal of Children and Media* 1 (2): 105–125. doi:10.1080/17482790701339118.

Milliken, Christie. 2002. The Pixel Visions of Sadie Benning. In *Sugar, Spice, and Everything Nice: Cinemas of Girlhood*, ed. Frances Gateward and Murray Pomerance, 285–302. Detroit, MI: Wayne State University Press.

Parrish, Julie. 2010. Back to the Woods: Narrative Revisions in *New Moon* Fan Fiction at Twilighted.net. In *Bitten By Twilight: Youth, Media, and the Vampire Franchise*, ed. Melissa A. Click, Jennifer Stevens Aubrey, and Elizabeth Behm-Morawitz, 173–188. New York: Peter Lang Publishing.

Piepmeier, Alison. 2009. *Girl Zines: Making Media, Doing Feminism*. New York and London: New York University Press.

Pike, Kirsten. 2011. "The New Activists": Girls and Discourses of Citizenship, Liberation, and Femininity in *Seventeen*, 1968–1977. In *Mediated Girlhoods: New Explorations of Girls' Media Culture*, ed. Mary Celeste Kearney, 55–73. New York: Peter Lang.

Pomerantz, Shauna. 2008. *Girls, Style, and School Identities: Dressing the Part*. New York and Basingstoke: Palgrave Macmillan.

Projansky, Sarah. 2014. *Spectacular Girls: Media Fascination and Celebrity Culture*. New York and London: New York University Press.

Sandahl, Carrie. 2003. Cripping the Queer? Intersections of Queer and Crip Identities in Solo Autobiographical Performance. *GLQ* 9 (1): 25–56. http://muse.jhu.edu/journals/journal_oflesbian_and_gay_studies/v009/9.1sandahl.html.

Turner, Victor. 1982. *From Ritual to Theatre: The Human Seriousness of Play.* New York: Performing Arts Journal Publications.

Warner, Marina. 1995. *From the Beast to the Blonde: On Fairy Tales and their Tellers.* London: Vintage.

Filmography

Aquamarine. Dir. Elizabeth Allen. 2006.

Barbe Bleue. Dir. Catherine Breillat. 2009.

Beauty and the Beast. Dir. Bill Condon. 2017.

La Belle Endormie. Dir. Catherine Breillat. 2010.

A Cinderella Story. Dir. Mark Rosman. 2004.

Girl Asleep. Dir. Rosemary Myers. 2015

Gossip Girl. The CW. 2007–2012.

The Lure. Dir. Agnieszka Smoczynska. 2015.

Pan's Labyrinth. Dir. Guillermo del Toro. 2006.

Ponyo. Dir. Hayao Miyazaki. 2008.

Pretty Little Liars. ABC Family. 2010–.

The Princess Diaries. Dir. Garry Marshall. 2001.

Rosaline. Dir. Daniel Errico. 2016.

Sleeping Beauties. Dir. Jamie Babbit. 1999.

Sin-de-rel-la. Dir. Man-dae Bong. 2006.

The Tale of the Princess Kaguya. Dir. Isao Takahata. 2013.

A Tale of Two Sisters. Dir. Jee-woon Kim. 2003.

When Animals Dream. Dir. Jonas Alexander Arnby. 2014.

INDEX

A

'... And Although the Little Mermaid Sacrificed Everything to Win the Love of the Prince, the Prince (Alas) Decided to Wed Another' (Judith Viorst, 1984), 190

Andersen, Hans Christian, 1, 189, 230

Andersen, Victoria, 129

'... And Then The Prince Knelt Down and Tried to Put the Glass Slipper on Cinderella's Foot' (Judith Viorst, [1982] 1986), 148

Ang, Ien, 109

'Ashputtle' (Angela Carter, [1993] 1996), 148

Aquamarine (Alice Hoffman, 2001), 189

Aquamarine (Elizabeth Allen, 2006), 1

Atwood, Margaret, 5, 107

B

Bacchilega, Christina, 2, 5, 6, 14, 39, 50, 107, 120, 228, 234, 235

Badlands (Terrence Malick, 1973), 58

Bakhtin, Mikhail, 30

Barbe Bleue (Catherine Breillat, 2009), 107, 236

Bartky, Sandra Lee, 77, 198

Basile, Giambattista, 75

Baudry, Jean Louis, 142

Bavidge, Jenny, 14

Beastly (Daniel Barnz, 2011), 2

Beauty and the Beast (Bill Condon, 2017), 2

Beauty and the Beast (The CW, 2012–2016), 2

Bedroom culture, 81

Benjamin, Walter, 174

Berridge, Susan, 237

Bettelheim, Bruno, 71

Blackford, Holly Virginia, 41

Black, Rebecca W., 14, 237

Blood and Chocolate (Katja von Garnier, 2007), 37

The Bloody Chamber and Other Stories (Angela Carter, 1979), 107

'The Bloody Chamber' (Angela Carter, [1979] 1996), 107

'Bluebeard' (Charles Perrault, [1697] 2001), 15

© The Editor(s) (if applicable) and The Author(s) 2017
A. Bellas, *Fairy Tales on the Teen Screen*,
DOI 10.1007/978-3-319-64973-3

243

'Bluebeard's Egg' (Margaret Atwood, [1983] 1986), 107

Bordo, Susan, 94, 198

Boy who Cried Werewolf (Eric Bross, 2010), 37

Brake, Mike, 174

Brave (Mark Andrews, Brenda Chapman, Steve Purcell, 2012), 2

Breaking Dawn part 1 (Sean Condon, 2011), 88, 100

Breaking Dawn part 2 (Sean Condon, 2012), 100

'Briar Rose' (Grimm, Jacob and Wilhelm, [1857] 2001), 77

'Briar Rose' (Jane Yolen 1992), 70

'Briar Rose' (Sleeping Beauty), (Ann Sexton, [1971] 1986), 70

Brickman, Barbara Jane, 57

Brolin, Brent C., 142

Brownmiller, Susan, 42

Bruzzi, Stella, 100, 162

Buck-Morss, Susan, 184

Buffy the Vampire Slayer (The WB, 1997–2003), 2, 37

Burgess, Allison, 238

Burwell, Catherine, 13

Butler, Judith, 12, 151

Byers, Michelle, 14, 65

C

Cagney and Lacey (CBS 1981–1988), 123

Campbell, Joseph, 48

Carpenter, Laura M., 82, 108

Carter, Angela, 5, 37, 70, 107, 148

Carter, Erica, 175

Carter, Mia, 237

Cassell, Justine and Meg Cramer, 126

'Cinderella' (Ann Sexton, 1971), 148

Cinderella (Clyde Geronimi, Wilfred Jackson, Hamilton Luske, 1950), 153

Cinderella (Kenneth Branagh, 2015), 2

A Cinderella Story (Mark Rosman, 2004), 2

'Cinderella, or the Little Glass Slipper' (Charles Perrault, [1697] 1982), 153

Cinderella (Robert Iscove, 1997), 148

Clover, Carol J., 108

Communitas, 23, 27–29, 100, 108, 111–114, 120–122, 125–129, 134–138, 140–142, 149, 152, 155, 158, 162–164, 167, 170, 174, 176, 177, 179, 180, 182, 191, 192, 194, 206, 207, 214, 216–219, 221, 233

Comolli, Jean-Louis and Jean Narboni, 25, 93, 231

'The Company of Wolves' (Angela Carter, [1979] 1996), 37

The Company of Wolves (Neil Jordan, 1984), 2, 37

Cornelius, Michael G., 110

Cowdy, Cheryl, 195

Cowie, Elizabeth, 46, 73

Craik, Jennifer, 161

Crary, Jonathan, 177

Creed, Barbara, 49

Criminal Minds (CBS 2005–), 69

Crowley, Karlyn and John Pennington, 234

CSI (CBS 2000–2015), 69

Currie, Dawn H., 12, 151, 201, 232

Cursed (Wes Craven, 2005), 37

D

Day, Sarah K, 237

DeLamotte, Eugenia C., 40

de Lauretis, Teresa, 46

DeVaney, Ann, 212

Dickinson, Kay, 94

Dilley, Kimberly J., 113

Disney, 2, 3, 70, 147–149, 153, 155, 180, 189, 190, 195, 196, 218, 228, 236
Doane, Mary Ann, 55, 116, 155, 196
Do-it-yourself (DIY), 10, 28, 149, 155, 159–161, 163, 165, 167, 173, 177, 180–184, 238
Donoghue, Emma, 5, 148, 190
Driscoll, Catherine, 11, 40, 83, 151, 232
Driver, Susan, 238
Duggan, Anne E., 78
Dunn, Leslie and Nancy A. Jones, 207

E
Eclipse (David Slade, 2010), 100
Edward Scissorhands (Tim Burton, 1990), 2
Ella Enchanted (Gail Carson Levine, 1997), 148
Ella Enchanted (Tommy O'Haver, 2004), 2
Enchanted (Kevin Lima, 2007), 2
Evans, Caroline, 94
Ever After: A Cinderella Story (Andy Tennant, 1998), 148
Everett, Anna, 177

F
Fairy tales
   canonical versions of, 44, 76
   Disney's versions of, 196, 228
   feminist revisions of, 148, 190
Faludi, Susan, 8
Fashion, 8, 10, 12, 24, 28, 149, 152, 153, 159–163, 165, 166, 172, 179, 182, 183, 198, 209, 213, 231
Fay, Carolyn, 77, 86
Final girl, the, 108, 137

Fiske, John, 206
flânerie, 155, 173–177, 182–184
flâneuse, the, 174, 175, 178
Fleenor, Juliann E., 47
Foucault, Michel, 16, 51, 232
Fox-Kales, Emily, 212
Freeway (Matthew Bright, 1996), 2
Friedberg, Anne, 135
Frith, Simon, 174
Frozen (Chris Buck and Jennifer Lee, 2013), 2

G
Gaines, Jane, 93, 155, 209
Galt, Rosalind, 24, 75, 129, 212
Gamman, Lorraine, 123
Garber, Jenny, 81
Garcia, Maria, 16
Gateward, Frances, 16
Gennep, Arnold van, 18
Genz, Stéphanie, 9
Gilligan, Carol, 90
Gill, Rosalind, 9
Ginger Snaps (John Fawcett, 2000), 2, 37
The Glass House (Daniel Sackheim, 2001), 108
Gledhill, Christine, 132
Golden, Stephanie, 196
Gonick, Marnina, 11, 60, 203
Gordon, Rae Beth, 132
Gordon, Tuula, 113
Gossip Girl (The CW, 2017–2012), 1, 141
Gothic genre, 55
Gottschall, Kristina, Susanne Gannon, Jo Lampert, and Kelli McGraw, 97
Greenhill, Pauline, 4
Grimm, Jacob and Wilhelm, 38, 71

H

Haines, Rebecca, 54, 63
Halloween (John Carpenter, 1978), 108
Hanna (Joe Wright, 2011), 38
Hard Candy (David Slade, 2005), 38
Harris, Anita, 9, 81
Hawes, Janice, 84
Hayton, Natalie, 48
Hayward, Jennifer, 80, 154
Heath, Stephen, 142
Heatwole, Alexandra, 147
Heller, Dana, 184
Hennard Dutheil de la Rochère, Martine, 86
Hey, Valerie, 60, 124
Hoffman, Alice, 189
H2O Just Add Water (ABC, 2006–2010), 189
Hollinger, Karen, 56
H2O: Mermaid Adventures (Netflix, 2015–), 189
Huang, Mei, 155
Hunt, Samantha, 190

I

Inness, Sherrie A., 16
In the Cut (Jane Campion, 2003), 107
Into the Woods (Rob Marshall, 2014), 2

J

Jones, Leisha, 11, 110, 111, 128

K

Kaveney, Roz, 14
Kearney, Mary Celeste, 22, 57, 122, 149, 213, 230, 232
Keller, Susan, 174, 175

Kelly, Deirdre M., 9, 60, 72, 211
Klinger, Barbara, 89
Kolbenschlag, Madonna, 74, 75
Kotz, Liz, 210
Kramar, Margaret, 89
Kuhn, Annette, 46

L

La Belle Endormie (Catherine Breillat, 2010), 70, 236
'The Lady of the House of Love' (Angela Carter, [1979] 1996), 70
Lamb, Sharon and Lyn Mikel Brown, 90
Lawrence, Amy, 199, 200
Leavenworth, Maria Lindgren, 80
Lesko, Nancy, 22, 74
Levine, Gail Carson, 148
Lewis, Lisa A., 14
Lieberman, Marcia K, 71, 74, 75
Liminality, 15, 18, 19, 21–23, 26–30, 38, 39, 41, 54, 64, 72, 97, 98, 112, 114, 149, 152, 153, 155, 159, 166, 167, 173, 179, 180, 183, 191, 192, 201, 209, 217–219, 227, 228, 233, 235
  permanent, 28, 39, 191, 217, 218
  public, 28, 149, 153, 155, 159, 166, 167, 172, 180, 201
  temporary, 21. *See also* Ultraliminality
The Little Mermaid (Chris Bouchard and Blake Harris, 2017), 189
'The Little Mermaid' (Hans Christian Anderson, [1837] 2008), 189
The Little Mermaid (Ron Clements and John Musker, 1989), 189
'Little Red Cap' (Jacob and Wilhelm Grimm, [1857] 2001), 44
'Little Red Riding Hood' (Charles Perrault, [1697] 2001), 38

Luckett, Moya, 150, 238
The Lure (Agnieszka Smoczynska, 2015), 190, 236

M

Magazines, 203, 205, 206, 216, 237
Makeovers, 8, 150, 171, 184
Mako: Island of Secrets (ZDF Enterprises. 2013–), 189
Maleficent (Robert Stromberg, 2014), 2, 70
Marshall, Elizabeth, 44
Martin, Adrian, 22
Martin, Deborah, 61
Masquerade, 10, 18, 21, 28, 141, 142, 149–155, 167–173, 179–183
Matrix, Sydney Eve, 4
Mazzarella, Sharon R. and Norma Pecora, 237
McMahon-Coleman, Kimberley and Roslyn Weaver, 61
McRobbie, Angela, 80, 203
Melodrama, 132
Mermaids (Ian Barry, 2003), 189
A Mermaid's Tale (Dustin Rikert 2016), 189
Meyer, Stephenie, 71
Milliken, Christie, 237
Modleski, Tania, 46
Monomyth, 48, 49, 65. *See also* Neomyth
Morawski, Jill G., 19
Moseley, Rachel, 149, 213
Mulvey, Laura, 19, 116, 166
My So-Called Life (ABC 1994–1995), 65

N

Nancy Drew (Andrew Fleming, 2007), 108

Nash, Ilana, 3, 153
Negra, Diane, 72
Negrin, Llewellyn, 131
Neomyth, 49. *See also* Monomyth
The Neon Demon (Nicolas Winding Refn, 2016), 69
Neumann, Iver, 18
New Moon (Chris Weitz, 2010), 72
A Nightmare on Elm Street (Wes Craven, 1984), 108
Nochimson, Martha, 109
Norris, Pamela, 197

O

Ohmer, Susan, 156
Orenstein, Catherine, 43

P

Palmer, Gareth, 184
Panopticon, 51. *See also* Michel Foucault
Pan's Labyrinth (Guillermo del Toro, 2006), 236
Parrish, Julie, 237
The Passion of Joan of Arc (Carl Theodore Dreyer, 1928), 50
Payne, Jenny Gunnarsson, 142
Penelope (Mark Palansky, 2006), 2
Performativity, 18, 151, 155, 162, 165, 169, 170, 181, 182, 193, 210. *See also* Judith Butler
Perrault, Charles, 1, 38, 71, 107, 148, 230
The Piano (Jane Campion, 1994), 222
Piepmeier, Alison, 237
Pike, Kirsten, 160, 238
Pipher, Mary, 90
Platt, Carrie Anne, 71, 80
Polak, Michele, 14
Pomerance, Murray, 16, 127

Pomerantz, Shauna, 17, 160, 175, 232
Ponyo (Hayao Miyazaki, 2008), 236
Postfeminism, 3, 8–10
Postliminality, 19, 26, 27, 72, 88, 98
Poststructuralism, 17, 232
Preston, Cathy Lynn, 14
Pretty, the, 24, 25, 28, 46, 91, 94, 99,
        112, 129–131, 133, 136, 140,
        194, 208, 212, 215–217, 231
Pretty Little Liars (ABC Family,
        2010–), 1, 27
Pretty in Pink (Howard Deutsch,
        1986), 4
The Prince and Me (Martha Coolidge,
        2004), 147
Princess culture, 3, 8, 148, 153, 228
The Princess Diaries (Garry Marshall,
        2001), 147
Projansky, Sarah, 13, 71, 148
Purkiss, Diane, 2

R
Raby, Rebecca, 8, 9
Red Riding Hood (Catherine
        Hardwicke, 2011), 1, 26
Renold, Emma, 193
Rich, B. Ruby, 46
Ringrose, Jessica, 60, 193
Riot grrrl, 166, 184, 237
Robbins, Alexandra, 156
Romance
    and 'one true love', 6
Rosaline (Daniel Errico, 2016), 236
Ross, Sharon Marie, 13
Rowe, Karen E., 74, 75, 156
Rowe, Kathleen, 19, 155, 158, 199
Rowe Karlyn, Kathleen, 80, 175
Rudy, Jill Terry, 3
'Russalka, or The Seacoast of
        Bohemia' (Joanna Russ, [1978]
        1986), 190

Russ, Joanna, 190

S
Sabrina the Teenage Witch (ABC,
        1996–-2003), 2
Sandahl, Carrie, 238
Scheiner, Georganne, 2
Schoenfeld, Bethe, 110
School uniforms, 161, 165
Schor, Naomi, 130
'The Sea Hag' (Melissa Lee Shaw,
        1999), 190
The Seas (Samantha Hunt, 2004), 190
Secret Beyond the Door (Fritz Lang,
        1947), 117
The Secret Circle (The CW, 2011–
        2012), 2
Seifert, Christine, 71
Sells, Laura, 3, 194, 217
Seriality, 79, 97, 150
Sex and the City (HBO, 1998–2004),
        174
Sexton, Ann, 5, 70, 148
Shaw, Melissa Lee, 190
She's All That (Robert Iscove, 1999),
        147
Shopping, 85, 127, 174, 175, 177,
        182
Short, Sue, 38
Silverman, Kaja, 196
Sin-de-rel-la (Man-dae Bong, 2006),
        236
Sjorgen, Britta, 200
Skeggs, Beverley, 149
Sleeping Beauties (Jamie Babbit,
        1999), 70, 236
'Sleeping Beauty' (Charles Perrault,
        [1697] 2001), 71
Sleeping Beauty (Julia Leigh, 2011), 70
Slumber Party Massacre (Amy Holden
        Jones, 1982), 108

'The Snow Queen' (Hans Christian Andersen [1845] 2008), 2
Snow White and the Huntsman (Rupert Sanders, 2012), 1
Soap opera, 108, 109
Sparke, Penny, 212
Spectacle, 21, 24, 43, 45, 56, 71, 75–77, 79, 88–95, 99, 131, 147–149, 155, 156, 158, 159, 162, 163, 166, 168, 172, 180, 181, 209, 211, 214, 231. *See also* Fashion
  and colour, 208
  and pattern, 93
  and sparkles, 99, 213
Speed, Lesley, 199
Stacey, Jackie, 46
Stacey, Judith, 9
Stefanik, Andrea, 8, 9, 45
Steiner, Wendy, 132
Stein, Louisa, 164
Street culture, 173, 174, 176, 179, 182
Studlar, Gaylyn, 155
'Sun, Moon, and Talia' (Giambattista Basile, [1634] 2001, 75
Sydney White (Joe Nussbaum, 2007), 2
Szakolczai, Arpad, 217

T
The Tale of the Princess Kaguya. Dir. Isao Takahata. 2013, 236
'The Tale of the Shoe' (Emma Donoghue, 1997), 148
'The Tale of the Voice' (Emma Donoghue, 1997), 190
A Tale of Two Sisters (Jee-woon Kim, 2003), 236
Tangled (Nathan Greno and Byron Howard, 2010), 2
Tasker, Yvonne, 9, 122

Tatar, Maria, 14, 69, 110
Taylor, Anthea, 72
Teen Wolf (MTV, 2011–), 2, 37
Thelma and Louise (Ridley Scott, 1991), 50
Time
  and delay, 85
  and progress, 80, 86
  suspension of, 70, 79, 81, 86
Trites, Roberta, 196
Turner, Victor, 18, 39, 112, 152, 192, 233
Twilight (Catherine Hardwick, 2008), 1
The Two Mrs Carrolls (Peter Godfrey, 1947), 142

U
Ultraliminality, 28, 40, 191, 192, 194, 208, 214, 216–222, 229
The Uninvited (The Guard Brothers, 2009), 108

V
The Vampire Diaries (The CW, 2010–2017), 2, 37
Vampires, 2, 27, 37, 38, 71, 83, 88, 94
Veronica Mars (UPN, 2004–2007), 108
Viorst, Judith, 148, 190
Voice, 24, 26, 29, 38, 39, 42, 49, 54–60, 64, 65, 110, 113, 127, 128, 190, 194–202, 206–208, 219, 220, 231
  and shouting, 29, 194, 206, 208, 220, 231
  and singing, 194, 199. *See also* Voice-over
Voice-over, 26, 55, 57–60, 200

W
Walkerdine, Valerie, 74
Wallace, Diana and Andrew Smith, 47
Walton, Priscilla L. and Manina Jones, 110, 111, 128
Warner, Marina, 7, 61, 108, 114, 190, 227
Waters, Melanie, 9
Weber, Brenda R., 184
Werewolves, 37–38
When Animals Dream (Jonas Alexander Arnby, 2014), 37, 236
When a Stranger Calls (Simon West, 2006), 108
White, Susan, 189

Williams, Christy, 148, 198
Williams, Linda, 46
Willis, Jessica Laureltree, 72
Wilson, Natalie, 89
Witches, 3, 214, 229

Y
Yolen, Jane, 70
Yue, Genevieve, 70

Z
Zipes, Jack, 4, 29, 43, 78

MIX
Papier aus verantwortungsvollen Quellen
Paper from responsible sources
FSC® C105338

Printed by Libri Plureos GmbH
in Hamburg, Germany